QUICK HITS FOR
TEACHING WITH
DIGITAL HUMANITIES

QUICK HITS FOR TEACHING WITH DIGITAL HUMANITIES

Successful Strategies from Award-Winning Teachers

—⁂—

EDITED BY

CHRISTOPHER J. YOUNG, MICHAEL MORRONE,
THOMAS C. WILSON, AND EMMA ANNETTE WILSON

FOREWORD BY

EDWARD L. AYERS

INDIANA UNIVERSITY PRESS

This book is a publication of

Indiana University Press
Office of Scholarly Publishing
Herman B Wells Library 350
1320 East 10th Street
Bloomington, Indiana 47405 USA

iupress.org

Manufactured in the United States of America

Cataloging information is available from the Library of Congress.

ISBN 978-0-253-05021-2 (paperback)
ISBN 978-0-253-05022-9 (ebook)

1 2 3 4 5   25 24 23 22 21 20

Dedicated to the Memory of
Mary T. Ferone Young (1939–2018)
and
Robert K. Young (1936–2018)

CONTENTS

DIRECTOR'S WELCOME

The Quick Hits series of books began as a collection of proven teaching tips shared at FACET's Third Annual Retreat. Twenty-eight years later FACET members continue to come together for an annual retreat to recognize, celebrate, and promote effective teaching and learning. While the retreat is a hallmark event of the FACET experience, the community of dynamic teachers dedicated to excellence in teaching and learning continuously advocates pedagogical innovation, inspires growth and reflection, cultivates the Scholarship of Teaching and Learning, and fosters personal renewal in the commitment to student learning.

FACET and its membership vigilantly attend to the present and future of pedagogy in the pursuit of student success. In that vein, *Quick Hits for Teaching with Digital Humanities* marks the ninth installment in the Quick Hits series: *Quick Hits, More Quick Hits, Quick Hits for New Faculty, Quick Hits for Educating Citizens, Quick Hits for Service Learning, Quick Hits for Teaching with Technology, Quick Hits for Adjunct Faculty,* and *Quick Hits for Teaching and Learning with Canvas* (available on IU Expand). Each of these volumes features techniques and strategies that have proven effective in the classroom; more recent volumes of Quick Hits have also focused on the scholarship underlying these tips and strategies. The current volume follows this trend of longer Quick Hits with thirty-six case studies. A number of them include images that add perspective on the discussed topic.

As with previous Quick Hits, dedication to pedagogical innovation and effectiveness underlies the volume's topic, digital humanities. The articles in this book demonstrate how technological capabilities and access to rich archival resources open possibilities for pedagogical creativity and new avenues of community engagement. Personally, as I read these chapters, I feel inspired by the teachers who push the disciplines forward, who collaborate across disciplines, often with our librarian colleagues, and who empower students to make their good work visible beyond the classroom and university walls. I also feel challenged: our students have so much information at their fingertips and technological opportunity to shape the world around them, but they face a turbulent marketplace of ideas. The projects and works discussed in these essays, by and large, involve complexity, carefulness, creativity, critical thinking, and collaboration. The outcomes are often impressive signature works. The digital humanities, in other words, offer a way to prepare our students to have meaningful lives.

While this volume continues a publishing tradition for FACET, it does break new ground. For the first time a Quick Hits volume includes editors from beyond Indiana University. Emma Annette Wilson from Southern Methodist University and Thomas C. Wilson from the University of Alabama join FACET member Christopher J. Young, Professor of History and Assistant Vice Chancellor for Academic Affairs at Indiana University Northwest, and myself as editors. I appreciate deeply your contributions to this project. I also want to thank Edward Ayers from the University of Richmond for writing the volume's foreword. Finally, I am grateful to Karissa Rector, FACET's Program Coordinator, whose technical and organizational skills helped bring this project to completion.

Michael Morrone
University Director, Faculty Academy on
Excellence in Teaching, Indiana University

FOREWORD

EDWARD L. AYERS
Recipient of the National Humanities Medal for
"Making Our History Accessible in New Ways"
University of Richmond

AN EMBARRASSING VIDEO RECENTLY TURNED up: a 1995 promotional piece from the University of Virginia about the promise for the humanities of the then-new World Wide Web. It seems a virtual parody now, with the words "information superhighway" accompanied by an image of an actual highway. Students are clearly uncomfortable with the mouse and navigating a screen. One scene on the cutting-room floor showed a student running the mouse over the screen of the huge beige monitor hulking before her, not an illogical assumption at the time.

Despite the cruel documentation of the passage of time, the video attests to an early and enduring faith that those of us who teach about the past will find ways to take advantage of the opportunities of the present. In the quarter century since that video was shot, teachers and scholars have continued to experiment, to find new ways to connect students with the record of the human experience.

The essays in this book attest to that spirit of imagination and engagement. They chronicle a range of experiments to see how we might best use the powerful new means suddenly available to us, outpacing even the rhetoric of the early days of the web. This book, and the projects that underlie it, speaks to the commitment of dedicated scholars and teachers to make the most of our own moment in time, to share with the students the excitement of learning in new ways. It is a heartening and inspiring book.

QUICK HITS FOR
TEACHING WITH
DIGITAL HUMANITIES

PART I

OVERVIEW OF WAYS TO TEACH WITH DIGITAL HUMANITIES

ONE

Social Network Analysis

Visualizing the Salem Witch Trials

ELIZABETH MATELSKI
Endicott College

STUDENTS IN MY SALEM WITCH Trials class at Endicott College in Beverly, Massachusetts (only a few miles from the city of Salem), worked together to create a visualization—a sociogram—of the persons involved in the Salem witch trials of 1692.[1] Once constructed, they manipulated and interpreted this visual map both to ask questions and make new observations about the Salem witch crisis and to use this quantitative evidence to challenge previous Salem scholarship. This scaffolded project spanned several weeks, helping students become familiar with various technologies including online annotation software and social network analysis.

SALEM HISTORIOGRAPHY

The history of the Salem witch trials is one of the most contested historiographies in the Western world. More has been written about the events of 1692 with less agreement than just about any other historical subject, particularly in the history of early America. Starting with Cotton Mather's *The Wonders of the Invisible World* in 1693, scholars have tried to make sense of the hysteria that engulfed an entire region.[2] Early academics who studied this event concerned themselves chiefly with assessing blame. Who should be held accountable, they asked, for the mass hysteria that resulted in at least 160 arrests and 25 deaths? The so-called afflicted girls? The church ministry? Court officials? Or perhaps the nature of Puritan religion itself?[3]

Inspired by the "new" social history, later scholarship moved away from identifying the parties most responsible for the crisis. These authors sought to understand how this could have happened, or, in particular, what set the trials in Salem apart from other contemporary witch hunts.[4] Today, academics are less concerned about finding fault or assessing blame and instead recognize that there was not a single cause but rather a variety of reasons why the Salem witch trials occurred. Moving beyond why it happened or who or what was to blame, historians now use the example of Salem as a reflection of larger themes in colonial life.[5] Digital history—the latest trend in historiography—provides the opportunity to challenge or confirm previous scholarship and also to ask new questions.[6]

SOCIAL NETWORK ANALYSIS OF THE SALEM WITCHCRAFT PAPERS

The Salem witchcraft papers, which include testimonies, court transcripts, depositions, and arrest warrants, are an invaluable primary source that provides a key window into this historical moment. In 1938, President Roosevelt's Works Progress Administration provided funding for an extensive new compilation of Salem witchcraft materials. Under the supervision of historian Archie N. Frost, multiple archives were searched and their handwritten records transcribed. Forty years later, in 1977, historians Paul Boyer and Stephen Nissenbaum refined and published these transcriptions in *The Salem Witchcraft Papers: Verbatim Transcripts of the Salem Witchcraft Outbreak of 1692*.[7] In the early 2000s, Boyer and Nissenbaum's transcripts were digitized by the University of Virginia, making them even more accessible to historians today.[8]

For the students to complete a sociogram, they first had to complete a social network analysis of the Salem Witchcraft Papers. A social network analysis is the study of structure and relationships within communities. The mode of analysis has a long history in sociology and mathematics and is a recent addition to the humanities and history. Social network analysis concentrates on relations among members of a community rather than on individual attributes of those members. The objects of the study (persons, institutions, airports, etc.) are commonly referred to as actors or *nodes*. In this assignment, the nodes were individual persons involved in the Salem witch trials—that is, anyone who appeared in the court transcripts, depositions, warrants, and other primary documents that make up the Salem Witchcraft Papers. The lines that connect the nodes to each other represent relationships. These ties, also referred to as *edges*, can represent specific kinds of relationships. For this assignment, students labeled each relationship between various actors in one of five ways— accuser, coaccused, witness against, witness for, or court official. (See fig. 1.1.)

INTERPRETING CHALLENGING DOCUMENTS

Before students could close read the Salem Witchcraft Papers to construct a data set needed to create the visual map of nodes and edges, they first required instruction on how to better comprehend these seventeenth-century documents. Although the original handwritten documents had previously been transcribed, these were verbatim transcriptions. Early American printers often capitalized the first letters of words in ways that can appear quite arbitrary to a modern reader. Spelling and grammar could also get creative as no standardized spelling existed in 1692. Misspellings, contractions, and sentences that run on for many lines with little or no punctuation can become unwieldy. Moreover, documents that were not originally meant for public consumption tend to be more erratic in their spelling, grammar, and use of capitalization. This is particularly true of legal documents, like those from a court proceeding, many of which were hastily recorded and under considerable stress.

To assist with this task, students were responsible for annotating court transcripts and depositions regarding Bridget Bishop, the first accused witch to be executed during the Salem witch trials. A number of free annotation software programs are available online. Annotation software allows students to highlight and paraphrase discrete lines in a challenging text for stronger and more active reading comprehension. Students in my class used MIT's Annotation Studio (http://www.annotationstudio.org/). It should be noted, however, that one does not have to use specific annotation software for this part of the assignment; even copying and pasting the documents to be interpreted into Google Docs works for this task. In fact, a tool like Google Docs that many students are already familiar with may be even more useful. The goal of this part of the assignment is not to teach how to use a new computer program but to practice a skill—in this case, the annotation of arcane court documents—that can become internalized after considerable practice.

PRELIMINARY PAPER

After obtaining firsthand experience reading and successfully interpreting seventeenth-century documents, each student chose one of the accused witches and wrote a short paper (two to three pages) on this individual.

+
−

Facet   Timeline   Timespan   You have no active filters

Students used the digitized court documents as the basis of their evidence to respond to two questions. First, why did people think this person was a witch? And, second, how did he or she respond to those accusations? Students were not allowed to write about Bridget Bishop because they had already annotated documents from her court docket. This necessitated additional annotation of different primary sources in order to complete the short-response essay.

MINING THE DATA

The third step in this scaffolded project was the creation of a large data set from which we as a class could begin to analyze the connections and ties among individuals involved in the Salem witch trials. Each student was assigned another accused witch—ideally, one they had not written about in the previous assignment; they then read through all of the digitized documents related to that individual and recorded data on an Excel spreadsheet. Their task was to record each person named in their specific documents and identify how that person was connected to their accused witch. Were they the individuals who made the accusation? Were they accused of witchcraft in the same document? Were they mentioned as someone who was injured by the accused witch? Were they a petitioner who defied the court in declaring that this individual was not a witch? Other information such as gender, age, marital status, and place of residence was also recorded as network attributes. Students were provided with a template in Excel to help them keep track of this information and remind them of what information they needed to record. In later class discussions, students identified even more categories beyond those provided on the Excel template that could help historians ask questions beyond the Salem trials in a study of general colonial life in New England. Overall, 30 students were able to record the information for nearly 600 different actors (nodes) and over 1,900 relationships (edges) between those actors.[9]

After merging students' data into one master Excel file, we were ready to create a sociogram of the recorded connections and attributes of individual actors. We used Palladio—a free online visualization tool in active development by Stanford University.[10] Like Annotation Studio, Palladio runs on all

Figure 1.1. Zoomed in, using Palladio, to the center of the sociogram of individuals involved with the Salem witch trials. The larger the node (circle), the more often that individual appears in the court documents. The darker nodes belong to individuals accused of witchcraft.

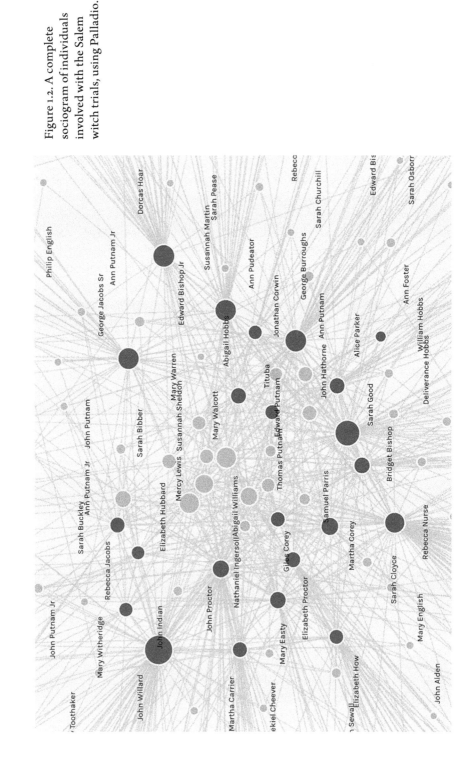

Figure 1.2. A complete sociogram of individuals involved with the Salem witch trials, using Palladio.

internet browsers and is, therefore, platform-independent. The website offers helpful tutorials for those wishing to learn the program, which is fairly intuitive compared to other social network analysis programs. For example, other programs require a separate file for nodes and one for edges; in Palladio, the master data set need only be saved as a single .csv file and then dragged and dropped into the program's data window. My goal was not to make students experts at Palladio in a few weeks' time but to familiarize them enough with the program's filter functions so they could manipulate the visual map we had created and make some preliminary observations. (See fig. 1.2.)

FINAL ASSESSMENT

As the fourth and final assessment, students composed a longer (five to six pages) paper. This paper asked students to blend traditional qualitative sources (i.e., the Salem court documents) with analysis of their quantitative data. Like all good history papers, the research essay began with curiosity and a question. Once students had annotated trial documents and mined a substantial amount of data from those sources, they could begin to ask questions of their primary materials through social network analysis. Some options included but were not limited to: Who was most central or most important to the Salem witch trials? What was the role of gender and/or age or residency in determining the accusers, accused, and witnesses for and against? If they continued with the individual they identified for the preliminary paper, what was their importance/level of centrality in the witch trials? They could also challenge or confirm previous Salem scholarship (i.e., theses proposed by historians John Demos or Paul Boyer and Stephen Nissenbaum). Students continued to refine their working theses, revising as necessary based on additional findings from court documents in the Salem Witchcraft Papers and observations from social network analysis.

By now, in this process, students will have had more experience bringing qualitative sources, like court documents, into a persuasive essay to support a thesis. A separate class period where they received instruction and then practiced interpreting and writing about general quantitative sources (tables, charts, graphs, etc.) proved useful. Similar to the annotation activity at the front end of the assignment, this extra practice familiarized students with the kinds of skills they were expected to command in their longer research paper.

The skills employed in this multicomponent assignment are certainly not singular to the Salem witch trials. Annotation of challenging documents provides students with the tools and the confidence to interpret a variety of primary sources. Similarly, social network analysis has been used in disciplines other than history, for instance, to show connections between characters in books, television series, or movies. The creation of a visual map or graph of connections and relationships among historical figures could easily be translated to a variety of historical events or moments and be made all the more rewarding when it is the students themselves who are working together as a class to mine the data and create the final visualization.

NOTES

1. Social network analysis utilizes sociograms—a graph or picture of a network's relations. A map that shows an airline's flights and the airports it connects to is an example of a sociogram.

2. Cotton Mather, *The Wonders of the Invisible World: Being an Account of the Tryals of Several Witches Lately Executed in New-England and of Several Remarkable Curiosities Therein Occurring* (London: John Dunton, 1693).

3. For example, Chadwick Hansen, *Witchcraft at Salem* (New York: Signet, 1969); Perry Miller, *The New England Mind: The Seventeenth Century* (Cambridge, MA: Harvard University Press, 1954); Charles W. Upham, *Salem Witchcraft: With an Account of Salem Village and a History of Opinions on Witchcraft and Kindred Subjects*, 2 vols. (Boston, 1867).

4. See Paul Boyer and Stephen Nissenbaum, *Salem Possessed: The Social Origins of Witchcraft* (Cambridge, MA: Harvard University Press, 1975); John Demos, *Entertaining Satan: Witchcraft and the Culture of Early New England* (Oxford: Oxford University Press, 1982); Richard Godbeer, *Escaping Salem: The Other Witch Hunt of 1692* (Oxford: Oxford University Press, 2005); Carol F. Karlsen, *The Devil in the Shape of a Woman* (New York: W. W. Norton, 1987); Mary Beth Norton, *In the Devil's Snare* (New York: Vintage Books, 2002).

5. For a well-respected and more recent work, see Emerson W. Baker's *A Storm of Witchcraft: The Salem Witch Trials and the American Experience* (Oxford: Oxford University Press, 2014).

6. Geographic information systems (GIS) software has already been applied to the events of 1692 to confirm the suspected location of Gallows Hill—the location where convicted witches were publicly executed. Benjamin C. Ray also utilized GIS to challenge Boyer and Nissenbaum's prominent Salem thesis regarding the economic and geographic relationship between the accused and their accusers. See, Benjamin C. Ray, "The Geography of Witchcraft Accusations in 1692 Salem Village," *William and Mary Quarterly* 65, no. 3 (July 2008): 449–478.

7. Stephen Nissenbaum and Paul S. Boyer, *The Salem Witchcraft Papers: Verbatim Transcripts of the Legal Documents of the Salem Witchcraft Outbreak of 1692* (New York: Da Capo Press, 1977).

8. Benjamin Ray, *Salem Witch Trials Documentary Archive,* The University of Virginia. Accessed February 12, 2020. http://salem.lib.virginia.edu/home.html.

9. It should be noted that consistency and correct spelling across students is essential. This can prove challenging since the Salem Witchcraft Papers have a number of different spellings for the same persons. For example, Ann Putnam's name might also be spelled Anne Putnam, Ann Putman, etc. Before individual student's data sets can be merged successfully, it is necessary to have uniformity in name spellings. This can be a tedious and time-consuming task for the instructor, but it needs to be accomplished for this part of the assignment to work.

10. Humanities + Design, *Palladio* (version 1.2.4), Stanford University, Accessed February 12, 2020. https://hdlab.stanford.edu/palladio/.

TWO

—ɯ—

Close Reading and Coding with the Seward Family Digital Archive

Digital Documentary Editing in the Undergraduate History Classroom

CAMDEN BURD

Andrew W. Mellon Postdoctoral Research Fellow
at the New York Botanical Garden

THE SEWARD FAMILY DIGITAL ARCHIVE is a digital documentary-editing project based at the University of Rochester that focuses on the family papers of nineteenth-century politician and diplomat William Henry Seward. The project features several thousand digitized, transcribed, and annotated letters spanning three generations of the Seward family. Unlike other documentary-editing projects, the Seward Family Digital Archive is a truly collaborative endeavor that relies on contributions from faculty, graduate and undergraduate students, and volunteers.[1] As the Text Encoding Initiative (TEI) and Technologies manager for the Seward Family Digital Archive, I maintain the project's TEI standards and introduce students to the technological skills needed to contribute to the digital documentary-editing project. In this chapter, I describe the structure of project-related courses and the methods by which students contribute innovatively to the Seward Family Digital Archive through a combination of seminar-style readings, historical research, and coding.

HISTORY OF THE SEWARD FAMILY DIGITAL ARCHIVE

Since the Seward Family Digital Archive began in 2013, Professor Thomas Slaughter, along with project managers, designed a series of courses exploring themes found within the family letters. Although we planned to incorporate digital tools into the curriculum, we never described them as "digital history" courses.[2] We do not emphasize the use of new technology, a focus on "tool training," or advanced digital concepts as defining components of the courses. Rather, the project-related curriculum resembles that of many reading seminars.[3] Students engage with secondary readings and discuss particular themes relating to the nineteenth-century correspondence: family, friendship, gender, and adolescence in the nineteenth century. The assigned readings and subsequent discussions prepare students for the themes found within the correspondence and provide them with the foundations to be informed digital documentary editors. Students receive eight to ten digital copies of Seward correspondence to supplement their readings. As written into the requirements of the course, we task students to transcribe, annotate, and mark up the letters using extensible markup language (XML), in preparation for publication in the digital archive.

COURSE DESIGN

The structure of the course emphasizes an in-depth study of the family's correspondence through a method of "close reading." Designed for studying the many layers of a particular document, close reading is a method of literary criticism that encourages a deeper engagement into a smaller number of texts. One group of scholars defines close reading as "the analysis of individuals, events, and ideas, [and] their development and interaction" within a given text.[4] The methods used in close reading resemble many of the elements identified in the Reading VALUE Rubric compiled by the Association of American Colleges and Universities, including comprehension, relationship to text, analysis, interpretation, and readers' voice. Historians utilize close reading as a method for examining all elements of a historical document. Students explore the contents of a letter in its historical context. Who wrote the letter? Where was the letter written? Who and what was mentioned in the correspondence? How does knowing the recipient shape or change how the letter was originally written? Students rely on primary source research in order to answer the questions embedded in each document. As they comb through census records, government documents, newspapers, and books, students must identify and annotate the individuals, places, and bodies of literature mentioned within their assigned correspondence.

As students undergo the process of historical research, they begin to unravel the many layers of personal connections of this prominent nineteenth-century family. We ask them to discuss the significant themes in letters and the

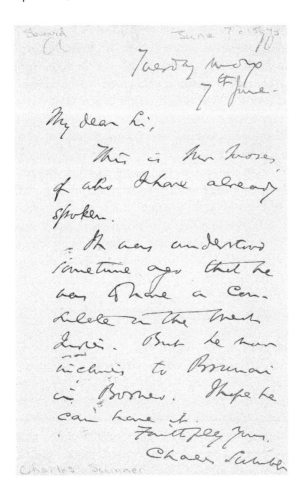

Figure 2.1. Letter from Charles Sumner to William Henry Seward, June 7, 1864. Seward Family Archives, University of Rochester.

personal connections behind them. Is a named individual a religious leader, politician, neighbor, distant family member, or simply an acquaintance? How does that affect how the author or recipient might discuss slavery, politics, or business? Students follow traces of town gossip, political happenings, physical ailments, business plans, and the varying aspects of family life as they appear in the correspondence. The seminar-style readings, assigned throughout the semester, help place the individual themes and named individuals into a larger historical context. The combination of close reading and seminar discussions allows students to fully grasp the Seward family in their social, cultural, and political milieu.

The students' research also contributes to the overall structure of the Seward Family Digital Archive. Every time they identify new individuals, books, or geographic locations, they enter the information into our extensive databases of nearly 5,000 individuals, 1,300 geographic locations, and 4,000 published works. Student research offers a unique opportunity to discuss the production and distribution of historical information in the digital age. Students quickly become aware of the inherent biases of the historical record when they struggle to find supplemental documentation for house servants, slaves, and freedmen mentioned in the correspondence during the research process. Additionally, students realize the difficulty of identifying the young, unmarried women mentioned in their letters due to nineteenth-century naming conventions. Although census records, birth and death certificates, church records, and county histories offer insights in some cases, students are forced to identify these individuals as "unknown." Through a close read and research of the assigned correspondence, students recognize the potential shortcomings of digital documentary-editing projects that still rely on traditional sources to share information—an important lesson that demonstrates the limits of technology in the digital age.

FINDING THE APPROPRIATE XML TAGS

In addition to research, students of varying technical and disciplinary backgrounds learn basic coding in order to publish their historical findings in the archive.[5] Digital humanists favor TEI due to its limited set of XML tags used to describe literary texts, historical documents, and other materials that might be of interest to scholars. TEI tags describe the contents of a text rather than the document's appearance on the web. Digital projects maintain unique project guidelines based on the larger standards supported by the TEI consortium. Although every project focuses on different aspects of the documents, they each follow a set of rules laid out by the TEI consortium.[6] Using a basic coding schema, students in project-related courses transform their transcriptions into digitized and machine-readable documents. XML, in particular, provides an entry point for undergraduate students. Although the structure of the code is similar to more advanced languages, the vocabulary is straightforward and legible to students with less coding experience. After spending one class discussing the most common tags used to identify individual people (<persName>), places (<placeName>), and bodies of literature (<bib>), students begin to mark up their XML files only referring back to the Seward Family Digital Archive guidelines for the less common editorial elements. We dedicate an additional four class sessions for collaborative markup and to discuss the code's structure and capabilities. Unlike many humanities courses that focus on isolated archival research, the Seward Family Digital Archive encourages collaboration and group dialogue throughout the research and digital-editing process. Undergraduate students come to rely on one another through peer learning in order to troubleshoot certain elements of code and complete the markup of their letters. Through collaboration and group coding sessions, students successfully research, transcribe, annotate, and mark up their assigned correspondence. Before the semester ends, students are able to view their published letters on the Seward Family Digital Archive.

CONCLUSION

The Seward Family Digital Archive serves as a model for those historians looking to incorporate digital tools into the classroom. Through a close read of nineteenth-century correspondence, students engage in historical research methods familiar to traditional history courses. Rather than assign students a conventional research paper, though, we provide a platform for undergraduates to contribute to a grant-funded and collaborative digital documentary-editing project. The incorporation of TEI and XML coding into the classroom allows students to engage with course material and share their research in innovative ways. Additionally, by introducing basic coding into the undergraduate classroom, students discover, learn, and master new digital skills necessary to share this unique collection with a wider audience—skills that students will be expected to know in an increasingly digital age. Over the past three years, the Seward Family Digital Archive has successfully incorporated digital tools into the classroom as a means of deepening historical study while providing a platform for introducing students to new technological concepts and tools.

NOTES

1. Seward Family Digital Archive Project, University of Rochester, Seward Family Digital Archive, https://sewardproject.org/. On the impact of digital projects as a collaborative work, see Matthew K. Gold and Jim Groom, "Looking for Whitman: A Grand, Aggregated Experiment," *Debates in the Digital Humanities* (Minneapolis: University of Minnesota Press, 2012), 406–408.

2. William Pannapacker, "Stop Calling It 'Digital Humanities': And 9 Other Strategies to Help Liberal Arts Colleges Join the Movement," *Chronicle of Higher Education*, February 18, 2013, accessed May 12, 2018, https://www.chronicle.com /article/Stop-Calling-It-Digital/137325.

3. Kara Kennedy, "A Long Belated Welcome: Accepting Digital Humanities Methods into Non-DH Classrooms," *Digital Humanities Quarterly* 11, no. 3

(2017), accessed May 12, 2018, http://www.digitalhumanities.org/dhq/vol/11/3/000315/000315.html.

4. Stefan Jänicke, Greta Franzini, Muhammad Faisal Cheema, and Gerik Scheuermann, "On Close and Distant Reading in Digital Humanities: A Survey and Future Challenges," in *Eurographics Conference on Visualization, 2015,* accessed May 12, 2018, https://diglib.eg.org/handle/10.2312/eurovisstar.20151113.083-103; Kate Singer, "Digital Close Reading: TEI for Teaching Poetic Vocabularies," *Journal of Interactive Technology and Pedagogy* 3 (2013), accessed May 12, 2018, https://jitp.commons.gc.cuny.edu/table-of-contents-issue-three/.

5. Neil Selwyn, "The Digital Native—Myth and Reality," *Aslib Proceedings* 61, no. 4 (2009): 364–379.

6. *Text Encoding Initiative,* accessed February 11, 2020, https://tei-c.org/.

THREE

Teaching with Digital Humanities

Engaging Your Audience

ROBERT VOSS

Northwest Missouri State University

THE BROAD SCOPE OF THE digital humanities requires significant attention to what we are attempting to do in our classes and what we expect our students to take away from the course. Many others have written on the value of engaging students early and often with digital humanities (DH) for the most impact on the students and professors. Teaching students through a program that has digital humanities interwoven throughout each course has been successful in developing interesting research ideas, revealing student interests, and even engaging high school students with entry-level DH work. Undergraduate work in DH can develop interactive timelines, multilayered textual analysis of documents, social network mapping, and cross-referenced maps and timelines. Developing ways DH tools work together across various courses allows educators to increase their teaching effectiveness.

Over the past several years, I have developed student and faculty interest in the digital humanities by using a four-step approach: (1) exposing them to DH through simple projects; (2) using DH in a collaborative setting; (3) refining the desired skills while streamlining student interests; and (4) having students create their own DH projects. This broad structure, spanning several courses and multiple interactions, has yielded significant understanding of digital humanities, interest in DH projects, and new student-based digital projects.

As undergraduates have the ability to understand, analyze, and develop digital humanities projects, our task is to develop the programs and courses that can best inculcate the students' growth as humanists. Removing the barriers that stand between the humanities and the science, technology, engineering, and math (STEM) fields is also possible through teaching with DH. By bridging digital humanities teaching across several courses, faculty can teach using DH in multiple formats and drive overall student interest in the humanities.

Digital humanities can be broadly understood as research, writing, and publication utilizing computers in ways that cannot be done in traditional paper formats. DH work generally consists of data, display, analysis, and teaching that interact in various capacities to develop new understandings of the human condition. The vast array of DH projects is inspiring and demonstrates the multitude of ways computers can be used in the study of the humanities. Digital humanities projects, for example, may include sources or data that use "big data" to ask and answer difficult questions. The "Six Degrees of Sir Francis Bacon" project is a great example of the effective use of complex data by creating a social network of early modern England. This project is a digital reconstruction of the expected social map of early modern England using information contributed from multiple sources.[1] Digital humanities also may include novel methods of interaction and display such as the digital project "Mapping Occupation" that reveals in maps and timelines a new understanding of the American South during the era of Reconstruction.[2] In other ways, digital humanists created digital tools such as Voyant and Token X to give new means of analysis to existing texts, allowing the users to "see" texts in a new way.[3] DH also can include digital teaching tools that demonstrate ways to use existing websites for a primary or secondary classroom purpose. The large digital repository "Railroads and the Making of Modern America," for example, includes a "Teaching Materials" link that includes lesson plans and ways to incorporate the site into classrooms.[4]

Teaching with DH is effective when instructors are intentional with the material and method of teaching. The first interactions with DH should be for exposure. A simple, single-class assignment, using a class-wide collaborative framework, can both generate new findings and expose students to the possibilities of DH. The challenge is to engage students and draw them into a deeper interest in the liberal arts and in digital humanities. Engaging new students with low-level interactions can generate new projects and develop new humanists.

One of the challenges of teaching with DH is to maintain course structure while integrating digital components into the course. Data are key to each

DH project. As students come to understand the foundations of data, they can then develop interactions with such information. Data entry, while somewhat tedious, can engage students and produce amazing results while not veering too far from the traditional course design. This data entry allows students to think about the process of building DH projects and to understand that they are not intimidating. Creating spreadsheets helps students understand the value of data sets and how to use them, even discovering new relationships within data. Several platforms allow for online collaboration for spreadsheets. As of this writing, Google Sheets, a spreadsheet program, allows multiple users to collaborate at once using their Google account.[5] Using Google Sheets as a foundation, TimelineJS builds an interactive timeline that can include images, videos, and various links to online material.[6] In a similar, but more robust iteration, Exhibit from the MIT Libraries in collaboration with the MIT Computer Science and Artificial Intelligence Lab (CSAIL) MIT Labs also uses Google Sheets.[7] Exhibit generates maps, timelines, and charts of information. At this stage of introduction to DH, it is valuable to remember that students do not need to be graded on all assignments—sometimes assignments are simply for exposure to the concepts and results.

It is possible to take a TimelineJS project or an Exhibit project and crowd-source the material in a single-class setting. For example, a history professor might ask the class to log on to a previously created Google Sheets template of the American Revolution and ask students to develop a timeline. Using mostly Wikipedia, pairs of students are able to develop a timeline of many events of the American Revolution. Students can then interrogate the results, seek relationships within the material, and ask new questions of the information. Of course, a quick project like this can have problems, but it also provides a great learning opportunity.

Using DH in the classroom should be followed up with a discussion of the merits of using these kinds of tools. Students tend to criticize much at the university level. They can turn that criticism to an analysis of DH. Following the example of the American Revolution timeline, instructors can tease out the values and challenges of creating historical projects like this—including the various skills that are needed to build an online experience. This can reveal new ways for them to write and research. Writing and presenting using Exhibit or TimelineJS can build a connection to student DH projects, even if they are not in a permanent online location.

DH in student research utilizing a collaborative structure is the second of four steps in teaching with DH. Teaching with DH should encourage students to interact, analyze, and produce DH projects. Many students have no problems building websites. Digital content creation is much different from teaching with DH. A website creation experience is, of course, valuable to the application of DH, but it is not essential.

Application and collaboration build student interest and understanding of the process of DH projects. While students have been exposed to the key components of what makes DH projects valuable, they need to experience the creation of those types of projects. Most students have preferences on collaborative projects, and DH requires teams for the most effective projects. Students often despise collaboration and group work—mostly for perceived workload imbalances. In building teams, it is important to have students hold each other accountable for their work. Student buy-in is essential in this stage of development. If possible, it is also valuable either to publish student work or for students to self-publish their DH projects. Students tend to develop their projects for their intended audiences, including the public. If students understand that they are working on digital projects that are for the general public, their work quality changes to reflect that.

Collaboration and application are not as important when the project being worked on is relatively rudimentary. Instead, students need to be pushed to ask larger "what if" questions. They need to develop the keys of humanistic inquiry, the questions and arguments that follow a viable topic. According to historian Jim Cullen, "Good questions have the power to turn meaningless information into meaningful answers."[8] Choosing strong research questions provokes students into working through the topic.

Closely related to collaboration and application are skills and streamlining, tools that reveal how DH is more than website design. After students have been exposed to some of the basics of DH and they have used it in a structured, collaborative environment, it is valuable to push them to refine their skills and find the tools that they may need in their own work. The skills acquired in this component are often more in-depth and specific to certain platforms and projects as opposed to general tools. Skills and streamlining are part of establishing a set of digital tools for the students' DH toolbox to use beyond the university setting.

Students gain an independence in their research and often take ownership of DH as they are gaining skills and streamlining their approaches. This is possibly the best area for extension outside of the traditional university classroom setting. Instead, as students progress toward independent projects they gain the ability to develop their own projects. The skills that make up the increasingly advanced and specialized parts of DH need to be the focus at this stage. Undergraduates can be introduced to the components of

DH projects that seek to answer complex questions. For example, utilizing social network analysis tools may allow students to develop new historical questions to ask of people of the past. Similarly, students may incorporate historical GIS into projects that seek answers to relationships between space and time. Choosing the right set of DH tools to address the questions being asked, or at least point to a way that the question might be answered, is important and a topic that should not be introduced too early but only when students are developing their interests. It is at this point that the "toolbox" is sufficiently full so the student can choose the right resource or skill to answer the question that they are seeking to answer. To expand on one of the examples above, students seeking to figure out a relationship between space and time will choose the tool that best suits them rather than being told which of the many resources to use.

Some digital humanists with advanced knowledge in the technical side of DH projects have developed tools for others to use that may be accessible to students, at some point, but might have been too complex if introduced too early. For example, one of the first technical textual analysis tools, TokenX, required a significant technical understanding for writing and publishing. The code and technical understanding demanded more skills than most undergraduates might have, yet the end product was widely usable. While the technological skills needed to create TokenX several years ago were rarely seen in humanists, today many humanities scholars have developed their own tools from their understanding of computers and programming languages. Many of these tools are available through GitHub and other repositories.[9]

Getting students to explore difficult topics using digital tools is interesting, but getting students to ask new questions and incorporate new digital tools is exciting. The "Programming Historian" began as a website to explain the technological side of digital humanities tools and has expanded into various programming languages in a peer-reviewed online publication.[10] William Turkel's original idea that understanding computers and applying them to the humanities can be collaborative and invigorating appeals to many who see the link between humanities and computing. Similarly, the DiRT Directory of digital research tools was an attempt to break down the barriers of humanities computing and digital needs.[11] The wide array of tools from website design to data management that was cataloged through the DiRT Directory allowed many humanities scholars to use digital tools of which they may not have been aware. While the DiRT Directory is no longer supported, the wiki is still available and useful. When projects like DiRT Directory and Programming Historian are combined, students will have access to skills and streamlining that they may need for their own projects.

As undergraduates begin refining their skills and streamlining their research interests, it is essential for them to be creating their own projects. Student projects in the digital humanities can ask innovative questions and seek bold answers that often go beyond the traditional research papers, yet the basic skills of humanities research and inquiry are essential. Students can interact with both traditional approaches and innovative applications of digital humanities. Students may be more comfortable writing traditional research papers than attempting to create digital humanities projects. When teaching with DH, it is important to ensure that the projects not be intimidating to students. Instead, DH can be applied after other research is completed. This way students may be interacting with the display and text of a DH project, for example, but not be using DH as a research component itself. In history classes, students can write a traditional research paper and apply DH tools after the initial project is completed.

When students engage with DH in gradually increasing measure, their long-term interaction will increase with their overall involvement. This process of "scaffolding" involves engaging DH students early with simple concepts and interactions and gradually getting those same students to apply and understand DH as a set of tools that the humanities can use to broaden research and understanding. The last step in the process of teaching with digital humanities is for students to create with DH. Student-generated projects should allow the student to develop a new idea but be based, initially, on prior research. This will be the culmination of the scaffolding effect on research. Students' work can then focus on the DH components.

For the final step in teaching with DH, students' previous research and technological understanding is foundational. Students need to learn more tools, but this might look more like the integration of various components. For example, one DH project might involve a timeline of the events surrounding John F. Kennedy's Bay of Pigs invasion. A secondary DH project of the same Bay of Pigs invasion could create a KML file using Google Earth.[12] At the end stage, the student might use a tool like MIT's Exhibit to blend the timeline and the map into one coherent piece. Shifting the work to a combined project would take more technological understanding, but a student with the background of two relatively simple DH projects should be able to develop a more complex project using an increased level of technological knowledge.

Teaching with digital humanities broadens the usage and exposure of already important humanities research while developing skills that students may apply outside of the classroom. Students and instructors alike can create new understandings of information through digital humanities that the public may appreciate more than student papers. Many students appreciate humanities classes more when they are learning through DH. Reaching a point of student work that is primarily digital, while a new idea, is one that colleges and universities are embracing, even if it is challenging the traditions of the humanities.

NOTES

1. "Francis Bacon Network [2, 1562–1626, 61–100%]," Six Degrees of Francis Bacon, accessed May 17, 2018, http://www.sixdegreesoffrancisbacon.com/?ids=10000473&min_confidence=60&type=network.

2. "Mapping Occupation," accessed May 17, 2019, http://www.mappingoccupation.org.

3. Stefan Sinclair and Geoffrey Rockwell, "Voyant Tools," 2016, accessed May 17, 2019, http://voyant-tools.org.

4. William G. Thomas III, "Railroads and the Making of Modern America," accessed May 21, 2018, http://railroads.unl.edu.

5. "Google Sheets," accessed May 21, 2019, https://docs.google.com/spreadsheets.

6. "TimelineJS," Northwestern University, accessed May 21, 2019, http://timeline.knightlab.com/#.

7. "Exhibit 3.0," Massachusetts Institute of Technology, accessed May 21, 2019, http://www.simile-widgets.org/exhibit3/.

8. Jim Cullen, *Essaying the Past: How to Read, Write, and Think about History*, 3rd ed. (Hoboken, NJ: Wiley-Blackwell, 2016), 30.

9. "GitHub," accessed May 21, 2019, https://github.com.

10. William Turkel, ed., "The Programming Historian," accessed May 21, 2019, https://programminghistorian.org.

11. "DiRT: Digital Research Tools," accessed May 21, 2019, https://digitalresearchtools.pbworks.com/w/page/17801672/FrontPage.

12. "KML Tutorial," Keyhole Markup Language, accessed May 21, 2019, https://developers.google.com/kml/documentation/kml_tut.

FOUR

—ᗰᗰ—

Teaching Text Encoding in the Madre María de San José (México 1656–1719) Digital Project

MARY ALEXANDER
University of Alabama

CONNIE JANIGA-PERKINS
University of Alabama

EMMA ANNETTE WILSON
Southern Methodist University

THE ALABAMA DIGITAL HUMANITIES CENTER, part of the University Libraries and located in the Amelia Gayle Gorgas Library at the heart of the University of Alabama campus, has played a prominent role in fostering both research and teaching using digital humanities. In the fall of both 2015 and 2016, Dr. Emma Wilson, Mary Alexander, and Dr. Connie Janiga-Perkins partnered to team teach the graduate course Readings in Women's Spiritual Autobiography: Language, Materiality, and Identity in Colonial Spanish American Texts using Digital Humanities.

The team-taught course was composed of four four-week segments that introduced students to the traditional literary research and paleography skills necessary to work with historic manuscripts and then to the thoroughly modern process of using text encoding with the Text Encoding Initiative (TEI) to translate student transcription and research into a digital edition of part of one of the texts they studied. The first segment consisted of an extensive study of history, literary criticism, and bibliography of and primary sources by women authors of the Spanish American colonial period and focused on the spiritual autobiographies of two Spanish American nuns. The first, Jerónima Nava y Saavedra (b. 1669), was a black-veiled sister in the Order of Poor Clares in Bogotá (Colombia). She resided in the Convent of Santa Clara her entire professed life until her death in 1727. María de San José (b. 1656, d. 1719) was an Augustinian Recollect nun from New Spain (México), who professed at the Convent of Santa Monica in Puebla and later founded the Convent of Soledad in Oaxaca.

Women such as María and Jerónima were taught that they were inferior in every way to men. From this early training as well as from other cultural and societal messages throughout their lives, women internalized a deep sense of inferiority, a belief that they were more given to emotion than logic, more deceptive than men, more capable of morally questionable behavior, and, therefore, in need of a stern, guiding (male) hand. Early in life that guidance was provided by the father of the family, or another strong male figure such as a grandfather or uncle. In adulthood, the honorable options for these (upper-class) women were marriage, the convent, and in some rare cases spinsterhood under the protection of a brother or another male family member.

María de San José and Jerónima Nava y Saavedra chose the convent, where they confronted not only a strong system of female authority but the "heavy male hand" of their confessors and the church hierarchy. Their autobiographical accounts portray their lives, both spiritual and worldly, and show the maturing of their agency despite often-harsh treatment by their confessors. The survival of these women's writing depended exclusively on the male authority exercised within the colonial church. Since few authenticated manuscripts of this type survive from the colonial era, it is especially important to create new opportunities for both their preservation and their dissemination.

The second segment concentrated on the art and theory of critical editing, with in-depth rereading of the primary sources from what Stuart Hall calls negotiated positioning.[1] Emphasis was placed on readings by Peter Shillingburg, Leah Marcus, David Greetham, Leroy Searle, John Lennard, and Zachary Lesser. Segment three consisted of a study of basic paleography and transcription techniques appropriate for women's writing in the seventeenth and eighteenth centuries in Spanish America. After a bit of practice, the project began. The classes transcribed unpublished portions of *The Life Story* of María de San José. We are grateful to the John Carter Brown Library in Providence, Rhode Island, for the 1,200-page manuscript.

In the fourth and final segment of the courses, the class moved to the Alabama Digital Humanities Center, where Mary Alexander and Dr. Emma Wilson taught the students text encoding and how to make a digital edition. (See fig. 4.1.)

Figure 4.1. Manuscript page from Maria de San Jose Oaxaca Manuscript 87R.

ENCODING A DIGITAL EDITION

The Environment

The Alabama Digital Humanities Center provided tools needed to encode a digital edition. The Macs had oXygen, an extensible markup language (XML) editor, installed on them. Big screens displayed slides and oXygen's screen. A whiteboard was used to record discussion points. This facility provided an ideal group learning environment.

The Team

The students were divided into groups of twos or threes. They would switch roles of encoder and proofreader. Mary Alexander led the instruction in using oXygen as an encoder and in the metadata principles governing TEI; Connie Janiga-Perkins led the literary research questions and conundrums presented by transcribing and encoding the text, specifically with regard to making the transition between the manuscript itself and a digital version; and Emma Annette Wilson mediated the discussions, asking questions about the links between the choices being made within the encoding, the transcription, and the original manuscript itself and extrapolating broader principles of digital scholarship at work within the scenario.

Teaching TEI

The TEI's customized schema, TEI Lite, was the best fit for the project with its set of basic elements for encoding a digital edition, a strong community of members, and its tools to support the creation of digital editions. Students were instructed to open an oXygen TEI P5 Lite template that provided the root element, list of namespaces, TEI header, and body sections in a valid TEI document. After discussion on the purpose of the namespaces, we started immediately encoding the text body. TEI header work was scheduled for the last class.

The students were instructed to paste the transcription in between the opening and closing tags of the paragraph element. A lesson on the importance of opening and closing tags in a well-formed document included information about the XML, an independent language used to store and transport data, the foundation of TEI's syntax. The line break element (<lb/>) was needed at the beginning of each prose line to mark a boundary point separating sections of text. Students were introduced to an XML syntax called milestones in TEI. oXygen's abilities as an XML editor with its internal support for TEI was demonstrated as it automatically provided a closing tag before students could finish typing the complete tag.

The groups of students were assigned pages of the diary to encode. Elements were needed for diacritics, strikethroughs, and superscripts to indicate abbreviations in the manuscript. Students learned about the UTF-8 character set. When a character with a diacritic was not supported by this character set, it would need additional inquiry for identification. Beginning with this unidentified character, a list of characters with unresolved encodings was compiled for future reference. Meanwhile, the class progressed from simple encodings to complex nested elements and elements with attributes. These gave the students opportunities to learn correct syntax for sustaining a well-formed and valid document.

The class discussions centered on possible encodings. Some thought that an element should be used to emphasize strikethroughs with thick dark markings, to indicate text being emphatically crossed out. The discussion on bold strikethroughs segued into a discussion about the meaning of diplomatic edition, an encoded text that is a literal transcription of the original document, including its physical structure and its variations. In this way, the digital teaching approach illuminated traditional editorial debates, bringing them to life afresh for a modern student group.

Within the manuscript, marginalia included words in the left margin, Arabic number with an alpha character in the right margin, and a drawing of a cross in the center. All were encoded to represent the original text layout. The words in the left margin were encoded as a segment as it was decided earlier that the document did not have text divisions. The cross required a glyph element to contain the URL to the cross's image. The students decided to use the glyph's subelement, desc (description) in which they supplied the basic description, "Religious cross." The glyph and desc elements served as an introduction to the larger TEI P5 standard, as they were beyond TEI Lite's schema. The TEI community's ROMA tool was introduced to produce a customized schema with the glyph element and its subelement for validation and documentation. With each additional element outside TEI Lite, the ROMA tool provided the needed documentation. This example of advanced encoding was crucial in allowing students hands-on experience of the possibilities opened up by TEI.

oXygen's feature to transform the encoded text to a web page display served as an aid for proofreading and visualization of the digital edition's layout. It was a favorite of one student based on her remarks and repeated use of it.

The TEI header elements are similar to a library catalog record with more elements. The header contained a source description element for describing the digital edition. For this element, the students thoughtfully crafted statements about their edition, and in this part of the class they had an opportunity to formalize some of the editorial principles that they had been discussing during their encoding sessions. The header include an annotated bibliography compiled by the students.

These encodings will be part of the iteration performed on the remaining raw text until it is completely transformed into a digital edition by future classes. The last class will perform final proofreading and edits.

OUTCOMES AND ONWARD

Team teaching this iterative graduate class is enabling students to engage in the creation of original research that will result in a substantive, lasting outcome once the digital edition is launched. Students were able to benefit from combined expertise in Hispanist studies and in digital techniques, and the sum of that experience generated a detailed knowledge both of their early colonial manuscript and its nuances and of the editorial dilemmas faced within a scholarly digital environment. The union of very traditional paleography and bibliography skills with cutting-edge digital techniques gives students a good foundation in both areas of their chosen field, preparing them for both onward research and, pragmatically, the job market.

Team teaching also made it possible for the students to cover a lot of ground in a relatively short period of time, as their discussions were mediated by the voices and research specializations of all three faculty members leading the class sessions. This setup created a truly immersive environment for the students, one that precisely models a modern research collaboration in the humanities and also that embodies the dynamics of a professional conference in the field. These intellectual experiences provide valuable professionalization opportunities for students that go beyond tangible skills of text encoding and into broader intellectual benefits, such as gaining confidence in speaking with professors on an equal footing as a fellow researcher and arguing for your point of view when particular encoding decisions had to be made. Team teaching can be administratively difficult, but it is well worth advocating for in order to give students an immersive, wide-ranging learning experience. In this instance, students' work will, down the road, be visible online as part of the completed digital edition of the spiritual manuscript, giving them a lasting testament to their research and enabling them to have their first taste of contributing to their field in a permanent way, and it was all made possible via collaboration.

NOTE

1. Stuart Hall, "Encoding/Decoding." *Culture, Media, Language: Working Papers in Cultural Studies 1972–79*. Birmingham, UK: Centre for Contemporary Cultural Studies (1980: 128—38). Hall espouses three possible approaches or means a reader can use to position himself or herself when decoding a text: the dominant or hegemonic, the negotiated, and the oppositional. For Hall, decoding a work using the negotiated approach lets readers acknowledge the hegemonic definitions at work in the process while reserving the right to make a more negotiated examination of the text. Such an approach allows us to decode María's Vida in a manner that takes into account the situational level, where we may find exceptions to the hegemonic reading and/or create new ground rules for approaching the text (137–38).

FIVE

—〰—

Teaching with Trials

Using Digital Humanities to Flip the Humanities Classroom

ADAM CLULOW

University of Texas at Austin

BERNARD Z. KEO

Monash University

SAMUEL HOREWOOD

Duke University

THE PROCESS OF STAGING MOCK trials is a familiar element of most law school classrooms. Based on extensive research either on real or hypothetical cases, teams of students present arguments and evidence before a panel of judges. Such exercises are incorporated into legal curricula in universities across the world, and there are a range of domestic and international events that allow students to compete directly with each other in this format. This model is far less common in the humanities classroom, even though it presents valuable opportunities to facilitate student engagement with a range of sources and to promote interactive learning.

Beginning in 2017, we experimented with a new model for the flipped humanities classroom that we called Teaching with Trials. It was designed to create a mechanism for structured research, debate, and engagement by pairing a digital humanities platform with a three-week mock trial exercise. Students were challenged to work through large quantities of seventeenth-century primary source material online before taking on one of four roles—as members of a prosecution or defense legal team, witnesses, researchers, or judges—in a comprehensive restaging of a historical trial. Although the model is relatively new, it has so far produced outstanding results, generating a high degree of engagement while improving learning outcomes for students.

THE CASE

Our initial experiment with this format was constructed around a famous, and still controversial, seventeenth-century case, the Amboyna Conspiracy Trial.[1] This commenced on February 23, 1623, when a Japanese mercenary called Shichizō, in the employ of the Dutch East India Company (*Vereenigde Oost-Indische Compagnie* or VOC), was arrested for asking questions about the defenses of one of the company's forts on the island of Ambon (often referred to as Amboyna in this period) in modern-day Indonesia. When he failed to provide an adequate explanation, he was tortured using a technique we now know as waterboarding. The result was a confession that Shichizō had joined a plot orchestrated by a group of English merchants to seize control of the fortification and, ultimately, to rip the spice-rich island from the company's grasp. Armed with this information, the VOC governor proceeded to arrest, interrogate, and torture the remaining ten Japanese mercenaries in the garrison, all of whom eventually admitted to their involvement in the plot. A few days later, the governor's attention turned to the English. Under torture, they too confessed to a conspiracy aimed at seizing the fort and ejecting the Dutch from Ambon. On March 9, an improvised tribunal of VOC employees convened to render judgment on the conspirators. The result was an emphatic guilty verdict, and, shortly thereafter, ten English merchants and ten Japanese mercenaries were executed in the public square outside the fortress.

The Amboyna case became immediately and immensely controversial. When news of what had happened reached London at the end of May 1624, it sparked outrage from the directors of the English East India Company, the king, and, by all accounts, the general public. Passions were further inflamed by the publication of a slew of incendiary pamphlets produced by both sides that sought to either damn the Dutch as bloody tyrants or condemn the English as faithless traitors. The result was that, despite occurring thousands of miles away in an unfamiliar part of the world, the trial on Amboyna swiftly escalated to become one of the most famous legal cases of its age and the subject of a long-running dispute between the Dutch and English governments, which clashed bitterly over the twin issues of blame and compensation.

The controversies produced by Amboyna combined to generate a sprawling archive that runs to more than five thousand pages of original documents scattered across the British Library in London, the National Archives in Kew, and the Nationaal Archief in The Hague. Despite this vast trove of materials, there is as yet no consensus as to what actually happened on Amboyna. For close to four centuries, scholars have debated whether there was in fact a plot to seize control of the castle and, hence, if the English merchants and Japanese mercenaries on Amboyna were innocent or guilty of the charges against them. After years of wrestling with these questions, we decided to try a different approach to the Amboyna case by turning it into an interactive classroom exercise designed to generate student engagement.

AMBOYNA ONLINE

Inspired by the public reaction to the groundbreaking podcast *Serial*, which had succeeded in drawing unprecedented attention to a previously obscure murder case, we decided to put the case online. We created a new digital humanities platform, the Amboyna Conspiracy Trial (www.amboyna.org) with the Roy Rosenzweig Center for History and New Media at George Mason University. (See fig. 5.1.)

At the center of the site, we placed an interactive trial engine called *What's Your Verdict* that presented the most compelling evidence offered by the Dutch East India Company, which we dubbed the prosecution, and their English opponents, the defense. To make a complex trial accessible, we boiled the case down to six key questions that have to be answered one way or the other in order to come to a verdict. For each question, the site presents the arguments mobilized by the prosecution and defense in conjunction with their most important pieces of evidence. As part of the process, we asked a distinguished London-based barrister to work through the material. Generously agreeing to waive his fees, he reviewed an extensive series of Amboyna files and then sat through hour after hour of filmed interviews, in which he guided students through the key questions any prospective juror would have to wrestle with. Finally, we created a large repository of additional material and documents related to the case.

The site went online in 2016 and since then thousands of visitors have worked their way through the trial engine, with the results all recorded in our database. Once the site was functioning properly, we combined it with a new trials-based exercise intended for the undergraduate classroom.

RESTAGING A HISTORICAL TRIAL

The mock trial exercise was staged initially with a second-year history class consisting of approximately a hundred students, who were divided into five tutorials of around twenty students each. We assigned individual roles to each

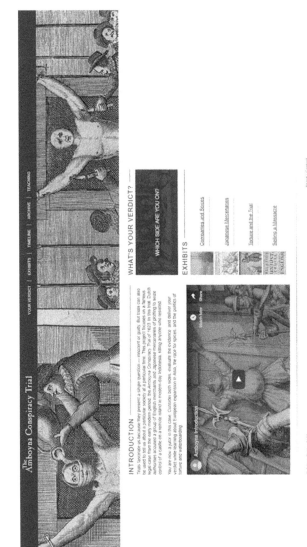

Figure 5.1. The Amboyna Conspiracy Trial website.

Table 5.1. Roles, Allocations, and Responsibilities for History Class Activity

Role	Allocations	Responsibilities
Attorney/Barrister	Three for prosecution	Prepare a briefing on key exhibits
	Three for defense	Interview witnesses during pretrial preparation
		Opening statements
		Examination and cross-examination of witnesses
		Closing statements
Researcher	Three for prosecution	Review and analyze evidence
	Three for defense	Prepare briefing papers for barristers
		Develop overall strategy
		Provide additional evidence and suggestions through the trial via notes
Witness	Two for prosecution	Research a specific historical character
	Two for defense	Work with either the prosecution or the defense
		Deliver testimony before the court and undergo questioning
Judge	Three to four total	Prepare for the trial, develop familiarity with the legal system of the period
		Keep order in the court, oversee barristers
		Ask questions of barristers and witnesses
		Deliver a verdict
		Prepare a written justification

of the students: three were judges, two were witnesses for the prosecution, two were witnesses for the defense, three were part of the legal team for the prosecution, three for the defense team, and the remaining students were assigned as researchers for the two sides. For the roles, allocations, and responsibilities, see table 5.1.

The mock trial exercise ran across three weeks. The first week was devoted to research and preparation as students started to work through the key materials.

During the second week, this process continued but the legal teams were also required to present oral arguments before the judges. These centered on a number of controversial exhibits including a legal justification of waterboarding prepared by a VOC official and an unverified note smuggled out from the original trial. The question before the judges was whether these exhibits, which significantly strengthened one of the two sides, should be admitted into the record. In this way, their inclusion or exclusion had the capacity to alter the overall course of the trial. In the third week, we staged the trial itself, which was divided into five stages: opening statements, witnesses for the prosecution, witnesses for the defense, closing statements, and verdict. When the trial concluded, the judges prepared a written statement explaining their verdict.

RESULTS

Although it required some initial explanation, the exercise proved highly successful. By tapping into students' competitive instincts, it generated a high level of engagement. Students who had previously been reluctant to look closely at weekly readings were willing to devote long hours outside the classroom to the case. Both the prosecution and the defense organized extensive meetings outside tutorial time to work through content, devise arguments, and prepare their legal strategies. This level of engagement extended across all four groups: researchers worked through all the documents on the website and then searched for further evidence; witnesses engaged deeply with their characters; legal teams prepared eloquent written statements and practiced their delivery; and the judges delved into the legal systems of the period and mastered the arcane rules regulating the use of torture in the seventeenth century. The overall experience proved enormously gratifying for us as instructors, and many students singled it out as the high point of the class.

IS IT REPLICABLE?

We believe this model can be easily replicated in a wide range of classroom settings. The Amboyna Conspiracy Trial started as a stand-alone website before we added a mock trial exercise. While the site is relatively sophisticated, it is also not strictly necessary for this exercise. On the most basic level, the trial exercise relies on a close reading of testimonies and legal documents. All that would be needed for the model to be replicated is a web page or even a simple online forum, such as Dropbox or a Google Drive folder, where a set of trial documents can be accessed. In our experience, the key is to place large amounts of information online but then to rely on students' competitive instincts to drive first independent investigation and then classroom discussion, hence making the most of limited time.

While the Amboyna trial exercise lends itself well to classes on the history of commodities or European expansion in Asia, there is no shortage of other trials with long paper trails that would serve equally well for a similar exercise. With relatively limited preparation, the Teaching with Trials model could be applied to diverse trials throughout history. Equally, there is no reason it could not be used for disciplines beyond history as the trial format could be applied to a wide range of subject material.

A review by Michael Prince of the literature on active learning reveals a consensus on the importance of interactive engagement and how it can improve student learning outcomes by facilitating a more hands-on learning experience.[2] As Richard Hake notes, interactive engagement is designed to "promote conceptual understanding through active engagement of students in heads-on (always) and hands-on (usually) activities which yield immediate feedback through discussion with peers and/or instructors."[3] Enabling student engagement requires teachers to create an environment in which there are repeated opportunities for students to interact both with their instructors and with their peers, all the time receiving continual feedback as they work through problems.[4] While the importance and value of the flipped classroom has long been noted, detailed studies have been confined mainly to the sciences, with far less research in the humanities.[5] As a result, there are fewer proven templates available for educators looking to flip the humanities classroom. We believe that the model sketched out in this chapter both is easily replicable and has multiple advantages. By using an accessible interdisciplinary approach that combines digital humanities with history and law, Teaching with Trials encourages active learning by students through ongoing collaboration with their peers while also promoting a deeper engagement with primary source materials. In particular, the model encourages students to engage in targeted research and develops their critical analysis skills by requiring them to closely examine a wide variety of sources in order to formulate a persuasive argument for their respective sides.

Our experiment with Teaching with Trials proved highly successful. Combining digital humanities platforms with the flipped classroom approach provides, we believe, an excellent means of engaging students and making the most of class time.

NOTES

1. Adam Clulow, *Amboina 1623: Conspiracy and Fear on the Edge of Empire* (New York: Columbia University Press, 2019).

2. Michael Prince, "Does Active Learning Work? A Review of the Research," *Journal of Engineering Education* 93, no. 3 (2004): 223–231.

3. Richard Hake, "Interactive-Engagement versus Traditional Methods: A Six-Thousand-Student Survey of Mechanics Test Data for Introductory Physics Courses," *American Journal of Physics* 66, no. 1 (1998): 64–74.

4. Todd Davis and Patricia Murrell, "A Structural Model of Perceived Academic, Personal and Vocational Gains Related to College Student Responsibility," *Research in Higher Education* 34, no. 3 (1993): 267–289.

5. For example, see Arthur Chickering and Zelda Gamson, "Seven Principles for Good Practice in Undergraduate Educations," *Biochemical Education* 17, no. 3 (1989): 140–141; Scott Freeman, Sarah Eddy, Miles McDonough, Michelle Smith, Nnadozie Okoroafor, Hannah Jordt, and Mary Pat Wenderoth, "Active Learning Increases Student Performance in Science, Engineering, and Mathematics," *Proceedings of the National Academy of the Sciences of the United States of America* 111, no. 23 (2014): 8410–8415; Edward Redish, Jeffery Saul, and Richard Steinberg, "On the Effectiveness of Active-Engagement Microcomputer-Based Laboratories," *American Journal of Physics* 65, no. 45 (1998): 45–54; Karl Smith, Sheri Shepard, David Johnson, and Roger Johnson, "Pedagogies of Engagement: Classroom-Based Practices," *Journal of Engineering Education* 94, no. 1 (2005): 87–101.

SIX

—⟨w⟩—

Corpus Visualization

High-Level Student Engagement on a Zero Budget

BRIAN KOKENSPARGER

Creighton University

WHILE PARTICIPATING IN THE EARLY Modern Digital Agendas (EMDA) 2015 institute at the Folger Shakespeare Library, I often spent my free time browsing the stacks.[1] Among a multitude of interesting rare books, I found a toy theater version of *Othello*.[2] Toy theater is a type of theatrical performance that was historically performed by juveniles and involved coloring and cutting out characters and scenery from a book to use when performing a provided script. I was immediately intrigued: How would a juvenile version of *Othello* deal with the "R-rated" racism, sex, and murder in one of Shakespeare's most intimately violent plays?

I read the toy theater and Folger Digital Online Text versions of the two scripts and decided to compare them.[3] What did Skelt leave in the toy theater version, and what did he take out? And how did he go about this task?

Figure 6.1 shows a small excerpt from the Skelt toy theater script for *Othello*.[4] It is the beginning of act 2, scene 2 in the Skelt script, and roughly covers act 1, scene 2 of the Folger Shakespeare Online version. The toy theater version roughly cuts some sixty-one spoken lines of the scene into nine lines, without (in my opinion) losing much of the flavor and dramatic purpose of the scene. In fact, the Skelt script in its entirety cuts the full version of the play into less than one-tenth of its size (in terms of spoken lines of text): 3,680

SCENE II.—No. 2.   *Another Street in Venice.*

Enter OTHELLO, pl. 2, IAGO, pl. 1, R. H.

Iago. Are you fast married, be sure of this, he will divorce you.

Oth. Let him do his spite, my services shall out tongue his complaints, for know Iago I love the gentle Desdemona. But look what lights come yonder.

Enter CASSIO, GIOVANNI, *and* LUCA, pl. 2, L. H.

Oth. The servants of the Duke, and my Lieutenant, what is the news.

Cas. The Duke requires your post haste appearance.

Oth. What is the matter.

Cas. Something from Cyprus.

Iago. Come Captain, will you go.

Oth. Have with you, stay, who have we here.

Iago. It is Brabantio.

Figure 6.1. A small excerpt from the Skelt toy theater version of *Othello*.

lines down to 317. But trying to balance two books and my notebook all at the same time to come to that conclusion was not easy. I found myself doing a large amount of transcription.

From my recent years of teaching college-level computer science and digital humanities courses, I was well aware that balancing a number of books and transcribing text were not activities that our current millennial students were even remotely interested in doing. I could barely get them to read a text; transcribing differences based on a tedious comparative analysis of two scripts in hard copy would have been an unpopular—if not impossible (for some)—assignment.

My go-to solution for this problem was to create an HTML5 and JavaScript web page tool to do all of the processing needed to visually compare the two scripts. My students could use this tool for the grunt work and then focus on analysis and conclusions—the activities most connected with my learning outcomes. Furthermore, why not have my advanced students make their own tools, to learn a skill that will provide a rich, flexible, and easy-to-use solution to any similar problem for them in the future? In either case, students who engaged themselves in the assignment were virtually guaranteed to learn about the subject matter—Shakespeare's *Othello*—simply by building and/or using the tool.

FROM DETACHED LABORERS TO SKILLED MAKERS

It is clear from the literature that experiential teaching methods improve learning in a number of ways.[5] However, experiential learning is expensive in terms of both time and money (for labs, equipment, consumables, etc.); college students expect it to happen in their courses, but university administrators are hesitant to pay for it. This dilemma calls for a low- or zero-budget solution, and HTML5 and JavaScript provide this solution with the additional benefit of a plethora of freely available tutorials and other resources.

HTML5 and JavaScript provide a learning lab environment with free browser software. All mainstream browsers on all popular OS platforms handle HTML5 and have native JavaScript interpreters, though some handle scripts more gracefully than others. Chances are that any device your students bring with them to the classroom will have fully functioning browsers that can handle any JavaScript problem that you throw at them. And because these interpreters are already installed, the software is not only free but requires no management and support from your end.

Faculty and students can learn JavaScript (especially as it interacts with HTML5) on numerous free tutorials on the internet. There are also inexpensive trade books for those students who may choose to be offline. Many of these are available for eAccess through school or public libraries.[6]

And although my area of work with students is in the digital humanities, any course or program that uses textual analysis as a major component of its student learning objectives can benefit from this assignment (or variations on it). Journalism (e.g., news stories, social media, blogs, transcriptions of talk radio), English literature and composition, modern language literature (as long as both versions of the text are of the same language and from the same era), and political science (speeches and debates) are just a few examples of programs that could benefit from using HTML5 and JavaScript to develop textual analysis or visualization tools. And, finally, developing the assignments for the classroom is not as difficult as you might think.

DEVELOPING AN HTML5/JAVASCRIPT LAB
FOR YOUR COURSE

Luckily, there are many online resources to help with the programming aspect of the assignment, so if you are not a coding wizard, you do not have to be. Do you know how to look up a specific task or problem on the web? Then that is all you need. What follows is a brief description of how I introduced and managed my HTML5/JavaScript project in the classroom.

It helps if the students already know a programming language—any programming language. Those students will know all the basic components and structures of programming, like creating and using variables, string functions, loops, conditional structures, and perhaps lists or arrays. For these students, all they need to know is the specific JavaScript syntax, which can be accessed through a trade book or online resource.

If students do not already know a programming language, it is not a deal breaker for the project. You will just have to scaffold a bit beforehand and give the students some basic introduction to working with HTML5 objects and JavaScript string manipulation. My experience with students is that, if they are motivated to learn something (and this project has the "cool" factor to provide plenty of that, I think), they will access online resources and learn what they need to learn "just in time." All you have to do is point them to safe, reliable resources and get out of their way.

When assigning a project like this one, students must start with "the stuff on the page." They cannot use HTML5 objects in your JavaScript code that do not yet exist in HTML code in the file. Urge them to look at their page designs and make sure everything shows up, and then encourage them to play with the objects to gain familiarity.

Next, they should add the JavaScript that does the work. Your approach can range from a description of what you want the students' scripts to do, followed by a "Now, go to it!" (for students who already know how to code, or for a second or third project in the semester class), to providing some base code and asking students to modify and augment it (for novice students or those in generally noncoding academic domains). It may very well be that you will have a classroom composed of both types of students; in those cases, I have found an "if you know what you are doing, go to it!" combined with an "if you don't know what to do, take this base code and watch me" seems to suit most needs for a classroom of mixed-skill students. Figure 6.2 shows a small excerpt of my approach at JavaScript code for solving a textCompare problem that we cover in the class.

In either case, it is of utmost importance to embrace creativity and let your own vision of the perfect tool go. This is not your tool. Look at it like an art teacher would: you would not be happy with students who simply copied your painting, would you? Do your own working version of the project before assigning it to your students, but keep it in your back pocket and let the students grow into their own versions.

```
var t2PrintList = [];
var t1PrintList = [];
var notFound = true;
var lastJ = 0;

alert("t1Tokens has " + t1Tokens.length + " and t2Tokens has " + t2Tokens.length);
for (var k=0;k<t1Tokens.length;k++){
    t1PrintList.push("\n"+k+"-"+t1Tokens[k]);
}
for (var i=0;i<t2Tokens.length;i++){
    for(var j=0;j<t1Tokens.length;j++){
        resp = simPhrases(t1Tokens[j],t2Tokens[i]);
        if(resp!=0){
            t2PrintList.push("\n"+j+"-"+resp+" ("+t2Tokens[i]+")");
            notFound = false;
            lastJ = j;
            continue;
        } // end if phrases are similar
    } // end for each line in large text box
    if(notFound==true){
        t2PrintList.push("\n"+(lastJ+1)+"-not found: ("+t2Tokens[i]+")");
        lastJ++;
    }
    notFound=true;
} //end for each line in small text box
```

Figure 6.2. Example of JavaScript code for the textCompare problem.

Next, display and gently critique exemplary student work during class. The ones who "got it" (and, therefore, whose works you choose to display) will be thrilled. The students who struggled will see that someone like them really can do this. If a member of the class has touted herself or himself as particularly adept at coding from the start, displaying and critiquing that student's work will be less helpful. It is better to choose the students with hidden talents that have blossomed during the class, as a kind of *EveryStudent*.

Figure 6.3 shows an example of JavaScript written by students for an interactive information form that generates new combo boxes based on user selections. Each student group was given an information knowledge base to model that would provide users with customized information based on their entered preferences. The JavaScript code in figure 6.3 was written early in the semester in a web programming course by a group of students who had already taken an introductory programming course but who otherwise had little prior experience with writing JavaScript code.

```
<title>EDGE Learning Communities</title>
<link rel="stylesheet" href="Assign2(2).css">
<script type="text/javascript">

function schoolYr(){

  if (document.getElementById('schoolYrChoice').value=="Freshman"){
      document.getElementById('outputDiv1').innerHTML =
      "<h4>Pre-Health Information Community:</h4><li>Students subscribe to online pre-health information for academic year.</li>";
      document.getElementById('outputDiv2').innerHTML =
      "<h4>Pre-Law Information Community:</h4><li>Students subscribe to online pre-law information for academic year.</li>";
      document.getElementById('outputDiv3').innerHTML =
      "<h4>Pre-Pharmacy Seminar (PRX 200)</h4><li>Friday 3:30-5:30 p.m. Rigge Science 120</li><li>PRX 200 - CRN: 5</li>";
      document.getElementById('outputDiv4').innerHTML =
      "";
      document.getElementById('outputDiv5').innerHTML =
      "";
      document.getElementById('outputDiv6').innerHTML =
      "";

  }

  if (document.getElementById('schoolYrChoice').value=="Sophomore"){
      document.getElementById('outputDiv1').innerHTML =
      "<h4>Pre-Health Seminar (PHLC 200)</h4><li>Sophomores interested in health careers. Friday 3:30-5:30 p.m. Rigge Science
120</li><li>PHLC 200 - CRN: 6</li>";
      document.getElementById('outputDiv2').innerHTML =
```

Figure 6.3. Example of student JavaScript code.

Finally, give them someplace to go from there. HTML5 and JavaScript are there for the taking. Literally, if students can figure out how to solve a problem in their heads, they can program a computer to solve the problem. It is important to help them realize that HTML5 and JavaScript are freely available to them at any time, in any place (even those places that do not have internet access), so how and when they engage problems on their own is totally up to them.

Figure 6.4 depicts the textCompare tool that I created to compare the Skelt and Folger versions of the *Othello* play.[7] Though it could stand some further refinement, it succeeded in allowing me (and my students) to compare, side by side, the two scripts and determine that Skelt used a strategy of erasure—starting with the full script and "erasing" large parts—to reduce the full *Othello* play down to a toy theater play that could be performed in under an hour. This determination would have been quite difficult to make while going back and forth between two hard copy scripts.

In cases where the students have few or no programming skills—and are reluctant to acquire them—you may have to provide your version of the tool for the students and just skip to the analysis part. This is sometimes necessary, because it assures you that every student will have adequate data to investigate in analysis. However, this approach perpetuates the computer programming as "magic" myth. In that scenario, students throw in text from two different sources, and "Abracabra!" a comparative visualization appears. How will they

Text Compare Tool

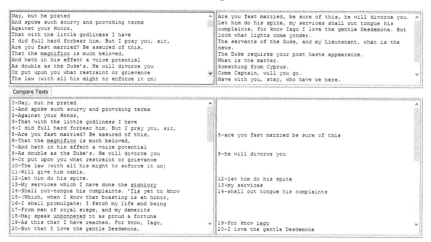

Figure 6.4. The working textCompare tool showing output.

truly be able to analyze the data unless they have at least a fundamental idea of how they were generated?

I have also used HTML5 and JavaScript tools to visualize linguistic complexity in Shakespeare's works and to classify genre-rich words among dramatic and fictional versions of Shakespeare's *Othello*. In addition to textarea and text objects, the canvas object (provided in HTML5) is a powerful tool that deserves more attention than I can provide here for its graphic display capabilities. Figure 6.5 is an example of a more complex tool using both the HTML5 document.getElementById attribute and canvas object for web pages. I developed this script during the EMDA 2015 institute at the Folger Shakespeare Library.

And this brings us to the most exciting part of using HTML5 and JavaScript in the classroom: students can use it to answer their own questions about literature (or any of the text-focused areas suggested above). Once they know how to get text into the tool, how to use textboxes or the coveted canvas object to get results out, and a few string processing methods, there is an immense amount of analysis that they can do entirely on their own!

If you need to assess your students, it is best to assess their analysis of the data provided by the tool. If you have two sections of the same course, try using this project in one section and have students do the book balancing and hand transcription assignment in the other. My bet is that those doing the coding

Linguistic Complexity Analysis Tool--Othello

Figure 6.5. Linguistic complexity visualization of *Othello*.

project will produce better analyses of the text and will have higher familiarity with the texts than those who simply compare the print copies and transcribe. I have not been able to gather assessment data to support this hypothesis, as I teach programming courses that require a programming approach, even in a digital humanities framework.

As a low-cost way to allow students to create their own tools to answer their own questions about their own text-based areas of interest, HTML5 and JavaScript cannot be beat in terms of their ubiquity, flexibility, and ease of use. Experiential learning on a zero budget is the direction to go in any text analysis–based course.

NOTES

1. I was accepted into and attended the "Early Modern Digital Agendas: Advanced Topics" institute at the Folger Shakespeare Library in 2015 through a National Endowment for the Humanities grant.

2. M&B Skelt, *Skelt's Characters and Scenes in Othello* (London: Theatrical Warehouse, 1823).

3. William Shakespeare, *The Tragedy of Othello, the Moor of Venice*, Folger Digital Online Texts, accessed (and downloaded) May 27, 2017, http://www.folgerdigitaltexts.org/?chapter=5&play=Oth&loc=p7.

4. Skelt, 6.

5. Educational scholarly research has produced a huge volume of scholarly support for experiential learning, beginning with Arthur Chickering's seminal

work on the method. See, Arthur W. Chickering, *Experience and Learning* (New York: Change Magazine, 1977). However, there is some recent discussion that current English literature teachers are not commonly using experiential methods to teach Shakespeare, as evidenced in Barrie Wade and John Sheppard, "How Teachers Teach Shakespeare," *Educational Review* 46, no. 1 (January 1, 1994): 21–28.

6. For example, my public library in Omaha, Nebraska, accessed May 7, 2018, https://omaha.bibliocommons.com/v2/search?query=JavaScript&searchTyp e=smart, showed thirty "Website or Online Data" sources, when I searched for JavaScript after logging on as a registered user.

7. Folger Shakespeare Library, stacks.

SEVEN

—ᴡᴡ—

Metadata in the Classroom

Fostering an Understanding of the Value of
Metadata in Digital Humanities

LISA M. McFALL

Hamilton College

DIGITAL HUMANITIES PROJECTS REQUIRE WIDE-RANGING skill sets and awareness of many tools and resources, including the Text Encoding Initiative (TEI), digitization practices, geographic information systems (GIS), data visualization, and metadata. While digital humanities projects are usually produced by the combined effort of a number of experts in these fields, it is still imperative to introduce those new to digital humanities to a broad overview of many of these topics so that they are aware of the role these resources play in digital humanities and how these tools can be used to benefit their projects.[1]

Metadata is a crucial part of digital humanities because it provides a way of accessing and organizing data. Metadata provides key terms and phrases for finding digital objects, ranging from newspaper articles and essays to interviews, photographs, and videos. Adding metadata allows objects in a repository to be findable and improves their discoverability. It can be used to supplement full-text searching and adds value by correcting misspellings, supplementing abbreviations so that they are searchable, and adding alternate spellings to facilitate searching.[2] Therefore, metadata is the foundation of the work that is done by scholars, allowing for the careful description of objects in ways that support new connections between objects and the analysis of items within a collection.

A basic understanding of metadata should be taught in all classes that are focused on developing skills in digital humanities in order to instill an early understanding of both the importance of metadata and the general principles of how to create metadata. In the past, metadata has been viewed primarily as librarians' work; however, developing skills in metadata will allow those embarking on a journey into digital humanities to develop a deeper understanding of their data. The usefulness of this information literacy extends beyond digital humanities into the broader topic of digital scholarship. Developing a clear understanding of metadata while having the opportunity to create metadata is crucial to the development of a foundation for digital humanities scholars at all levels.

The following is a general suggested approach for a one-shot metadata-centric session in a digital humanities class. It may be adapted for use by librarians and professors who are seeking to educate students on how metadata is an important part of the digital humanities research that is being done, regardless of topical areas. This grounding of the discussion of metadata into the larger context of digital humanities will allow students to develop more comprehensive insights into the digital humanities projects they have reviewed in class, providing them with the ability to see the role that metadata plays in digital humanities projects.

SETTING THE STAGE

It is imperative to set the stage for a discussion about metadata with undergraduate students who are enrolled in an introduction to digital humanities course. Students may be intimidated upon first hearing that they will be working with metadata. While students may know the basic definition of metadata (i.e., "data about data"), this definition is insufficient because the word *data* can be vague to those who are new to the field of information. Instead, starting with what is familiar when introducing the topic to them, and using scaffolding to help them build from what they know to the unknown, will more quickly gain their interest.

There are several ways to accomplish this. One way that is frequently successful as an initial overture toward making them feel more comfortable is to try incorporating an example of the everyday organization of information using metadata that they create, and organize by, without even realizing it. One favorite question to pose is, "How do you organize your closet?" There are numerous ways of doing this (e.g., by color, by type of clothing item, by season, by style, by outfit, as well as by some combination of these), and getting students to realize that they are already working with and organizing objects using metadata is an eye-opening experience for many of them.

Another example that gets students thinking about metadata and how it exists in different forms depending on the object is an example involving cookie cutters. To start the discussion, a photograph of a dozen or so cookie cutters in various shapes, sizes, and colors is shown. The students are then presented with the discussion prompt of how they might organize them. Some possibilities include by color, by season (e.g., Christmas cookie cutters, Valentine's Day cookie cutters), by size, and by type (e.g., depicting living animals, depicting humans, inanimate objects). This can also be done by dividing students into groups and having them physically manipulate the cookie cutters, which is especially useful for students who are tactile learners. These fun examples of organizing show students that creating metadata is not as intimidating as it might initially seem.

PRINCIPLES OF METADATA

Once the seed has been planted that students are already using metadata in their daily lives and that organizing information is the principle behind the creation of metadata, defining information is a good next step. One definition of information is the communication or reception of knowledge that exists in the mind of someone who understands the subject matter.[3] Using a definition such as this can lead to a discussion that information has characteristics (e.g., size, creator, title) and those characteristics can be used to organize the various pieces of information about an object. These characteristics are then used to build a metadata schema.

Metadata is used to describe objects and to build relationships between objects. The cartoon by John Norris is a perfect example of the benefits of using metadata. (See fig. 7.1.) The top panel of this cartoon shows a user looking through an interface at objects that are filed into folders in drawers. The user is forced to look through these drawers to try to find the desired item, with the user having to select a single drawer for an item that has the ability to fit into two different drawers or that perhaps does not match any of the drawers available. This process is an inefficient method that leads to user frustration at not easily finding the desired item(s).

The bottom panel of the cartoon illustrates the difference when metadata is used for organizing objects. Instead of hunting through folders for objects that can only live in one place, the user quickly locates relevant items because the metadata brings together related items no matter where they are stored.

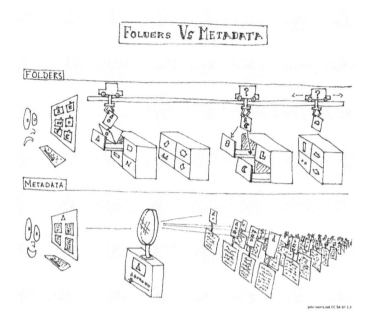

Figure 7.1. John Norris, Folders vs. Metadata, https://www.flickr.com/photos /john-norris/5865469840. Used under the Creative Commons Attribution-ShareAlike 2.0 Generic license. J. Norris, 2011, "Folders vs. Metadata—Document Organization," accessed June 22, 2018, http://john-norris.net/2011/06/23/document -organization-folders-vs-metadata/.

Combining the earlier closet and cookie cutter organizational discussions with the cartoon's illustrations allows the students to think about metadata through a more familiar lens and draws upon their personal experiences organizing information without realizing that they were already working with metadata.

TRADITIONAL METADATA EXAMPLES

Because the students are now comfortable with the idea of metadata, it is now possible to start looking at some of the more traditional uses and applications of metadata, such as in the library catalog and databases that students may frequently use. By teasing apart a record in the local library catalog to show the various pieces of metadata that describe the item (e.g., title, author name in a specific format, date), they have an opportunity to see metadata in action. This can then be expanded on to show how metadata is used to build relationships among objects and make comparisons. There are books that share an author, multiple resources about the same subject, materials that are published by the same publisher in the same year, and so on. The idea of making these connections to build a collection of related material ties directly into the idea of collection building in digital humanities. The library catalog example can also lead to a discussion with students about creating metadata with an eye toward other people using it.

Timothy W. Cole highlights what makes "good" metadata that helps students think about how to build metadata for collections. In Cole's words:

- "Good metadata should be appropriate to the materials in the collection, users of the collection, and intended, current and likely users of the digital object.
- Good metadata supports interoperability.
- Good metadata uses standard controlled vocabularies to reflect the what, where, when and who of the content.
- Good metadata includes a clear statement on the conditions and terms of use for the digital object.
- Good metadata records are objects themselves and therefore should have the qualities of good objects, including archivability, persistence, unique identification, etc. Good metadata should be authoritative and verifiable.
- Good metadata supports the long-term management of objects in collections."[4]

CREATING METADATA

The final portion of a session on metadata and digital humanities focuses on hands-on practice creating metadata for a series of objects. It is beneficial to discuss with the professor any class projects that are already built into the course to see if there is a way to create an in-class metadata lab that helps support another project. If there is not one available, designing a project that presents the students with a set of objects that have some relationship to one another, along with a list of metadata fields to use to describe each object, is a good way to contain the exercise so that students do not need to spend the time trying to locate objects to build a collection.

One way to accomplish this task is to select a popular song and locate related items. Possible examples for the minicollection that is presented for metadata creation include a CD containing the original version of the song by the original performer, the original music video by the original performer on YouTube, the sheet music for the song, a cover of the song on YouTube as performed by another artist, and a mash-up (i.e., a song containing the piece mixed with another piece in a unique way). Students then decide on the metadata, such as a title, who the primary people are involved in the piece, what type of file it is, who the publisher is, keywords/tags that can be used to describe the item, and what relationships this item has to the other items in the collection.

After some time working through this exercise, the group comes back together to discuss the decisions they made in creating the metadata. This process of practicing building metadata gives students a chance to work with objects, to think about how to describe them in a way that is useful to other people, and to understand how the creation of metadata is a subjective and valuable contribution to digital humanities projects.

CONCLUSIONS

Metadata is not a subject that has traditionally been taught in classrooms as part of the typical set of skills students learn; however, developing a skill set with metadata is valuable for undergraduate and graduate students, particularly those who are becoming active in the field of digital humanities. Introducing students to metadata will enable them to develop a firmer grounding in an understanding of how archives and collections are organized and findable through metadata. Certain students may even develop an interest in becoming involved in creating metadata for an active digital humanities project after this initial overview session. With a carefully guided approach that provides scaffolding to introduce students to metadata in familiar contexts through creating metadata for a preselected set of items, students can learn the value of metadata and develop a deeper understanding of the role it plays in digital humanities.

NOTES

1. Anne Burdick, Johanna Drucker, Peter Lunenfeld, Todd Presner, and Jeffrey Schnapp, *Digital Humanities* (Cambridge, MA: MIT Press, 2012).

2. Sheila Bair and Sharon Carlson, "Where Keywords Fail: Using Metadata to Facilitate Digital Humanities Scholarship," *Journal of Library Metadata* 8, no. 3 (2008): 249–262.

3. Daniel Joudrey, Arlene Taylor, and Katherine Wisser, *The Organization of Information*, 4th ed. (Santa Barbara, CA: Libraries Unlimited, 2017).

4. Timothy W. Cole, "Creating a Framework of Guidance for Building Good Digital Collections." *First Monday* 7, nos. 5–6 (2002).

EIGHT

Teaching the Philosophy of Computing Using the Raspberry Pi

MARY ANGELEC COOKSEY

Indiana University East

According to *ResourceEd*, "32% of educators are using technology to bring experts or experiences into the classroom virtually."[1]

CENTRAL TO THE CHALLENGE OF all forms of university teaching is bringing student learning to life. In the past, the tools provided to instructors with which to confront this challenge were limited. The blackboard, the whiteboard, the PowerPoint presentation—these were the staples that made up the tool kit, and this was especially true for disciplines like the humanities, and within the humanities, for subjects like philosophy. Of late, however, the tool kit of the philosophy teacher has become enlarged by more expansive and impactful teaching technologies. One such example is the creation of the Raspberry Pi kit, a low-priced set of components with which to build a computer, the act of which may hold great power to positively impact the teaching of courses like the Philosophy of Computing and the Ethics of Information and Privacy.

The hypothesis is that, in the end, much will be gleaned about the Philosophy of Computing from the student having the hands-on experience of building her own computer. Put another way, learning how the resistors and capacitors electronically create the virtual platform that makes the human communication of information—or disinformation—possible, greatly informs learning

54

about the metaphysical, epistemological, and ethical ideas that drive ideation and behavior online ... all made possible by the Raspberry Pi and using it as a teaching tool within the pedagogy of backward design.

One of the best characterizations of backward design is that put forth by Ruth Mitchell and Marilyn Willis in their work, *Learning in Overdrive: Designing Curriculum, Instruction, and Assessment from Standards,* originally published in 1995. In the introduction to a section of the book titled "Step Six: Mapping Backward from the Culminating Task to the Learning Sections," the authors invite the reader to imagine Christmas "in a little shack way out West—the kids snuggled together in the cold, crisp evening, dreaming of a sugarplum morning." They continue by pointing out that stories about these children and these holidays always include an orange or a tangerine being found in Christmas stockings the next day. The authors then pose the question: Can you imagine how complicated it was to move an orange tree all the way to Kansas in 1869? With that inquiry, the heart and soul of backward design is exposed ... and the structure of its architecture made accessible to be fully understood.[2]

First appearing in educational literature in the mid-twentieth century as the "mapping backward" strategy referenced in the paragraph above, backward design as a curricular design model is most generally attributed to the duo of Grant Wiggins and Jay McTighe. In their landmark publication *Understanding by Design,* originally published in 1998, Wiggins and McTighe define backward design as an approach to curricular design as "purposeful task analysis." They continue by noting that the logic of backward design "suggests a planning sequence for curriculum which has three stages: identification of desired results, the determination of acceptable evidence, and the planning of learning experiences and instruction."[3] Filtered through the lens and language of curriculum design, these steps have come to mean that quality course design begins with the determination of learning outcomes, settling on assessment strategies that will most effectively measure the attainment of those outcomes, and then making decisions about course content, learning activities, and signature assignments that will be most effective in connecting the dots for students.[4]

This process of beginning course design by "imagining when a course is over ... then asking: what is it I hope that students will have learned, that will still be there and have value several years after the course is over?" is a design model that may seem counterintuitive, but which has, in the end, proven to be highly effective in producing the desired results of increased student learning.[5] In fact, for Fink and many others, backward design is the backbone of creating the most significant learning experiences for students.

In the case of the digital humanities, backward design is especially significant as its application can lead to a transparency in teaching that can strongly support the most desirable of end goals—student attainment. In the case of the Philosophy of Computing, backward design becomes initiated by beginning with the premise of the utility of having students gain knowledge of hardware and software operation through interacting with all of the components and processes of the Raspberry Pi.

The Raspberry Pi, created by Eben Upton, is a credit card–sized computer originally designed for education, inspired by the 1981 BBC Micro. Upton's goal was to create a low-cost device that would improve programming skills and hardware understanding at the preuniversity level.[6]

The story of the Raspberry Pi actually began in 2006 when Upton and other faculty members at the University of Cambridge in Britain found that their incoming computer science students were ill-prepared for a high-tech education. While many students in the previous decade were experienced electronics hobbyists by the time they got to college, these freshmen were little more than skilled Web designers. A part of the reason for this was that easy to use, modern PCs hid most of the nuts and bolts behind a pleasing interface. So students were skillful navigators of applications but needed more experience with the architectural dimensions of what made those applications work.[7]

The Raspberry Pi—about 3 inches by 2 inches and less than an inch high— was intended to replace the expensive computers in school science labs. For less than the price of a new keyboard, a teacher could plug in the Pi and connect it to older peripherals that might be lying around. But because Pi initially ran only Linux, a free operating system popular with programmers and hobbyists, students would have a learning curve. Now, however, the Raspberry Pi foundation is pushing out a second version of the Pi that hopefully will be more accessible.[8] (See fig. 8.1.)

In part, what makes this tool so accessible to so many grade levels and disciplines is its "basic nature." The simplicity of the Raspberry Pi makes it easy to get started, helping students use basic digital, analog, and electromechanical components and instilling an awareness of simple programming concepts. The Raspberry Pi strips computing back to its basic elements. This "stripping down" is perfect from a pedagogical standpoint as well. In a course like the Philosophy of Computing, teachers want students to see what is going on with computing at its most basic level. When it comes to the educational benefits of the Raspberry Pi, it is not always just about the code.

By its very construction, the Raspberry Pi helps instill computational thinking and skills such as decomposition, pattern recognition, logical

Figure 8.1. Raspberry Pi 4 model b—side. Photo credit: Michael Henzler, accessed September 13, 2018, https:// commons.wikimedia.org /wiki/File:Raspberry_Pi _4_Model_B_-_Side .jpg(CC BY-SA 4.0).

thinking, reasoning, and problem-solving. These are the very skills most employed by those who unethically infiltrate systems and commit cyber-crimes. By learning more about these skills and how they combine with the hardware and software that make computers work, philosophy students will become far better equipped to understand the nature of these crimes, as well as the skill sets and work of those who perpetrate them.[9]

In order for the experience building their own computer using the Rasp-berry Pi kit to be as rich as possible, students need the freedom to experiment, hack, and collaborate. An instructor might explore a pedagogy like group work to support this freedom to create and to collaborate. Classroom layout is also important, and groups should be encouraged to work in spaces designed to promote collaborative learning and the sharing of ideas. Instructors might cre-ate collaborative teams that are well matched in skill level so that no student is left out. Rotating roles could also be given to students on a project-by-project basis (e.g., coder, builder, project manager, quality assurance, and others).[10]

In previous semesters of teaching the Philosophy of Computing, hands-on experiences have taken the form of assigning students "web quests," wherein they would be given sets of conditions to locate on websites in illustration of certain virtual attributes of good and bad moral representation or ethical positioning. Other times, these hands-on experiences took the form of asking for students' responses to case studies wherein real-life conditions would be described as variables for consideration in applying traditional or classic moral decision-making models to embedded, ethical problems. Simulation was as close as we could get to immersing students in the virtual world of cybercrime, hacking, and negative social influence. With the introduction of the Raspberry Pi within the pedagogy of backward design, the hope is that the richness of the immersion in "business" of the Philosophy of Computing will be to amplify learning and, in turn, enlarge and positively impact the student experience.

NOTES

1. "How Teachers Are Already Using Raspberry Pi in the Classroom," The State of Technology in Education: 2016, accessed September 13, 2018, https://resourced.prometheanworld.com/education-technology-report-2016.

2. R. Mitchell and M. Willis, *Learning in Overdrive: Designing Curriculum, Instruction, and Assessment from Standards: A Manual for Teachers* (Golden, CO: North American, 2003), 66.

3. G. P. Wiggins and J. McTighe, *Understanding by Design* (Alexandria, VA: Association for Supervision and Curriculum Development, 2003), 16–17.

4. L. D. Fink, *Creating Significant Learning Experiences: An Integrated Approach to Designing College Courses* (San Francisco, CA: Jossey-Bass, 2003), 63.

5. Ibid., 64.

6. John Biggs, "Personal Tech Toolkit: A Tiny Computer Attracts a Million Tinkerers," last modified September 30, 2013, accessed September 13, 2018.

7. Ibid.

8. Ibid.

9. "How Teachers Are Already Using Raspberry Pi in the Classroom."

10. Ibid.

NINE

—⚏—

Teaching Digital Humanities with TimelineJS

ROBERT VOSS

Northwest Missouri State University

TEACHING WITH DIGITAL HUMANITIES (DH) provides many opportunities for students and instructors to interact with new material in novel ways. One of the most consistent and transformative methods of teaching with DH is utilizing the TimelineJS product from Knight Labs at Northwestern University.[1] Teaching with DH includes both accessing material that has been digitized and encouraging students to create humanities projects that are digital in nature. TimelineJS is flexible enough to be used by both novice and expert digital humanists.

TimelineJS offers an intuitive method of interacting with historical information that can be either simplified for new students and introductory methods or made complex for advanced students. TimelineJS is a tool for creating visually rich, interactive timelines. The tool offers ways to create and embed timelines into a website or simply to view the timeline through the application. The interface is very straightforward, yet the ways of using the program in teaching can be as simple or as complex as the instructor would prefer.

Developing interest in DH often requires an exploratory experience. TimelineJS is perfect for this type of project. TimelineJS uses Google Sheets for data input. Since Google Sheets is collaborative, student groups or even the entire class can contribute to a single timeline. The timeline does not need to be published online or have a long life; it can serve a simple purpose of introduction to the process of DH work.

Formatting humanities lessons with TimelineJS depends on the instructor's focus. TimelineJS is most effective in a teaching environment when the students have a predetermined set of information and a restricted focus for their work. Rather than just telling students to "make a timeline," it is valuable to set parameters on what they should be doing. Teaching students the various components of the project before introducing the project is best. For example, each timeline entry needs to have a descriptive title, a clever subtitle, and an informative short paragraph of information. Students should understand that the best entries have been edited and reviewed by as many people as possible but also know that only a few people may actually review entries. Professors should not be the only reviewers. Students should review each other's work.

Constricting a research set of information is also valuable when teaching with TimelineJS. Using a database for information can assist in the restrictions. Using Umbra Search (umbrasearch.org) for African American history, for example, provides a wide set of information that has been curated by multiple archivists.[2] Umbra also yields over nine hundred thousand items to search within. A predetermined set of information allows students to spend their efforts on their projects, not on researching.

Teaching with DH also helps students understand how the public interacts with our work. Students creating a timeline should keep it under twenty entries to maintain a reader's focus. Similarly, if students understand that timelines tell stories, they should attempt to develop a story arc with a strong chronological narrative. Stories that jump around or are unrelated are not as strong as those with a larger narrative.

This is also where students can get the most out of a project. A story being told using TimelineJS should not just include major events; rather, the focus should be on those occurrences that led to the major events. That is, students should research and determine those smaller events that led to the major events. As part of the story arc, this allows readers to have a better connection to the material and a better understanding of the topic.

The process of actually creating the timeline digitally is very straightforward. First, the student builds a new Google Sheet using the provided template.[3] Using the template, the student fills in the appropriate columns such as begin date, end date, headline, body text, media, and other columns. After filling in material, the student selects "publish to the web" under the file menu. Copy the URL for the timeline from the browser's address bar. The student then copies and pastes the spreadsheet URL into the text box on the project's website (timeline.knightlab.com/#). The result is either a link directly to the timeline or an embed code to paste on your site where you want your timeline to appear.

The timeline content remains editable. Students can continue to manipulate their content after the timeline is published. The formatting is not alterable after publication, so it is important to make design decisions early since they are permanent.

For advanced users, the entire project is open source. An open source DH project reveals the source code so others can change it, if so desired. Many of us do not have the technical expertise to change the code, but since TimelineJS is so robust, little needs to be changed for the simplest project to be easily usable.

The TimelineJS tool was designed with a focus on a single user. There is no practical restriction on a single user working on a timeline so it may be used for group work or class projects.

Teaching with DH can be exhilarating and extremely useful for students and teachers alike. Students get hands-on experience with a digital tool in TimelineJS while also having the opportunity to show off their work to others. For instructors, they are able to demonstrate to others what is happening in their class rather than just sharing student papers. The collaborative nature of DH projects shines brightly when we teach with DH.

NOTES

1. "TimelineJS," TimelineJS, accessed February 18, 2020, http://timeline .knightlab.com.

2. "Umbra Search," Umbra Search, accessed February 18, 2020, https:// umbrasearch.org.

3. "Google Sheets," Google Sheets, accessed February 18, 2020, https://www .google.com/sheets/about/.

Authentic Instruction through Blogging

Increasing Student Engagement with Digital Humanities

KATHERINE WILLS

Indiana University-Purdue University Columbus

ROBIN D. FRITZ

Indiana University-Purdue University Columbus

The digital humanities today is about a scholarship (and a pedagogy) that is publicly visible in ways to which we are generally unaccustomed, a scholarship and pedagogy that are bound up with infrastructure in ways that are deeper and more explicit than we are generally accustomed to, a scholarship and pedagogy that are collaborative and depend on networks of people and that live an active 24/7 life online.

Matthew Kirschenbaum, "What Is Digital Humanities and What Is It Doing in English Departments?"[1]

CONTEXT

When James Hutton polished off the final edits of his life's treatise, *A Theory of the Earth with Proofs and Illustrations*, in 1795, his channels for dissemination were few and far between compared to those available to today's researchers. Had he had access to a blog or a website, perhaps his essential—but poorly written—understanding of plate tectonics would not have languished for another twenty years until his death, after which his assistant, John Playfair, believed he was finally free to craft his own latter-day SparkNotes version, ushering in our modern-day study of geography. One wonders if a few harsh tweets from Hutton's university rivals and a negative review on Reddit may have sped up the process.

But Hutton had few options, and his primary channel—essentially textbooks—lacked the widespread immediacy available today. Still, while writers, researchers, critics, students, and faculty now have access to easily disseminated means of communication, the ability to comprehend and be understood, much as it was in Hutton's day, is never a guarantee.

Thus, as viewed from sixty thousand feet, instructing students in the art of professional communication still requires sharing, organizing, and translating information and meaning, but as we faculty drill down into the drop zone of different courses and their specific objectives, it becomes necessary to add flexibility across channels, including digital channels, to that spectrum.

One such channel adapted into professional communication courses at Indiana University's Columbus campus with various degrees of success is a student-written course blog. On its surface, the assignment objectives are simple:

- Reinforce each lecture's subject with student-researched content that adds a practical perspective or shares a relevant example;
- Supplement and expand students' understanding of key issues affecting their ability to communicate effectively;
- Provide students with a platform for self-expression on a topic of interest to them;
- Instruct students in the art of writing short, but captivating, content;
- Practice presentation skills as each student leads a brief, in-class discussion, with Q&A, on his or her post; and
- Offer students creative opportunities to earn extra credit.

At its core, however, an additional value from a student-written course blog derives from elements that were not anticipated when the blog assignment was first introduced in 2011, including:

- The opportunity to reach and interact with a global audience, offering access to diverse cultures, viewpoints, and perspectives;
- An assignment with an authenticity and legitimacy that appeals to students, especially those who are millennials and from Generation Z;
- A desire on the part of students to revisit and revise their work, post publication, as a response to public interaction, peer feedback, etc.; and

- Pride in their work resulting from public visibility as well as competitiveness over comments received and views earned.

Today's W231 site began as a blog/website/space for communication and writing for students to explore workplace-oriented communication by using social media formats accessible to external audiences (https://x204project.blog/about/). The writing blog supports icons linking to Twitter, Facebook, and LinkedIn. Its posts can be *liked* by readers who choose to show appreciation for individual offerings. The flow of ideas is reflected in the changing topics from 2011's genres of writing to 2018's evolution of issues, including "Fake News."

APPLICATION

In terms of implementing the assignment, the framework remains constant semester to semester, but the application of it varies. Prior to the start of each semester, relevant communication trends and issues are researched, news sites are scanned for current events focusing on communication-driven conflict, and examples of epic successes and failures, whether they be presidential call-ins to Fox News or celebrity tweets that tank a company's stock, are sought out for student-led exploration.

Next, a spreadsheet of potential topics that coincide with intended lecture content is prepared. For instance, if the objective for the week is instructing students on how to effectively share negative information, one topic may ask a student to analyze Kylie Jenner's February 2018 tweet and its disastrous $1.3 billion impact on Snapchat. Yet another week, as students are instructed in the process of writing to persuade—gain attention, build interest, reduce resistance, and motivate action—another topic may require a student to break down the official movie trailer for Al Gore's documentary *An Inconvenient Truth*, as an example. And, if the topic is how to communicate as part of a team (as group projects are a regular component of many IUPUC courses), one student may discuss the differences between good conflict and bad conflict by means of an episode of *Survivor* while another student may compare and contrast leadership styles of different boat captains on *Deadliest Catch* (see fig. 10.1).

On the first day of each semester, students are presented with a handout detailing technical instructions on how to access the course blog and upload their individual posts as well as a wide-ranging list of potential topics and due dates for each. Potential topics always outnumber students, hence the extra credit opportunities, and each lecture may coincide with multiple ideas. Students are then allowed to choose their topics on a first-come basis and are also

W231 - Professional Writing

SOCIAL MEDIA/BLOG PROJECT

TOPICS

The following is a list of topics and pre-assigned due dates. Students may also submit other relevant topics for consideration. See me for more detail regarding any of the following topics:

Topic	Due
Compare and contrast how men and women communicate differently. Discuss the pros and cons of their different communication styles. Do so without bias towards your own sex and provide examples.	1/25
What is a "spoken-word" performance? Identify a "spoken-word" artist and relate what this individual does in terms of communication.	1/25
Can words change human behavior? Reflect on how words and communication affect us and those around us, both positively and negatively. Use examples.	2/1
Research, analyze, and discuss the Baby Boomer generation. How has their collective life experience impacted how they communicate, act, and react, especially with regard to technology?	2/1
Pick a well-known individual (actor, celebrity, sports figure, politician, etc.) Analyze this individual's frame of reference. How do you think this person's frame of reference impacts his or her actions? How does it impact how this individual communicates? Provide examples from his or her life which back up your analysis.	2/8
Compare and contrast net neutrality. What are the pros and cons with regard to online communication? Provide examples.	2/8
Research, analyze, and discuss the Millennial generation. How has their collective life experience impacted how they communicate, act, and react, especially with regard to technology?	2/15
Discuss the importance of listening and outline how individuals can improve their listening abilities.	2/15
Discuss how miscommunication can cause instances of malpractice in the medical field. Identify an example and walk through what happened and how it could have been avoided.	2/22
What is fake news? How can readers identify it? Where can readers go for real news that isn't biased?	2/22

Figure 10.1. Partial list of potential post topics for the blog from the spring 2018 semester.

afforded the opportunity to suggest their own topic ideas, pending approval and assigned due dates.

By week two, class conversations are focused on actively discussing how effective communication works—and fails—and students are knee-deep in writing that culminates in instruction on how to apply communication to a blog post. By week three of the semester, their first posts go live, and each class begins with short student presentations on their topics. After receiving feedback, students then revise their posts online.

When introducing such an assignment, however, one should first note the distinction between digital humanities (as applied here, an overarching intersection of ideas and their study/expression/application via digital outlets) and technology (as applied to communication courses at IUPUC, computing channels and tools that enhance course content rather than the actual science of creating such tools). For example, in their article, "To Podcast or Not to Podcast," Mark Urtel and Eugenia Fernandez do not dwell on the physical development of podcasting technology itself but rather on the creation and effective application of podcasting content.[2] Thus, with this blog assignment, the instructions for accessing the site and posting content are a means to, rather than the focus of instructions.

ENGAGEMENT

Because of its inherent authenticity, adopting a technology-based assignment with a real-world audience hungry for content elicits from many students a greater desire to put forth their best work. Since their efforts and results are not limited to their instructor's eyes only, students have tangible reasons to actively research their topics, implement the writing process, and invest significant effort into the revising and proofreading stages of their blog post assignments. In short, the very public nature of this assignment alone motivates many students to care deeply about the end result beyond merely receiving a good grade. In essence, with this assignment, many students strive to excel.

Moreover, as students are also required to present their topics to their classmates and then lead a Q&A discussion on the topic, the blog assignment forces an additional pedagogy of engagement since students must also support and defend their work verbally. Additionally, constructive feedback on how to improve individual presentations from a content and performance perspective is also shared among students, resulting in yet another opportunity for communication instruction.

As with any assignment, however, some students will give a minimal effort, even with a blog post on a topic of their choice published on a public forum. No matter the effort to pull participation out of unwilling individuals, it cannot be avoided. But, given the public nature of the content and the opportunity to share and promote individual posts via social media as well as division newsletters and school websites—culminating in comments and feedback from outside of the class, the university, even the country—student engagement and interest often exceeds that of less authentic assignments, including essays, emails, letters, memos, reports, PowerPoints, etc. By its visible nature, a student-written course blog, which supports 678 subscribers (and climbing) and with over seventy thousand views worldwide since 2011, has the potential to legitimize the study of communication by providing something writers have longed for since we first put chisel to rock, pen to paper—a living, breathing audience beyond that of the instructor.

DIGITAL TRAJECTORIES

Because technology—and channels for communicating—continues to change, one should expect future iterations of college-level communication courses to evolve to include more and more digital assignments like our blog posts. Whether it be drafting targeted content for websites or figuring out how to maximize social media via HootSuite, the essential nature of communication, that transmission of information and meaning, and its instruction will remain the focus. But the real challenge—engaging students in a way that excites and teaches while eliciting their best work—will remain as well. Digital channels, however, may be the key to unlocking that somewhat reluctant engagement.

NOTES

1. Matthew Kirschenbaum, "What Is Digital Humanities and What Is It Doing in English Departments," Debates in Digital Humanities (2012), accessed February 1, 2018, http://dhdebates.gc.cuny.edu/debates/text/38.

2. Mark Urtel and Eugenia Fernandez, "To Podcast or Not to Podcast," in *Quick Hits for Teaching with Technology: Successful Strategies by Award-winning Teachers*, ed. Robin K. Morgan and Kimberly Olivares (Bloomington: Indiana University Press, 2012), 37–38.

REFERENCE

Hutton, James. (1899). Theory of the Earth: Proofs and Illustrations. Sir Archibald Geikie (Ed.) Geological Society. Accessed at https://play.google.com/books/reader?id=M8YQAAAAIAAJ&hl=en&pg=GBS.PA1

PART II

SUPPORTING TEACHING AND LEARNING

ELEVEN

—w—

Capacity Building for DH Pedagogy Supports

An Ecological Approach

ARMANDA LEWIS

New York University

EVOLVING FROM ITS INITIAL FOCUS on research, digital humanities (DH) as a field now recognizes pedagogy as a valid approach for exploring new meanings in the humanities. The same experimentation, collaboration, and interdisciplinarity associated with DH scholarship is observed in teaching practices and creates synergies with trends in humanities education that have moved toward the acquisition of skills, collaborative learning, digital pedagogy techniques, and a broader connection of research to nonacademic spaces. Additionally, the same discourse that surrounds the potentials of DH for scholarship are applied to teaching.[1] Examples of DH pedagogy are varied and on the rise but remain a collection of individual anecdotes detailing the faculty-student experience. Less attention has been placed on the multitiered supports necessary for such courses to happen.

From an individual faculty perspective, supports involve design expertise, modest technological training, student support, and a peer-based community. From a departmental perspective, receiving support to promote curricula that stress project-based learning as a pedagogical approach is essential to giving humanists so-called twenty-first-century skills—collaboration, interdisciplinary knowledge, and creative critical thinking—that enable them to communicate with broader audiences and place their scholarship in both theoretical and practical terms. From an institutional perspective, creating external partnerships and multilayered incentives for existing faculty to model public humanities and conduct team-based research provides students with examples of how scholarship can reach beyond academic circles. Additionally, it is unclear how the success of programs does impact curricular decisions at the macro level. The ultimate purpose of this discussion is to leverage use cases that integrate educational technology tenets, organization theory, and humanities pedagogy to offer a series of DH support best practices.

Digital humanities pedagogical initiatives seek to infuse within liberal arts education rich opportunities for interactivity and innovation that mesh with the socioeconomic pressures about professional preparation and learning trends promoting twenty-first-century skills. Recalling the core knowledge and skills typically associated with the humanities, deep inquiry and critical thinking are at the top. The humanities have evolved throughout history. Most recently, the humanities have grown to incorporate new tools and methods that reflect, in part, the enormous quantity of humanistic work and exegesis and the growth of digital tools. The term *digital humanities* has multiple meanings but generally refers to the use of digital and computational tools to make sense of and glean patterns from humanist data from a range of media.[2] The use of these interdisciplinary tools and methods gives rise to activities that leverage project-based and computer-supported collaborative learning, and integrate data analysis and visualization, multimedia storytelling, programming, rapid prototyping, games, simulations, and physical computing, and other techniques.[3]

SUPPORTING INDIVIDUAL FACULTY MEMBERS' DH PEDAGOGICAL EFFORTS

Individual faculty, both on instructional and research tracks, have many commitments—advancing existing research, teaching undergraduate and/or graduate courses, and providing service to their institutions. It is recognized that expanding one's bandwidth to introduce unfamiliar pedagogical tools, methods, and domain knowledge takes considerable resources, with more incremental integration of DH approaches being more common.[4] We have no concrete evidence of how these individual efforts affect institutional culture in terms of the proliferation of DH pedagogical initiatives, though we can observe that the most successful DH pedagogical support streams for individual faculty take into account institutional culture and create an ecological framework for scaffolding progress.

Link DH Teaching to DH Research

One best practice to ensure ongoing DH pedagogical innovation is to facilitate translations of DH research into curricula and vice versa. Hamilton College has pioneered a humanist model for supporting teaching and research initiatives through the Digital Humanities Initiative (DHi), described as "a collaboratory . . . where new media and computing technologies are used to promote humanities-based teaching, research, and scholarship across the liberal arts."[5] Based on the principle of the atelier, DHi offers more general skills training but within the framework of specific projects that link teaching to research. Pedagogy and research are not opposing areas between which faculty must choose to commit their time. Participants are given phased support, with the idea that, over time, faculty will have more agency and can play more active roles in the learning and development process. This approach has several implications. In keeping with good instructional technology practices, the emphasis is kept on the research in question, and technologies are only a means of addressing that research. This means that uses of technologies are situational and grounded. In keeping with current theories of learning, faculty are provided scaffolded learning experiences with technology so that knowledge construction is incremental and manageable.[6] Another is based on active learning principles and the notion that humanist knowledge can be practical through the use of technology. Projects focus on interdisciplinary topics that would benefit from a range of methods and tools, including Comparative Japanese Film Archive, Jazz and the City, Sacred Centers in India, and Virtual Freedom Trail. These and other projects integrate student collaborators as full participants.

Examining how Hamilton College frames the DHi gives us important takeaways with respect to supporting individual faculty members' efforts to integrate DH into their teaching. Importantly, there is a process linked to the goals and methodologies of the initiative as well as a linking of these aims to the curriculum. Faculty are not merely individual grantees but rather part of a community of practice involving the use of digital research methods and tools. There are several additional best practices for supporting individual faculty that come from the DHi model.

Develop Scholars' Holistic Understanding of DH Pedagogy

There are many dimensions to integrating DH into teaching, and preparatory experiences for faculty must balance breadth with time considerations. Exposure to emerging and traditional pedagogical approaches that are associated with DH are important, especially for researchers who may not be familiar with formal pedagogy. Integrating DH into teaching, however, is not merely a matter of learning about pedagogy. Primers in digital humanities should give faculty an idea of the diversity of digital research projects, approaches, and teaching interventions as well as differentiate between small-scale individual projects, medium-sized efforts that cross departments and institutional units, and large-scale efforts that include teams from several institutions and complex infrastructure. Introductions to methods and tools are beneficial most when they are contextualized with disciplinary questions that can be tied naturally to a particular method or tool. These contextual overviews: (1) give all interested faculty a baseline of knowledge with which to be conversant; (2) offer a sense of the expertise required to complete certain projects; and (3) allow faculty to identify those methods or tools that they want to directly develop or for which they need to identify a collaborator. Beyond learning about the scope, tools, and methods of DH, faculty need exposure to project management skills. Deep knowledge is not necessary, but a sense of a project life cycle is useful to understanding how a DH research project is distinct from a non-DH project. Since many DH pedagogical interventions are project based and collaborative, understanding DH pedagogical projects as DH research projects is important to ensuring that class projects are designed to fit within an academic term or across multiple terms. Some DH class efforts require tools and resources that must be obtained, even if a budget is not necessary.

Make Visible Institutional Supports

There are many centralized offices and other resources that support pedagogical innovation. Depending on the structure of the institution, pedagogical innovation may be supported by offices dedicated to informational technology, educational technology, instructional design and production, teaching advancement, libraries, interdisciplinary studies, data analysis and advancement, and more. Publicizing the offices that have relevant staff and services according to project type will avoid overwhelming faculty and focus information. Also, being realistic about the services and level of support offered will prepare faculty as they determine what skills they must obtain directly and which they can access through partnerships.

BRIDGING DEPARTMENTAL EFFORTS

Departments and academic programs play an important bridge role in DH pedagogy and research. Best practices focus on leveraging the field-specific ties within a department or group of associated departments. Departments can:

- Encourage bottom-up initiatives like communities of practice with associated fields. They can take the lead on offering professional development experiences that contextualize DH for particular fields and engage undergraduates, graduate students, and teaching and research faculty.
- Sponsor cross-department curricular efforts. Cross listing DH courses provides a low-barrier way to promote DH curricula; sponsoring interdisciplinary and team-taught DH courses that attract students from diverse majors provides a more robust, labor-intensive link.
- Assist faculty in securing funds for and managing research projects.
- Recognize DH teaching efforts in the tenure review process. Scholars have reimagined how digital scholarship and innovative teaching could impact the tenure and promotion process.[7] Departments have a central role in shaping new guidelines that consider collaborative and digitally inflected scholarship and teaching practices.

CREATING INSTITUTIONAL ANCHORS TO SUSTAIN DH PEDAGOGICAL INNOVATION

Institutions play the central role of consolidating disparate DH efforts into a unified vision, for internal and external constituencies. They secure a range of resources as well as promote efforts beyond individual or departmental initiatives.

The Scholar's Lab at the University of Virginia (https://scholarslab.org/) offers a model for promoting and sustaining DH pedagogical and research efforts, and the lab is recognized internationally due to institutional efforts to build deep collaborations across disciplines, earmark physical space, and secure financial resources. DH figures prominently in several presidential priorities, including cross university collaboration and research portfolio growth. Linking the efforts of local DH research and teaching to strategic priorities communicates the primacy of the efforts to all stakeholders.

The development of the NewYorkScapes project at New York University (https://newyorkscapes.org/about-us/) reveals the role of the institution in sustaining nascent DH efforts. This emerging DH initiative has a scholarly and pedagogical focus and has grown into a research community dedicated to exploring humanistic location-based scholarship around the city of New York.

This effort began as a community of practice, and it was recognized early on that institutional buy-in was vital for sustainability of the project.[8] Technological infrastructure, for example, should be centrally hosted and managed; central support staff should be dedicated to the project long term; and faculty and staff should be recognized for their efforts.

Best practices reveal that the institution should:

- Develop messaging that promotes DH as an institutional priority. A review of sustainable DH efforts reveals organization-level promotional language that emphasizes interdisciplinarity, institutional commitment, and successful research and teaching examples. Such examples promote selected "big ideas" in the digital humanities that link teaching and research.
- Recognize the importance of physical space. Discipline- and department-based spaces prove inadequate for fostering collaborations suitable for widespread DH efforts, while centralized spaces dedicated to DH efforts communicate the institutional importance of the effort and bring together diverse communities. Research indicates the symbolic and functional importance of centralized physical spaces for increasing interdisciplinary collaborations.[9]
- Provide faculty with a range of top-down incentives. Stipends and course assistants for developing courses are important for recognizing the distinct preparations required of some DH curricular development. Showcasing faculty teaching efforts in the form of research support, conferences, and university awards communicates the importance of curricular innovation. Sponsoring professional development opportunities, working groups, and cluster hiring ties DH efforts to university strategic priorities.
- Assist faculty and departments in thinking of DH efforts in terms of life cycles, acknowledging varying scales, impacts, and persistence. Some DH efforts are purposely short lived and experimental, while others span beyond the university and are meant to persist as a stable institutional offering.

We have discussed the technical, infrastructural, and administrative best practices that are necessary to sustain faculty-led pedagogical DH initiatives and foster institution-wide capacity-building efforts. Viewing the efforts of individual faculty, departments, and institutions as three connected spheres highlights the various stakeholders and agendas represented. This ecological approach recognizes the complexity of resources required to build and sustain DH pedagogical initiatives.

NOTES

1. Brett D. Hirsch, ed., "Introduction: Digital Humanities and the Place of Pedagogy," in *Digital Humanities Pedagogy: Practices, Principles and Politics* (Cambridge, UK: Open Book, 2012), 3–30, accessed June 19, 2019, https://doi .org/10.11647/OBP.0024.

2. Matthew Gold, ed., *Debates in the Digital Humanities* (Minneapolis: University of Minnesota, 2012).

3. Katrin Becker, *Choosing and Using Digital Games in the Classroom* (Basel: Springer, 2016), doi:10.1007/978-3-319-12223-6_3. Lisa Spiro, "Opening Up Digital Humanities Education," in *Digital Humanities Pedagogy: Practices, Principles and Politics*, ed. Brett D. Hirsch (Cambridge, UK: Open Book, 2012), 331–364, accessed May 13, 2019, https://doi.org/10.11647/OBP.0024.

4. Funding for individual faculty tends to support projects (i.e., a National Endowment for the Humanities Digital Humanities Award) or knowledge expansion, with one notable example being the Andrew W. Mellon Foundation New Directions Fellowship, which offers a year of support for scholars to pursue advanced training in a different field and/or methodology.

5. Hamilton College Digital Humanities Initiative, accessed June 19, 2019, https://www.hamilton.edu/academics/centers/digital-humanities-initiative /about.

6. Jerome Bruner, *Acts of Meaning* (Cambridge, MA: Harvard University Press, 1990); Haoqi Zhang, Matthew W. Easterday, Elizabeth M. Gerber, Daniel Rees Lewis, and Leesha Maliakal, "Agile Research Studios," *Companion of the 2017 ACM Conference on Computer Supported Cooperative Work and Social Computing—CSCW '17 Companion*, 2017.

7. Deborah Lines Andersen, *Digital Scholarship in the Tenure, Promotion, and Review Process* (New York: Routledge, 2015); John Guillory, "Evaluating Scholarship in the Humanities: Principles and Procedures," *ADE Bulletin* 137 (2005): 18–33, 10.1632/ade.137.18.

8. Acacia Warren, *Project-Based Learning across the Disciplines: Plan, Manage, and Assess through +1 Pedagogy* (Thousand Oaks, CA: Corwin, a SAGE Company, 2016).

9. Michael S. Harris and Karri Holley, "Constructing the Interdisciplinary Ivory Tower: The Planning of Interdisciplinary Spaces on University Campuses," *Planning for Higher Education* 36, no. 3 (2008): 34–43.

TWELVE

—〜〜—

From Researcher to Curator

Reimagining Undergraduate Primary Source
Research with Omeka

JAMES ROUSSAIN

University of St. Michael's College

SILVIA VONG

University of St. Michael's College

IN 2011, THE PRINCIPAL OF the University of St. Michael's College envisioned the integration of the John M. Kelly Library Special Collections, which include the college's rare book and manuscript collections, into the Book and Media Studies program. He successfully received approval to create a course related to special collections and archival research. First considered temporary, the course was assigned a "special topics" code; if successful, the course would continue under this designation and would remain optional for students pursuing the Book and Media Studies major or minor options. In 2012, a librarian was assigned to teach the course, SMC300: Libraries, Special Collections, and Archives. The initial iteration of the course focused solely on producing a research paper using primary sources and maintained this format until 2014. After reevaluating the impact on learning and the major form of student assessment, it was determined that a traditional research paper was limiting students to a formulaic assignment they had encountered many times before. To challenge students to use and interpret special collections and archival materials and to introduce the idea that research can be presented in different formats, an exhibition proposal assignment was introduced in the fall of 2014. This assignment proved to challenge the students' notion of how research can be expressed and disseminated, and as a result, in the winter of 2017, the assignment was restructured so that students could translate their research papers into an online exhibition using a platform of their choice (e.g., Omeka, Blogger, WordPress). In 2017, an archivist was hired to coteach or teach the course, and in 2018, the archivist led SMC300 and limited students to the use of Omeka.

COURSE STRUCTURE

Meeting once weekly for twelve sessions, SMC300 is taught within the John M. Kelly Library with easy access to the library's special collections. Further to raising awareness of special collections and their uses, SMC300 has two main objectives: (1) to define and apply foundational concepts in library and archival science and (2) to apply critical thinking and research skills in the evaluation of primary sources to create a new work. While the exhibition assignment offers an opportunity to realize the latter, the first objective is met through lectures and class activities with content divided into three broad themes: (1) defining and using diplomatics and evaluating primary sources; (2) understanding archival theory and practices; and (3) applying archival theory to the use and preservation of materials.

Exposing students to a variety of special collections environments has recently emerged as a third goal of the course. The proximity of the Kelly Library's Special Collections reading room allows for easy integration of materials and facilities into class content. In the third week of classes, for example, students attend a tour of the Special Collections reading room, where staff offer a one-hour introduction to the space that touches on handling guidelines, how to request materials, and how to interpret finding aids. As Patrick Williams has recently noted, as compared to other spaces in academic libraries, special collections have far less frequently been the site of student instruction and most remain unaware of or, worse yet, intimidated by their use.[1] This valuable session helps disambiguate the reading room, breaking down access barriers to the use of materials.

Carrying this theme of raising awareness of special collections and their varied uses, students are not only toured through the Special Collections reading room but also offered behind-the-scenes visits to the City of Toronto Archives and the Internet Archive, the latter whose digitization facilities are located on the University of Toronto's downtown campus. The notion that archival and rare book materials can be used for purposes beyond "traditional"—or monograph-oriented—research (e.g., exhibitions, public outreach, digital preservation) is reiterated throughout. In reflecting on her own experience working with postsecondary students, Anna McNally writes that students' attention can be piqued by challenging their assumptions of archival research—white cotton gloves, an Indiana Jones–style storeroom of forgotten artifacts—to effectively engage them in course content.[2] Having students see how materials are used in nontraditional formats and settings helps lay the groundwork for the exhibition assignment.

ASSIGNMENT STRUCTURE

Embodying the views of noted Canadian archivist and archival theorist Hugh Taylor, the exhibition assignment is part of a larger project where paired students select a group of records and explore both their form and their content. There are no right or wrong answers, and as Taylor expressed in a seminal 1972 article, students are asked to "enter into a dialogue with these records . . . and ask your own questions and draw your own conclusions . . . see what happens."[3] Focusing on process rather than product, students review their records to extract a narrative of their choosing, while also noting their physicality (physical condition, organization, how produced, material composition, etc.). The assignment is open ended: tell a story based on what you discover. It is this story that is then presented in an online exhibition; students also submit a paper outlining their discoveries: the narrative they choose to present paired with a critique of the materiality and presentation of the records as informed by the theories learned in class.

To give context to the exhibition, students are prompted to prepare their project as though they were hired by the library to prepare an online exhibition highlighting a collection of records in an "accessible and engaging manner." Doing so establishes parameters for their project, including a defined audience and a known support network. Projects are graded according to the clarity and visual presentation of the narrative, the use of images and content from the materials studied, and a discussion of how they plan to promote their exhibition. The integrity of citations and copyright statements are also reviewed. In brief, this is a real-world application of the research process: students synthesize and distill their discoveries to an easily consumed message.

UNDERLYING PEDAGOGY

Both SMC300 and the exhibit assignment were designed with pedagogical features in mind to create an effective learning environment informed by information literacy principles, specifically primary source literacy.

As noted, this assignment involved students in the entire research process, from choosing sources to honing their research questions, extracting a narrative, and synthesizing their findings into an exhibition. George Kuh recently noted the value of allowing students to be actively involved in the inquiry cycle, where the greatest benefits "accrue to students who participate in determining the questions . . . collecting and analyzing the desired information, distilling the implications of the findings, and presenting the results and conclusions orally, in writing, or another demonstration form."[4] By being offered limited guidance on what the final product should be, students had to engage in the process and, in so doing, hone their critical thinking skills.[5]

When the course was first designed in 2012, the literature and standards were consulted to ensure that some elements of information literacy education were present. However, in 2015, the Association for College and Research Libraries (ACRL) released a document outlining key concepts for information literacy in higher education. In revising the assignment to complement these new models, it was noted that the assignment aligns with the concepts of Information Creation as Process, the idea that "information in any format is produced to convey a message and is shared via a selected delivery method. The iterative processes of research, revising, and disseminating information vary, and the resulting product reflects these differences" and Research as Inquiry, where "research is iterative and depends upon asking increasingly complex or new questions whose answers in turn develop additional questions or lines of inquiry in any field."[6]

Each concept in the ACRL framework has a set of knowledge practices (actions) and disposition (attitudes). In reviewing the two concepts noted above, the exhibit assignment aimed to develop in students their ability to "transfer knowledge of capabilities and constraints to new types of information products" and to "consider research as open-ended exploration and engagement with information,"[7] respectively, while understanding that the humanities discipline can disseminate and communicate research through various channels outside of traditional models of publishing.

In 2018, with SMC300 now led by an archivist, the pedagogical underpinnings of the course were again revisited, this time to draw on literature from the archival community specific to primary source literacy. While librarians have developed a culture of working in information literacy for more than twenty-five years, archivists have only recently begun to fully exploit their role as educators and have—for just over ten years—been looking at how to formalize methods for the teaching of primary source literacy as distinct from, but part of, larger information literacy programs.[8] Archivists and special collections librarians are playing catch-up.

While a comprehensive review of current literature is beyond the scope of this piece, the 2003 work of Elizabeth Yakel and Deborah Torres, "AI: Archival

Intelligence and User Expertise," succinctly identifies three types of knowledge necessary for the effective use of primary sources and is largely responsible for strengthening the discussion of archivists as educators.

In addition to subject knowledge, which is specific to the researcher's interests and beyond the scope of both our context and that of many other educators, Yakel and Torres identify "artifactual literacy" and "archival intelligence" as key skills. The first speaks directly to one's ability to understand, interpret, and analyze primary sources to assess their value as evidence. Archival intelligence, however, is a researcher's knowledge of archival principles, theories, and practices that underlie the rules and procedures unique to archival research, such as how records are arranged and described or how to understand the relationship between primary sources and their surrogates.[9] An awareness of these principles can greatly facilitate an individual's ability to locate and access relevant sources allowing the generation of research questions more attuned to available records.

While artifactual literacy—how to evaluate and interpret primary sources—is well represented under established information literacy approaches, the teaching of archival intelligence remains largely untouched, where, as Yakel and Torres argue, the "acquisition of archival intelligence is something that should be embraced by archivists as a role unique to them."[10] It is under this paradigm that the Kelly Library's Outreach and Instruction Archivist situates the exhibition assignment. By applying the diplomatics and archival theories discussed in class to their assignments, students exercised their artifactual literacy skills—evaluating and choosing relevant sources—facilitated by archival intelligence, or a knowledge of how to do archival research. Ultimately, such an approach creates a universal skill set easily applied to many different repositories or research contexts far beyond SMC300.

CREATING DIGITAL RESOURCES AS A CLASSROOM ACTIVITY

Johanna Drucker broadly defines digital humanities as a "set of conceptual and practical approaches to digital engagement with cultural materials."[11] The SMC300 exhibition project provides an introduction to the concept and procedures of creating a digital object while combining archival theory and practice, which has also been demonstrated by Lisa M. Sjoberg and Joy K. Lintelman. They write, "Our goal in designing these DH assignments has been to create collaborative projects that fuse theory with this practice of animating archives. In so doing, students authentically experience scholarship and the production of knowledge, particularly because their work is disseminated to the public."[12] Sjoberg and Lintelman valued and aimed to create a learning experience that mirrored the actual practice of scholarship in the humanities through digital humanities projects. Sarah Clayton and Jeffrey M. Widener also offered a similar DH assignment where critical thinking and curation were emphasized in collaboration with the course instructor.[13] Surprisingly, digital literacy skills were a challenge for the librarians and course instructor, which include procedural skills such as converting digital files as well as information literacy skills such as attribution, searching the library resources, and information bias.[14]

Similar to the experiences of Sjoberg and Lintelman, and Clayton and Widener, the digital exhibition project aimed to engage students in critical thinking, primary source literacy, and information literacy. While this can be taught through research papers, for the first few years of the course, students showed a lack of engagement with critical thinking, primary source literacy, and information literacy concepts. Students were unflinching when presented with a research paper. A common pattern began to emerge where students began to skip class or disengage in the lectures on archival research. Many of the students cited in the course evaluations that they were already familiar with writing research papers and felt disengaged with the coursework. In order to motivate students, it was vital to challenge them through unconventional assignments that activated a higher order of thinking. In the first version of the assignment, students were asked to create exhibition content as a proposal including elements of layout, condensed content, and an environmental assessment related to lectures on preservation; in the recent version, students were asked to create content and layout using Omeka as well as to present on their digital online exhibit. (See Table 12.1.) The Omeka platform was explored yet some students felt more comfortable with other platforms such as Blogger or WordPress. To help students understand the different forms, the research paper and an online exhibition, discussion around audience, style, and purpose were incorporated into the lectures and eventually one or two lectures were dedicated to training students on how to use Omeka and translate academic work into content for a general audience.

The tactile experience of creating or re-creating can leave a lasting impression on the students, as it requires them to engage in a higher level of thinking and skills. David R. Krathwohl explains that creation can involve generating, planning, and producing, which may require a student to draw from knowledge dimensions.[15] In this case, in order for students to produce the exhibit assignment, they would need to have factual, conceptual, and procedural

Table 12.1. First and Recent Versions of the Description for the Exhibit Assignment

	Description
2014: Exhibit Proposal	Apply your research skills in a real scenario. You are a librarian or archivist and have been tasked to design an exhibit to showcase one or two special items from the Rare Book Collection or Archives. If you do more than one item, the items must be connected by a common theme. Before you can proceed with creating the exhibit, you must submit a proposal to an exhibit committee. You must use items from the Kelly Library Special Collections and Archives.
	You must include the following in your proposal:
	• Introduction: Outline your theme, target audience, and purpose. • Content: Include the text that will accompany the item and images. You must include references or a works cited list. • Physical Layout of the Exhibit: Pick one or two cabinets and provide an initial layout of the cabinet cases, including item, image, or text/content locations. • Environmental Assessment: Visit the Kelly Library Exhibit Area and outline some preservation concerns.
2018: Online Exhibit and Presentation	Using your research findings and knowledge gained in the course, each group will prepare an online exhibit to tell the stories you discovered in the records. This online exhibit is an opportunity to present the findings you outlined in your final paper in a way that engages a broad audience.
	For this assignment, you will be applying your research skills to a work-related scenario:
	You have recently been hired by the John M. Kelly Library to promote their archival materials and have been asked to pull together an online exhibit to showcase a particular collection of records in an accessible and engaging manner. Before the new exhibit goes live, however, you have been asked to pitch a draft to your colleagues so they can provide feedback before you finalize it. Using an online platform, create an online exhibit with a central theme using your research findings.

Note: The first version of the assignment had a grade value of 20 percent, while the recent version has a grade value of 35 percent, which includes the online exhibit and presentation.

Table 12.2. Descriptions of the Knowledge Required for the Exhibit Assignment

Knowledge Dimension	Students will need to know . . .
Factual	Their research well enough to translate complex academic terms into shorter text as well as explain terms to academics or an audience from another field.
Conceptual	How to apply archival organization theory to develop an effective and discoverable online exhibit.
Procedural	How to create an online exhibit using the tool Omeka as well as understand other archival procedures related to organization such as assigning metadata to each online object or item.

Note: The full Bloom's Taxonomy matrix can be found in Anderson et al.'s *A Taxonomy for Learning, Teaching, and Assessing: A Revision of Bloom's Taxonomy of Educational Objectives.*

knowledge to succeed in translating their research papers into online exhibits. (See Table 12.2.)

CONCLUSION

Using the Omeka platform offered students enrolled in SMC300 the opportunity to actively engage in the research process and to think abstractly about how to effectively present their findings. By creating an exhibition, students had to consider how to structure and present a narrative, choose appropriate images and other multimedia items, and write in a style appropriate for a varied audience. The authors, having structured the final assignment in this way for the past two sessions, are pleased to see high levels of positive student engagement. In particular, students are keen to use visuals to tell a story and to present their research outside of the traditional research essay format: this proves to be a novelty and, as is one of the course objectives, illustrates that primary source research can support a variety of projects.

As with any assignment, however, ours is not without its challenges: namely, students were often overwhelmed with the workload and intricacies of archival research and grew frustrated with having to work with a partner throughout. Archival research is a slow and tedious process, and, in the spirit of engaging in an authentic experience, this process was unmediated: students experienced the true thrills of discovery paired with the endless frustrations of multiple dead ends and folder after folder of indecipherable handwriting. While students were encouraged to start their research early in the semester, many faced a time crunch as the semester waned; this assignment is best delivered over a whole term and evaluated through a scaffolded structure to keep students well paced. To motivate students and offer formal feedback on their research method and proposed topic, a research proposal was due midway through the semester.

Frustrations aside, recent course evaluations show that students appreciate the challenge and creativity involved in the assignment, noting that the project has allowed them to grasp and apply class content in a meaningful way. Marshall McLuhan, famed Canadian media theorist and himself once associated with St. Michael's College, would likely have supported our objective. As Taylor noted, McLuhan has convincingly shown "that the medium conveys its own powerful message over and above the content,"[16] and, by stressing the tactile experience of viewing the form of the records and then manipulating how their narrative is disseminated, we, too, are asking students to reflect on the same notion.

NOTES

1. Patrick Williams, "What Is Possible: Setting the Stage for Co-Exploration in Archives and Special Collections," in *Critical Library Pedagogy Handbook Volume 1: Essays and Workbook Activities* (Chicago: Association of College and Research Libraries, 2016), 113.

2. Anna McNally, "'The Archive' as Theory and Reality: Engaging with Students in Cultural and Critical Studies," in *Educational Programs: Innovative Practices for Archives and Special Collections* (Lanham, MD: Rowman and Littlefield, 2015), 65.

3. Hugh Taylor, "Clio in the Raw: Archival Materials and the Teaching of History," *American Archivist* 35, nos. 3–4 (July 1972): 329, https://doi.org /10.17723/aarc.35.3-4.x2626ht453850482.

4. George D. Kuh, "Adding Value to the Undergraduate Research Experience," in *Undergraduate Research and the Academic Librarian: Case Studies and Best Practices*, ed. Merinda Kaye Hensley and Stephanie Davis-Kahl (Chicago: Association of College and Research Libraries, 2017), xiii.

5. Elizabeth Yakel, "Information Literacy for Primary Sources: Creating a New Paradigm for Archival Researcher Education," *OCLC Systems and Services: International Digital Library Perspectives* 20, no. 2 (June 1, 2004): 62, https://doi .org/10.1108/10650750410539059.

6. Association of College and Research Libraries, *Framework for Information Literacy for Higher Education*, 2016, http://www.ala.org/acrl /standards/ilframework.

7. Association of College and Research Libraries.

8. Peter Carini, "Information Literacy for Archives and Special Collections: Defining Outcomes," *Portal: Libraries and the Academy* 16, no. 1 (2016): 191, https://doi.org/10.1353/pla.2016.0006.

9. Elizabeth Yakel and Deborah Torres, "AI: Archival Intelligence and User Expertise," *American Archivist* 66, no. 1 (January 1, 2003): 52, https://doi.org/10.17723/aarc.66.1.q022h85pn51n5800.

10. Ibid., 52.

11. Johanna Drucker, "Introduction to Digital Humanities," UCLA Center for Digital Humanities, 2014, http://dh101.humanities.ucla.edu/?page_id=8.

12. Lisa M. Sjoberg and Joy K. Lintelman, "Animating Archives: Embedding Archival Materials (and Archivists) into Digital History Projects," in *Educational Programs: Innovative Practices for Archives and Special Collections*, ed. Kate Theimer (Lanham, MD: Rowman and Littlefield, 2015), 104.

13. Sarah Clayton and Jeffrey M. Widener, "Beyond Embedded Librarianship: Co-Teaching with Faculty to Integrate Digital Scholarship in Undergraduate Research," in *Undergraduate Research and the Academic Librarian: Case Studies and Best Practices*, ed. Merinda Kaye Hensley and Stephanie Davis-Kahl (Chicago: Association of College and Research Libraries, 2017), 1–17.

14. Ibid., 5.

15. David R. Krathwohl, "A Revision of Bloom's Taxonomy: An Overview," *Theory into Practice* 41, no. 4 (2002): 212–218.

16. Taylor, "Clio in the Raw," 318.

THIRTEEN

—ₘ—

Teaching Together for the Digital Humanities Graduate Certificate

HÉLÈNE HUET

University of Florida

LAURIE N. TAYLOR

University of Florida

INTRODUCTION: CREATING UF'S DIGITAL
HUMANITIES GRADUATE CERTIFICATE PROGRAM

The University of Florida (UF) has a long tradition of work in the digital humanities (DH). As explained in "Intertwingularity with Digital Humanities at the University of Florida" and "Library Collaborative Networks Forging Scholarly Cyberinfrastructure and Radical Collaboration," this tradition often built from the strong community foundation of the libraries and librarians.[1] Activities include work by individuals and small groups for research, teaching, and programmatic community work to enable capacity for larger scale and longer term collaborative activities. The libraries and library faculty have been collaborative leaders in this work, notably with an internal grant in 2014 for the "'Developing Librarian' Digital Humanities Pilot Training Project"[2] that provided training for librarians on new tools and practices in the digital age, focusing on DH, who would then support training and teaching classes on DH. The experience of the training program complemented skills coming in with new hires in the libraries.

With expanded skills, librarians contributed as core UF community members who came together in 2015 to create the Digital Humanities Graduate

88

Certificate. As explained in the *UF Digital Humanities Graduate Certificate Memo and New Certificate Form*, the libraries and librarians were essential community collaborators and leaders for DH teaching.[3] The DH Graduate Certificate was made possible because of the earlier quick hit work in trainings and teaching by the libraries and the community of practice with so many people involved in DH at UF. The certificate itself required an extensive amount of work to create because it was the first of its kind in being led by faculty from multiple departments and colleges and, as a result, was not housed in any one of them. Importantly, however, this work put in place the structures for ongoing quick successes and further program growth. Additionally, the team was able to create the certificate by designing it to build on existing courses and to only add one new course. The structure for the certificate accomplished several core goals rapidly, with each of these goals supporting fast and strong future work:

- Creating a collaborative leadership team on DH teaching, with experts from multiple colleges and departments.
- Creating a process to evaluate and validate existing DH courses and to incorporate and connect them with broader DH teaching through the certificate.
- Building the community of practice for DH teaching by requiring all courses for the certificate to identify as either depth or breadth courses, thereby positioning faculty and their courses in relation to each other.
- Building flows across departments by requiring students to take at least one of the required courses out of their home department.
- Creating the DH Graduate Studio, a new course for extending and credentialing DH skills.

The DH Graduate Studio was created as a new capstone course, one that embodied collaborative DH practices. The studio builds on the work done in other courses and serves to refine skills as connected across different disciplines, as public scholarship, and as part of the professional skills and portfolio development for students.

STUDIO CAPSTONE COURSE

The DH Graduate Studio course is open to any student at UF who is enrolled in a master's or PhD program. It is designed to be interdisciplinary and for students who already have experience with the field of digital humanities.

What makes the studio course unique is twofold. First, it offers an opportunity for students to apply their own research and teaching interests to the creation of a digital project. Indeed, in addition to more traditional readings, discussions, and presentations, students are required to produce a digital portfolio, where one of the major elements is either a traditional research project (e.g., thesis, dissertation chapter, scholarly article, exhibit, or scholarly presentation) or a course syllabus that relates to the student's digital projects. Second, the course is cotaught by a faculty member from one of the affiliated departments and colleges and a librarian from the George A. Smathers Libraries. This experience benefits students and faculty members on many levels. Not only does it strengthen ties between humanities, arts, and science departments and the libraries, between faculty members and librarians, and between students and librarians but also it highlights to students the important role librarians have in the creation of digital projects as well as their knowledge of the DH field. Librarians often help faculty and students with their digital projects, but they also have projects of their own and present them at various DH conferences. This capstone course is thus a great way to shed light on the too often hidden work and scholarship of librarians. Further, the course also showcases additional career opportunities for graduate students, supporting job placements.

The DH Graduate Studio has been offered every spring semester since 2016. A librarian and a faculty member always co-teach it together. While the faculty members rotate every year, the librarians usually teach the class two years in a row. Thus far, the syllabus has been mostly identical for all four years the class has been offered, but it is easily modifiable depending on the number of students, their interests, and their experience.

The course follows John Dewey's model of experiential learning, meaning that students (and teachers alike) learn through experience and by collaborating together. A lot of the class time is dedicated to intensive group discussion of individual and collaborative student work. This allows students to familiarize themselves with the work of their colleagues as well as to hone their interpretation and analysis skills. This is also a great way for them to practice professionally presenting their digital projects.

Another important aspect of the course is that it serves as a creative space where students get to collaborate with other researchers in and outside the class. This is why the course is taught in the libraries, "in a laboratory space that can serve as a physical hub of the course's undertakings." The course also uses "virtual environments for supporting asynchronous collaboration, such as wikis, blogs, etc."[4] In fact, the content of the course (e.g., syllabus, articles to read, summary of what has been discussed during class time) is available on a Scalar site in one of the course iterations.

Students collaborate within the class by contributing recommendations for readings, leading and coleading discussions, participating as trainers where they teach and serve as expert aids for technologies and tools they know, and participating as part of a studio environment. Within the studio framework, students present their project ideas to the group, contribute with constructive criticism and recommendations, brainstorm, and workshop projects and work together.

As we mentioned previously, students need to have developed a digital project by the end of the DH Graduate Studio. For instance, for the spring 2019 class, Madeline Gangnes, a PhD candidate from the Department of English, created the (De)collected War of the Worlds,[5] a public-facing online project that exemplifies ways in which historical and material contexts of serialized texts might be made more approachable and accessible. The project incorporates facsimiles, illustrations, paratexts, and historical information. Most crucially, it houses transcripts of the serialized version of the novel that are text-to-speech compatible and interspersed with detailed descriptions of image-heavy materials. These transcripts are augmented with scholarly annotations to create a critical digital "edition" of the text. This project aims to (1) demonstrate that rejecting notions of origin and completeness affords opportunities to (re)discover un- or underdiscussed meanings surrounding serialized texts; (2) offer an accessible critical resource for scholarship and pedagogy related to this novel; and (3) provide a model for similar projects related to other serialized texts, especially lesser-known works.

Some of the challenges of teaching the DH Graduate Studio have been the varied levels of experience from the students as well as the huge difference in the number of students taking the class every semester the course if offered. While students are required to have taken a Digital Breadth seminar and a Digital Depth seminar before being able to take the DH Graduate Studio, we have found that the students' experience with digital tools and their needs in terms of digital research and projects are extremely different, which can make working in groups or evaluating the work rather challenging.

Moreover, we had to adapt the syllabus dramatically in the spring of 2018 because only one student registered for the class. We, therefore, could not do the planned group projects or presentations. Instead, because the student was still unsure as to what exactly she wanted to work on in terms of the digital project, the coteachers arranged to have presentations of various digital tools from colleagues in the libraries, discussed current DH topics/issues, required mandatory attendance for the THATCamp conference taking place at the university in order for her to discover new digital projects and network, and provided feedback and support on the person's potential digital project that will eventually be part of her dissertation. The student learned a lot in the course and appreciated the flexibility of the teachers to rearrange the syllabus to fit her needs. But it was a bit of a challenge for the teachers, who had never worked together before, to have to rethink the assignments and requirements of the course.

CONCLUSION: LIBRARY FACULTY PERSPECTIVES

As the two library faculty members who have taught the studio course and served on the DH Certificate Board, our experiences cover the past, present, and potential futures for the course, certificate, and new opportunities with DH teaching, for fast successes and meaningful change.

The certificate and the studio are both still rather new, and we are still making changes to them as more and more students become interested. For instance, we have been asked whether it would be possible to offer the studio as an online class, something we had not considered originally. Moreover, with recent hirings in the libraries and at the university, there are now more faculty members doing digital scholarship. This means that in the future, we will be able to offer more courses for the certificate and have rotating teachers for the studio. UF's Digital Humanities Graduate Certificate offers one example of a quick hit in terms of building from existing courses, adding a single new course with the studio, and the many quick hit successes that the studio and the certificate have made possible. The UF DH community is collaborating more closely now because of the certificate, students are benefiting from the program, and UF overall is better positioned to support students, faculty, and new projects and work in research, teaching, and service.

NOTES

1. Laurie N. Taylor and Blake Landor, "Intertwingularity with Digital Humanities at the University of Florida," July 23, 2014, *dh+lib: Where the Digital Humanities and Librarianship Meet,* http://acrl.ala.org/dh/2014/07/23 /intertwingularity-digital-humanities-university-florida/; Laurie N. Taylor, Suzan Alteri, Val (Davis) Minson, Ben Walker, Haven Hawley, Chelsea Dinsmore, and Rebecca Jefferson, "Library Collaborative Networks Forging Scholarly Cyberinfrastructure and Radical Collaboration," in *Technology-Centered Academic*

Library Partnerships and Collaborations, ed. Brian Doherty (Hershey, PA: IGI Global, 2016), 1–30.

2. Blake Landor, Laurie N. Taylor, Richard Freeman, Missy Clapp, and Peggy McBride, "'Developing Librarian' Digital Humanities Pilot Training Project" (Gainesville: George A. Smathers Libraries, University of Florida, 2014), http://ufdc.ufl.edu/AA00022054/00001.

3. Digital Humanities Graduate Certificate Committee (Elizabeth Dale, Terry Harpold, Jack Stenner, Dhanashree Thorat, Laurie N. Taylor, Sophia Krzys Acord, Eleni Bozia, Leah Rosenberg, Kenneth B. Kidd, Shelley Arlen, Blake Landor, Laurie Ellen Gries), 2015, *UF Digital Humanities (DH) Graduate Certificate Memo and New Certificate Form* (Gainesville: University of Florida), http://ufdc.ufl.edu/AA00032330/00001.

4. Elizabeth R. Dale and Laurie N. Taylor, *Digital Humanities Graduate Studio HUM 6836 Syllabus* (Gainesville: University of Florida, 2016–2017), http://ufdc.ufl.edu/AA00038077/00001/allvolumes.

5. Madeline Gangnes, *The (De)collected War of the Worlds,* http://decollected.net.

FOURTEEN

—ᴍ—

Graduate Training in the Digital Archive

SERENITY SUTHERLAND

State University of New York, Oswego

USING THE CONCEPT OF THE digital humanities project as a "basic unit," this chapter contributes to ongoing discussions about how digital archive projects deliver graduate student education in two forms: pedagogical training and skill development via project building.[1] Digital projects also introduce graduate students to the importance of networks and networking within the DH collaborative work space where librarians, archivists, web designers, programmers, students, and faculty come together in order to produce a successful DH project.

For graduate students, DH projects can be useful vantage points from which to look out at the wider academic system—how to write grant applications, how to navigate administrative concerns about resources, how to address some of the challenging topics that orbit DH work, namely increases in adjunct labor, destigmatizing careers outside the traditional academic path (commonly referred to as alternative academic, or alt-ac, careers), and fair compensation for DH staff and librarians. None of these issues are unique to the digital humanities—and the context at each institution and department can differ—but given the intense criticism and enthusiasm surrounding the emerging field of DH, grad students see the bones of university culture laid bare. In a practical way, DH projects also offer specific skill sets and work experience to help graduate students gain professional development. As Ashley Reed and others have noted, the digital project exists as a space for mentorship and apprentice-like skill building.[2] Graduate students who work as managers of digital archives also learn how to set deadlines and determine what it means to be "finished" with a digital project, although perhaps not necessarily how to go about finishing.[3] Digital projects also demonstrate to graduate students the importance of collaboration with other scholars, library professionals, and archivists and the need to fight for inclusion of archivists and librarians as equal project members. Thus, digital projects are "projective," by causing a shift in humanities education and signaling the need for collaborative digital pedagogy and equal investment in the digital archive on the part of librarians, academics, and archivists.[4] Training graduate students in these aspects from the ground up instills that DH affords the ethos of academic egalitarianism, openness, and ingrained collaboration.

In my own experience as a graduate student manager on the Seward Family Digital Archive (SFDA) at the University of Rochester, I found the digital project to be useful for both understanding the discipline of the digital humanities and gaining skills deployable to the job market.[5] I began working on the project during my graduate studies, first as the transcription, annotation and editing manager and then as the project manager.[6] The SFDA consists of letters between members of William Henry Seward's family, including his wife Frances, sons Gus, Fred and Will Jr., and daughter Fanny. Seward is perhaps best known for his purchase of Alaska and as President Abraham Lincoln's secretary of state. Before that he was governor of New York and worked as a lawyer, land company manager, and even volunteer militiaman. William Henry Seward, affectionately known to the family as "Henry," was always traveling, much to Frances Seward's irritation. Henry hardly chose to stay home; however, this produced regular correspondence between the late 1820s and the 1870s, resulting in about four thousand family letters. The documents are stored in the department of Rare Books, Special Collections, and Preservation at the University of Rochester.

Built into the foundation of the SFDA workflow is the training of undergraduate and graduate students through class seminars and paid employment. The heart of the work done is transcription, annotation, and editing of letters by instructing team members in guidelines and providing them with the education necessary to understand the context of the time period. Because pedagogy is so crucial to the function of the project, the students train each other in their specialty areas at the project level. For example, the graduate student in charge of transcription policies instructs all other students on the guidelines, even writing and updating the guidelines as necessary.[7] Within the classroom setting, which enrolls both undergraduate and graduate students, a graduate student member of the project officially TAs the course, while other graduate students employed by the project guest lecture on topics such as online mapping, mark up in TEI (text encoding initiative—an XML language), and documentary editing. This trains graduate students in the power of DH pedagogy, which includes incorporating archives into the classroom, training undergraduate students in both skills and theory associated with DH, and how to organize project-based learning. In my experience, I discovered the most powerful promise of the digital archive is its pedagogical capabilities of experiential learning and professional development.

Depending on team member interest, students might work on individual research projects such as mapping in GIS, cataloging the massive library of books owned by the Seward family, creating a glossary of nineteenth-century words, or tagging in TEI. Through such work, students see that the digital humanities are impossible without collaboration from information technology specialists, librarians, faculty members, and other students, as well as institutions such the Seward House Museum in Auburn, New York, and the Rare Books and Special Collections at the University of Rochester. Thus, students begin to break down barriers between faculty, librarians, staff, and technologists, especially as every task on the project is collaborative and would not be successful without the help of specialists outside of academia and the professoriat. Graduate students learn the value of networking within a diverse field of DH specialists as well as how to talk about their DH research to both academic and general audiences. Writing descriptions for site content, preparing academic papers for conferences, and composing transcription guidelines for retired volunteers at a local community center are tasks that members of the project undertake.

Aside from developing specific pedagogical and project-building skills, DH projects are situated within a larger network of the academy that graduate students encounter through their management and pedagogical roles. This positionality affords graduate students a bird's-eye view into university culture, and can open a broader discussion about neoliberalism within the university generally, and more specifically, about how the "dark side of the digital humanities" rears its neoliberal head.[8] At the university level, the success of DH programs is tested in undergraduate and graduate curriculum and marketed, perhaps not disingenuously, as "the next big thing." This leaves graduate students, in particular, bearing the brunt of experimentation within the field. Students invest the foundational moments of their careers in an exciting but precarious field that places graduate student futures on the chopping block if the experiment of digital humanities does not pan out.[9] Some graduate students, as Ryan Cordell notes, come into graduate programs not even aware of what DH is and may exhibit skepticism toward the field's aims.[10] This is not to be dismissed, according to Cordell, as it can help graduate students see how the structure of the institutionalized university is "fundamentally networked."[11] Indeed, seeing how DH exists within the university network as a multilayered phenomenon can help graduate students assess key theoretical issues, which they themselves maybe experiencing, such as the politicization of academic labor. DH work depends on networking with dedicated specialists beyond just the professorat—folks like librarians, archivists, volunteers, museum professionals, and students—while also operating within an academic framework that relies on the university culture and system.

Johanna Drucker reminds us that a network can refer to an infrastructure that makes computers and digital devices "connect" while also referring to the people and practitioners who create the relationships that are involved in actually "doing" and "producing" the work of the digital humanities.[12] The network of people essential to the rigorous work of the digital humanities became vividly clear to me as a graduate student manager at SFDA. The website would not load in an acceptable time frame without the collaboration of our programmers, the user experience would be disrupted by disorganized menus without the advice of web designers, many difficult cursive words and other archaic language would be transcribed in error without the dedication of our volunteers from a local retirement community, and our project would lack the required funding without the advice of our granting officer. These are just a few of the nodes within the university network that I was part of facilitating and that benefited the project, as well as myself. Working on the digital project made these nodes of the university system more apparent to me than I experienced while writing my dissertation.

On the project level, networking via collaboration resulted in positive outcomes given the project's ethos of fair and equal partnership with university staff, librarians, archivists, and community volunteers. SFDA employees are compensated generously and viewed as valuable members of the team, from undergraduate students to graduate managers. Within the project, our team modeled what equitable DH work could look like. This offered a useful contrast to the larger academic system wherein I was attempting to find a job, working as an adjunct laborer, and concerned about the issue of unequal recognition librarians and staff receive when compared to faculty engaged in DH work.

As a graduate student, I learned to navigate the spaces of our DH project embedded within the larger university system, seeking volunteers to grow the Seward Family Digital Archive and collaborating with librarians and archivists for a smooth-running day-to-day operation, while simultaneously teaching DH courses as an adjunct, wondering if all this DH work would result in any kind of future employment at the university level. Jentery Sayers argues that "ideal teaching and learning" for graduate students is an "entanglement of theory with practice, resulting in practitioner knowledge" of DH discourse and concepts.[13] Part of developing this practitioner knowledge is an understanding of the university system as part and parcel of the researching and teaching that graduate students are trained to do. Digital projects are well positioned to offer this type of day-to-day training and perhaps prepare a cadre of graduate students primed to disrupt the inequality of academic labor while upholding the validity of the digital humanities as an academically rigorous and necessary field of study.

NOTES

1. Anne Burdick, Johanna Drucker, Peter Lunenfeld, Todd Presner, Jeffrey Schnapp, *Digital_Humanities* (Cambridge, MA: MIT Press, 2012); Peter M. W. Robinson, "Project-Based Digital Humanities and Social, Digital, and Scholarly Editions," *Digital Scholarship in the Humanities* 31, no. 4 (December 2016): 875–889; Stephen Brier, "Where's the Pedagogy? The Role of Teaching and Learning the Digital Humanities," in *Debates in the Digital Humanities* (Minneapolis: University of Minnesota Press, 2016), ed. Matthew K. Gold.

2. Peter M. W. Robinson, "Project Based Digital Humanities"; Ashley Reed, "Managing an Established Digital Humanities Project: Principles and Practices Form the Twentieth Year of the William Blake Archive," *DHQ* 8, no. 1 (2014); Lydia Bello, Madelynn Dickerson, Margaret Hogarth, Ashley Sanders, "Librarians Doing DH: A Team and Project-Based Approach to Digital Humanities in the Library," *Collaborative Librarianship* 9, no. 2 (May 2017): 97–103.

3. Matthew Kirschenbaum, "Done: Finishing Projects in the Digital Humanities," *DHQ* 3, no. 2 (2009); Reed, "Managing an Established Digital Humanities Project. The standards for what it means to be done with an academic, digital project are in flux, and, indeed, being "done" and "finished" with a digital project are not the same thing. Folks at the University of Victoria are working on strategies for preserving digital projects once they have ended. See https://projectendings.github.io/ (accessed 2/17/2020) for the Endings Project details.

4. Burdick et al., *Digital_Humanities*.

5. See www.sewardproject.org (accessed 2/17/2020).

6. A 2014–2016 Andrew W. Mellon Fellowship in the Digital Humanities at the University of Rochester also helped support my DH graduate training.

7. For examples of project guidelines, see the Seward Family Digital Archive, https://sewardproject.org/ProjectStandardsGuidelines (accessed 2/17/2020).

8. Wendy Hui Kyong Chun, Richard Grusin, Patrick Jagoda, and Rita Raley, "The Dark Side of the Digital Humanities," in *Debates in the Digital Humanities,* ed. Matthew K. Gold (2016); Daniel Allington, Sarah Brouillette, and David Golumbia, "Neoliberal Tools (and Archives): A Political History of Digital Humanities," *Los Angeles Review of Books,* May 1, 2016.

9. Leonard Cassuto raises the point that the DH job market moment is not a sustainable phenomenon and will likely fizzle out. According to Cassuto, those graduate students receiving DH training late in the game may find the DH "job-market moment" passes them by. Leonard Cassuto, "The Job-Market Moment of Digital Humanities," *The Chronicle of Higher Education,* January 22, 2017, https://www.chronicle.com/article/The-Job-Market-Moment-of/238944 (accessed 2/17/2020).

10. Ryan Cordell, "How to Not Teach the Digital Humanities," in *Debates in the Digital Humanities,* ed. Matthew K. Gold, 2016.

11. Chun et al. "Dark Side of the Digital Humanities."

12. Johanna Drucker, *Introduction to Digital Humanities: Concepts, Methods, and Tutorials,* 2013, http://dh101.humanities.ucla.edu/ (accessed 2/17/2020).

13. Jentery Sayers, "Locating Praxis in Digital Studies: Designing Courses for Graduate Students," presentation at the Simpson Center for the Humanities at University of Washington, April 26, 2018, https://jentery.github.io/uw/.

FIFTEEN

—⟋⟍⟍—

Digital Humanities and Undergraduate Research for Undergraduates

DAVID AINSWORTH

University of Alabama

NOW THAT THE DIGITAL HUMANITIES has found its way into the classroom, teachers and digital humanists should do more with the specific advantages it offers. Digital platforms and digital projects can easily and cheaply project student work into the wider world or preserve it for the use of future classes. And yet, much of this potential goes unrealized: students in an advanced literature class may be asked to put up a project on YouTube or to present a Prezi, but the audience for this work remains restricted to a single classroom of students. Even the best of undergraduates may not be doing digital projects and research of interest to a specialized scholarly audience, but their work can be of great use to other students. Given that student papers and presentations can be easily and cheaply made available for other groups of students, instructors should make use of that resource, with the students' permission, in the name of helping students learn from each other.

While this chapter discusses specific ways in which undergraduates in an English program can produce digital research aimed at an undergraduate audience, the principles here can be extended to almost any academic discipline that supports an undergraduate program. If students can develop a sufficient level of expertise in a particular course about a topic of interest to undergraduates who are at a similar point in the program or to a general student audience outside of the program, then they can produce digital research and other materials to help those other students learn and think about that same topic. Most digital research projects developed for students to undertake within the bounds of a single course in a single semester can be adapted into projects that extend outside of those bounds. Though I offer some concrete examples of projects that my own students have completed, these represent a starting point; the possibilities are almost as limitless as those for digital humanities research as a whole.

Paulo Freire's work on critical pedagogy argues that students should be empowered agents within the classroom; while his theories have not been universally adopted, they underlie much of the work that we do as instructors of literature. The notion that our students have something to say, that they can learn by talking with and hearing from each other, underlies a wide variety of classroom practices including peer review, student-led discussion, and in-class presentations. Nevertheless, instructors almost always conceive of this intellectual labor as limited to a single course. A student working on a senior thesis might be drawing on past written work to do so, but the work will either be that of scholarly professionals or their own, not that of their fellow students. In the 1970s, nobody needed to make an effort to confine student work to the classroom, because both practice and a wide range of constraints kept it there. Those constraints have since been lifted; changing our classroom practices, then, can empower students to make deliberate intellectual contributions to each other's learning while underlining its value beyond receiving the diploma.

Undergraduates can usually expect that any written work or research they conduct for a particular course will matter only within that course and that semester. On rare occasions, a student's essay might end up becoming an undergraduate thesis or a writing sample as part of an application to a graduate program; even more rarely, an undergraduate may publish in a professional journal either as sole or coauthor. Digital humanities projects changed that expectation to a small degree, as DH allows for undergraduates to work on pieces of a larger project, whether that work involves transcribing early modern broadside ballads or producing an online edition of John Milton's poetry and prose.[1] Participation in these projects can be a source of pride for students as well as an item on their CVs. As yet, however, the full pedagogical potential of digital platforms has not been tapped, in part because of a disjuncture between the research expectations of academics and the capacities and experience of undergraduates. I suggest that many more students can be offered opportunities to do academic work of lasting value if instructors specifically create such opportunities with an undergraduate audience in mind. Doing so allows these students' work to mean something beyond the effect it has upon themselves.

I have taught at both small liberal arts colleges and large state schools; in both settings, faculty sometimes made use of anonymized student papers to talk with their current students about how to perform research or write strong analytic essays. While these examples were undoubtedly useful for their students, I suspect that the authors of these papers did not derive as much satisfaction from their continued usage as a typical academic might upon finding that someone has cited one of her articles or books; these essays were not only dissociated from their authors but also approached from a formal perspective, with only secondary emphasis placed on their ideas. They were not being engaged with in the ways that academics engage with each other's work. Collaborative DH research does not usually offer undergraduates the opportunity to have their contributions engaged with academically, either, even in cases where the overall work ends up being used by many people. At best, students might present their research at an undergraduate research fair or conference. Why should English majors be denied one of the greatest pleasures of our discipline, that of having one's work be of value to future scholars, when good undergraduate research can be of immediate use to other undergraduates?

Over the past nine years, I have offered that pleasure to students in my annual undergraduate course on John Milton as part of a digital platform I titled The Edifice Project. Students in my class write an argumentative essay addressing a prompt on a specific topic that changes every year: "Good and Evil," for example, or "Milton's Satan." I then select the best or most promising essays to be revised, expanded, and posted to the Edifice Project Research Library.[2] Each of these essays, as well as the research papers written by other members of the class, must engage with at least one of the existing essays from the Edifice Project Research Library. Students can expect that their essays, once posted, will influence the thinking of future classmates; I know of at least one instructor at another university who sent his students to do research on the Edifice Project library. These students can thus experience some of the rewards of single-author scholarship, while knowing that their intellectual work matters to people outside their immediate classroom.

While the digital research library takes advantage of a digital platform to make available traditional print texts (in electronic form), our students can also benefit from the opportunity to produce "born digital" materials, which will matter beyond the confines of their own classrooms. For example, advanced undergraduates could work in collaboration with their instructors to produce materials useful to students outside their majors. Many colleges and universities offer literature surveys aimed at a general student audience; whether designed as a historical survey or a great books course, these classes often cover a great deal of challenging material at a high rate of speed. As a scholar of John Milton, I know how difficult and intimidating his writing can be; in my dedicated Edifice Project Milton course, I usually expect my students to feel some degree of comfort and proficiency with his work around the ninth week of the semester. Literary surveys typically spend no more than a week or two reading brief excerpts of his work. As a result, students with less expertise are asked to gather some degree of knowledge about his poetry in a very short period of time. Those teaching these surveys may themselves find Milton's work difficult. While there are some resources online, which could help students develop some degree of understanding or appreciation of Milton's writing, they may be aimed at a general audience (like Wikipedia) or at students looking for a very specific kind of help (like SparkNotes). And yet, students in my advanced course on Milton possess the basic knowledge needed to provide assistance to those taking a survey course; indeed, given that most of these same student-scholars will have taken that survey them-selves, they understand the needs of that audience very well indeed. Scholarly sources rarely present to someone grappling and struggling to understand a difficult text; summaries and quick references imply that a complex poem can be reduced to easily understood notes. Student-scholars are in a unique position to demonstrate the process of developing an understanding of a text; by asking them to do so, we as instructors provide them the opportunity to deepen their own learning while assisting others. By asking our students to generate digital materials that will help other students learn, we engage them in the kind of active learning so valued in today's academy.

In the spring of 2013, I experimented with having my students record group podcasts about Book Nine of Milton's *Paradise Lost.* The students selected four important passages from this section of the poem (thirty to forty lines). The four passages were read aloud by students, with a focus on the sound and meaning of the lines, and those readings uploaded to my Edifice Project site. The students then split into groups of two or three, with each group choosing two words or phrases of particular significance from the available passages. They were responsible for establishing the context of these words or phrases as well as offering three differing interpretations of them or their significance to the poem as a whole. After doing so, each group recorded a brief conversation (five to ten minutes) about that passage, which they then submitted to me. I linked each discussion to the words or phrases in the passages. In one instance, two groups discussed the same passage; I linked both discussions to it. Dur-ing interviews I conduct at the end of the semester, my students called out this project as having been especially useful to them, forcing them to think more deeply about interpreting this poem as well as more broadly about the nature of literary interpretation. At the time, I had no clear idea of an audience for these Milton podcasts, but I am now preparing to duplicate them as resources for students in our early British literature survey course. By selecting passages covered by the majority of our survey instructors, I can ensure that these conversations have relevance to students in the surveys. By discussing meaning and significa- tion within these passages, these learners can develop their understanding of the poem, and my students will know that their work will remain valuable to future students for years to come.

Advanced undergraduates can be effective mentors for their peers, but, as digital humanists, we need to do more to break down the artificial boundaries of the college classroom and to open up opportunities for our students to do work that matters to others. Doing so will only improve learning and generate a stronger sense of collegiality and community among students. A single class meeting, for example, could be dedicated to discussing a past student's writing with him or her: the class would read the paper as homework, and the returning student would appear either in person or electronically to talk with the current students. In the long run, creating a stronger sense of intellectual legacy and connection may prove vital to the survival of the academy, both by chipping away at the solipsistic image of the ivory tower academic and by maintaining a connection with those who graduate but do not eventually join the professor- ate. The resources and techniques of the digital humanities are especially well suited to accomplishing this task.

NOTES

1. See the English Broadside Ballad Archive site, at https://ebba.english .ucsb.edu/, and the John Milton Reading Room, at https://www.dartmouth.edu /~milton/reading_room/contents/text.shtml/.

2. The Edifice Project Research Library can be found at http://edificeproject .ua.edu/?page_id=64.

SIXTEEN

Pay It Forward

Collaboration and DH Capacity Building at the University of Toronto Scarborough

KIRSTA STAPELFELDT
CHRISTINE BERKOWITZ
CHAD CRICHTON
ANNE MILNE
ALEJANDRO PAZ
NATALIE ROTHMAN
ANYA TAFLIOVICH
University of Toronto Scarborough

THE UNIVERSITY OF TORONTO SCARBOROUGH (UTSC) is a suburban campus of the University of Toronto, Canada, with over thirteen thousand undergraduate students. The campus emphasizes experiential learning, promising strong co-op and service-learning placement opportunities and "real-world experiences."[1] UTSC also self-identifies as an "anchor" institution, rooted in and benefiting the diverse communities of eastern Toronto.[2] These characteristics of the campus align with an active, local digital humanities (DH) teaching and research community. The following briefly highlights several examples of DH embedded in UTSC courses, focusing on instances where faculty partnered with the UTSC library's Digital Scholarship Unit (DSU). In addition to partnering with local faculty, the library's DSU collaborates with campus-based and central IT services to develop and maintain infrastructure in support of campus digital scholarship and local digital special collections. The library's DSU also works with the library's subject librarian (liaison librarian) program to support undergraduate DH teaching through reusable, open learning objects, documentation, and the training of TAs and faculty. Also of crucial importance is the DSU's involvement in larger open-source communities, notably Islandora, where UTSC contributes to and benefits from open-source applications used in the international GLAM (Galleries, Libraries, Archives, and Museums) community. As the diverse examples below highlight, collaboration not only facilitates DH methods and practice in the undergraduate classroom but also lays the foundation for ever-improving support within an institution (and larger community) for DH work.

ANNOTATING THE EIGHTEENTH-CENTURY: HOGARTH IN CONTEXT (2015–2018)

Average class size: Thirty students
Offered in: Junior (third) and Senior (fourth) year
Department: English
The Hogarth in Context project is an online, multimedia deep-dive into the works of William Hogarth, led and managed since 2015 by Anne Milne.[3] Students in Milne's third- and fourth-year courses contribute, through graded assignments, to a collection of online resources about the English painter and engraver William Hogarth (1697–1764). The primary resources for the project are digital copies of William Hogarth's engraved plates, sourced from Wikimedia Commons. Hogarth's engravings present perspectives on life in eighteenth-century London, particularly on issues such as sexual assault, substance abuse, poverty, animal cruelty, disease, and morality. Prior to the start of term, librarians upload images from one of these sequences into the underlying repository and provide basic metadata for the images. At the time of writing, published series include *A Harlot's Progress*, *A Rake's Progress*, *The Four Stages of Cruelty*, *Industry and Idleness*, and *Marriage a-la-Mode*. Students are introduced to the platform very early in the course, and it becomes both source material and publication platform for coursework. The assignment structure and the ways in which the students interact and contribute to Hogarth in Context has evolved over time, as Milne has responded to the feedback from students as well as adjusting work to the makeup of her classrooms and the evolution of the software supporting the site.

Assignments are scaffolded, with students being introduced by the liaison librarian (Chad Crichton) to online historical research via a curated research guide of relevant material. More advanced features of Zotero (an online, open-source bibliographic management system) are used by the students who create and interact with group bibliographies. Based on the research completed by the students, students write longer works, as well as annotations that overlay the image and describe details of the plates, providing context for details whose significance may go unnoticed by most modern audiences. Anne Milne has also partnered with the UTSC Centre for Teaching and Learning to provide students with instruction on writing for the web and how it differs from essay writing. Once the text of annotations has been reviewed, students publish the work themselves, during class time, with training and support provided by librarians. All students are credited for their work and may request to have material removed. For many English majors, this course represents the only encounter they will have during their undergraduate degree with the creation of digital scholarship. This assignment can be labor intensive—Milne acts as perpetual editor, publishing only works of sufficient quality to add to the value of the resource. She has also presented on these experiences, particularly on challenges in locally sourcing expertise for instructing students about writing scholarly, web-based material.[4]

The library's DSU seeks to build generalized applications that can be sustained by a wide user base, rather than creating bespoke software. This means that Milne, along with many library's DSU collaborators, weathered the construction of the software and showed a willingness to compromise a set of dream features in order to support long-term sustainability. Image annotation on the web remains a topic of intense interest and activity in digital scholarship communities, and the library's DSU developed Hogarth in Context's tools to adhere to emerging standards and practices, and as part of this larger dialogue.[5] The resulting annotation software has been published for use by others and lays a foundation for annotation work at UTSC and in other institutions using Islandora.[6]

AUTHORING ORAL HISTORIES: NEARBY
STUDIES/NEARBY HISTORIES (2013–2018)

Average class size: Twelve to thirty students
Offered in: Senior (fourth) year
Department: Historical and Cultural Studies, Women's and Gender Studies, and Geography
The Nearby Studies project is a multifaceted initiative developed in 2013 between the UTSC History and Women's and Gender Studies programs

in the Department of Historical and Cultural Studies, and the City Studies program in the UTSC Department of Human Geography, led by Christine Berkowitz.[7] The project develops partnerships with community groups on topics of local interest and teaches interdisciplinary courses with an emphasis on community-based participatory research methods and digital projects as well as "the acquisition and development of online and material collections."[8] Course offerings over the years have involved research/teaching collaborations between the departments of History, Women's and Gender Studies, City Studies, Sociology, and Anthropology. Through coursework, students gain an awareness of the significance of local and oral histories[9] as well as the richness of Scarborough's historical and cultural landscape. Students write blog posts and collect, analyze, and interpret data all while developing an understanding of both the methods and the responsibilities related to the collection and preservation of oral histories and the dissemination of digital products for a public audience. A grant-funded exhibit specific to the history of UTSC has made some of the material public, and the project hopes to launch a larger public collection in the future.[10] Students begin submitting blog posts to the platform and commenting on the posts of others early in the term. These assignments encourage students to reflect on the material in the repository and their learning experiences, both theoretical and practical, and are classified using an ever-evolving controlled vocabulary and archived after term. The basic structure of the blogging assignment and final digital assignment predate the current system and Berkowitz's partnership with the library's DSU, though assignments continue to evolve alongside the Nearby Studies platform. Development has focused on making assignment administration less laborious and producing better structured (and easier to preserve) outputs. For example, the library's DSU is currently working on an application that will permit students in this course (and others) to catalog, license, and submit complex oral history materials directly into a workflow where they can be reviewed by an instructor and published directly to the course repository. This process is currently manual. Students will also soon have the ability to annotate video and audio content directly in the interface (a development with origins in the Hogarth in Context project).

As students progress toward their final assignment, they receive tool-based instruction for the production of videos and audio files from the UTSC Centre for Teaching and Learning as well as other campus experts from partnering departments. The liaison librarian for the department of Historical and Cultural Studies (Whitney Kemble) provides instruction on Zotero and conducting online library research. In a complementary course, students take service-learning placements with community organizations and institutions, where they contribute to the creation, repair, or dissemination of content (often through digitizing or other digitally mediated efforts). The library's DSU has also provided placements for students. Many institutions are dealing with similar challenges providing support for the authorship, dissemination, and stewardship of oral histories. Challenges include multilingual transcription and annotation of audio/video content, as well as interlinking and describing the unpredictable formats and structures of these materials. When Berkowitz approached the DSU for support, she offered personal grant funds to pay for an external developer to work with the DSU on prototype software. That commitment fostered open-source software that is now in use by several international institutions with local audio/video repositories and Oral History projects.[11] The software was a significant topic of discussion in an "Islandora Interest Group," with members from nine institutions, many of whom use the software in their own institutions.[12] The library's DSU has also published and presented on the technical dimensions of the project.[13]

DIGITAL HISTORY: REMEDIATING RYCAUT'S *PRESENT STATE OF THE OTTOMAN EMPIRE* (2014)

Average class size: Usually capped at fifteen students
Offered in: Senior (fourth) year
Department: Historical and Cultural Studies
Digital History is a fourth-year course taught in the Historical and Cultural Studies department. The inaugural version taught by Natalie Rothman focused on Paul Rycaut's *Present State of the Ottoman Empire*.[14] Rycaut's text is a product of the widespread international diplomatic and commercial interest in the Ottoman Empire through the sixteenth and seventeenth centuries and is a rich source for scholars of the period. Among the course learning objectives, Rothman sought to emphasize the value (and limitations) of digital methodologies and collaboration. Rothman worked with librarians and archivists to bring students into the University of Toronto Fisher Rare Book Library at the start of the term to view the original text. After students reflected on this experience, they were provided with a digital copy (including facsimile scans and digital full text), created in partnership with the Toronto Libraries and the Internet Archive. As the course progressed, weekly tutorials highlighted common approaches to computer-based inquiry and considered their implications for producing insights about the text. Throughout the course, students submitted blog posts to an online system reflecting on their own learning process as well as the outcomes of their assignment. Tutorials focused on encoding, annotation, mapping, and image analysis. Working in groups, students made heavy

use of the Google ecosystem, including Drive (for text cleanup and encoding), Sheets, and Fusion Tables (for mapping and other visualizations). Students also used Etherpad for collaborative note-taking, Voyant to explore text analysis, and Zotero for collaborative bibliographic management. The platform hosting student work and interaction is called Serai and is hosted by the library's DSU, though it was developed by Rothman's team using an Early Researcher Award from the Ontario Ministry of Research and Innovation (2012–2016). Serai self-defines as a "free and open online collaboratory for scholarship on premodern encounters across ethnolinguistic and religious divides, combining regional expertise with a keen interest in the transformative potential of digital scholarship."[15] The course also benefited from a local grant from the UTSC Centre for Teaching and Learning.[16] In addition to facilitating reusable learning materials, the instructional team Rothman put together used other methods, such as online surveys, to glean insight into student perceptions and skills and their development through the course. Most of the course tutorials became a set of Creative Commons licensed slides, maintained by the library's DSU for the use of other course instructors teaching digital research methods in the classroom.[17]

INTRODUCTION TO SOFTWARE ENGINEERING AND THE MEDIACAT PROJECT FALL 2014–PRESENT

Average class size: 100–125 students across sections
Offered in: Junior (third) year
Department: Computer and Mathematical Sciences
UTSC Department of Anthropology faculty member Alejandro Paz studies the evolution of public discourse through the digitization of media and transformation of online news reporting. In 2014, Paz began working with the library to explore application-based support to aid him in tracking and recording real-time development of news stories as they emerge online, as well as the cross-referencing of materials between news outlets and individuals using platforms such as Twitter. Across campus, Anya Tafliovich teaches multiple courses in the UTSC Computer Science program, including the popular Introduction to Software Engineering. In this course, students are introduced to methodologies for software development and project management. In smaller groups, students design an application for a client, collecting specifications and working together to provide an end product. Tafliovich and her teaching team review submissions for the top applications, which students then present to the client(s), Tafliovich, and other judges on a final-day event. The top application wins a prize and is often adopted by the client. Tafliovich has offered

additional summer courses to students who wish to refine their application further or explore other aspects of application architecture.

Tafliovich seeks out real-world challenges that would benefit from programming capacity and eschews private industry, enabling students to keep credit for their work and build knowledge of open software initiatives. Paz's proposed research application met this standard and introduced Tafliovich's class to the world of humanities computing research methods. The combination of the liaison librarian program and the library's DSU serendipitously connected Paz with Tafliovich, as the DSU librarians are also liaison librarians for Computer Science. The resulting meetings and coursework produced an application called MediaCAT. MediaCAT combines a customizable crawler with a custom search engine to collect information from news websites and Twitter accounts, including citations and hyperlinks. The information is stored "in preparation for an advanced analysis of the relations across the digital news-scape."[18] This open-source application is still in active development, with subsequent students developing it through paid work placements funded by Paz, who intends to use some of the material collected by the application as source work for students in his own future teaching. MediaCat has already fostered cross-disciplinary work, created a tool for use by researchers at UTSC and elsewhere, and introduced Paz to more formalized software development methods, and it continues to provide students with a practical project for education and course credit, for which they receive real-world recognition. It is reasonable to suggest that embedding humanities computing in undergraduate classrooms may inspire students to seek similar work in the future, enriching the field with new skills and perspectives. In addition, students working collaboratively in courses with obvious cross departmental collaboration may better understand the research (and professional) environment into which they are graduating.

A common problem for digital humanists is one of access—access to tools and skills as well as the primary and human resources required to mount DH assignments. These examples of collaboration add fuel to the oft-stoked engine of discourse surrounding the significance of collaboration, particularly for accessing and sustaining faculty access to resources. Notably, they reflect how a successful classroom project may provide not only enrichment to students but material for study and praxis across several disciplines.

NOTES

1. Utsc.utoronto.ca, "Experiential Learning Vice Principal Academic and Dean," accessed August 15, 2018, https://www.utsc.utoronto.ca/vpdean /experiential-learning.

2. Utsc.utoronto.ca, "Partnerships and Community Engagement Anchor Strategy," accessed August 15, 2018, https://www.utsc.utoronto.ca/partnerships /anchor-strategy.

3. Hogarth.digitalscholarship.utsc.utoronto.ca, "Home," accessed August 15, 2018, https://hogarth.digitalscholarship.utsc.utoronto.ca.

4. Anne Milne, "Unexpected Illiteracies and Clunkiness: Imagining 'Writing for the Web' for English Majors," paper presented at Digital Pedagogy and the Student Experience, Toronto, Ontario, August 19–21, 2015, accessed August 15, 2018, https://www.utsc.utoronto.ca/conferences/dpi/session/anne-milne-utsc.

5. M. E. Barnes, N. Ledchumykanthan, K. Pham, and K. Stapelfeldt, "Annotation-Based Enrichment of Digital Objects Using Open-Source Frameworks," *Code4Lib* 37 (July 18, 2017), https://journal.code4lib.org/articles /12582.

6. Digital Scholarship Unit, Islandora Web Annotations, GitHub, accessed August 15, 2018, https://github.com/digitalutsc/islandora_web_annotations 10.5281/zenado.1198880.

7. Utsc.utoronto.ca, Nearby Studies "Home," accessed August 15, 2018, https://nearby-studies.digitalscholarship.utsc.utoronto.ca.

8. Utsc.utoronto.ca, Nearby Studies "About," accessed August 15, 2018, http://nearby-studies.digitalscholarship.utsc.utoronto.ca/about.

9. Nearby Studies is an interdisciplinary research project and as such the collaborations include disciplines engaged in community-based participatory qualitative research that despite some differences in name involve similar approaches based on interview methodologies—oral history, ethnography, life stories, interviews. We substitute "oral history" for our purposes here to simplify the narrative only.

10. Storiesofutsc.ca, Scarborough Oral Histories Project, accessed August 15, 2018, https://storiesofutsc.ca.

11. Islandora Labs, Islandora Oral Histories Solution Pack, GitHub, accessed August 15, 2018, https://github.com/Islandora-Labs/islandora_solution_ pack_oralhistories.

12. Islandora Oral Histories Interest Group, Islandora Oral Histories Interest Group, GitHub, accessed August 15, 2018, https://github.com/islandora -interest-groups/Islandora-Oral-Histories-Interest-Group.

13. M. E. Barnes, N. Ledchumykanthan, K. Pham, and K. Stapelfeldt, "Supporting Oral Histories in Islandora," *Code4Lib* 35 (January 30, 2017), http:// journal.code4lib.org/articles/12176.

14. Paul Rycaut, *The present state of the Ottoman Empire. Containing the maxims of the Turkish politie, the most material points of the Mahometan religion, their sects and heresies, their convents and religious votaries, their military discipline, with an exact computation of their forces both by land and sea. Illustrated with divers pieces*

of sculpture, representing the variety of habits amongst the Turks. In three books: Sir Paul Rycaut, 1628–1700: free download, borrow, and streaming: internet archive, accessed August 15, 2018, https://archive.org/details/presentstateofotooryca.

15. Serai.digitalscholarship.utsc.utoronto.ca, "Home," accessed August 15, 2018, https://serai.digitalscholarship.utsc.utoronto.ca.

16. Utsc.utoronto.ca, Digital Scholarship Unit UTSC Library Pedagogy Project, accessed August 15, 2018, https://digitalscholarship.utsc.utoronto.ca/content/utsc-library-pedagogy-project.

17. Serai.digitalscholarship.utsc.utoronto.ca, HISD18 Digital History, accessed August 15, 2018, https://serai.digitalscholarship.utsc.utoronto.ca/hisd18-digital-history?page=5.

18. Utsc.utoronto.ca, Mediacat Welcome to Mediacat, accessed August 15, 2018, http://mediacat.utsc.utoronto.ca.

SEVENTEEN

—⚉—

Visualeyes This

Using Interactive Visualization Tools to Engage Students in Historical Research and Digital Humanities R&D

SCOT A. FRENCH

University of Central Florida

FOR THE PAST TWENTY YEARS, first at the University of Virginia (UVA) and more recently at the University of Central Florida (UCF), I have been incorporating digital tools into my undergraduate and graduate history seminars as low-risk, high-reward "adventures" in digital humanities. Students in my early courses learned basic HTML coding in order to create simple web exhibits and share their community-engaged research projects with the public. (Some of their hand-coded projects, hosted by the UVA, remain accessible to this day.) Later, through my coteaching collaborations with visualization specialist Bill Ferster, students participated in the development of a dynamic, open-access web-authoring tool called VisualEyes. Examples of our students' published work with VisualEyes can be found in the Jefferson's Travels digital mapping project funded by the National Endowment for the Humanities (NEH), the K–12 instructional materials for UCF's National Cemetery Administration–funded Veterans Legacy Program, and Sarah Schneider's web project, Searching for Home: Migrations of the Château de la Guette Children during and after the Holocaust.[1]

Our embrace of digital tools in the classroom has been enabled by rapid advances in web-authoring technology yet constrained at times by institutional factors beyond our control. At the UVA, for example, where I taught

114

undergraduate digital history seminars from 2000 to 2011, I had the benefit of a robust cyberinfrastructural support network and the freedom to teach upper-level digital history courses of my own design. There, the greatest constraint was a department chair's stubborn insistence that capstone history courses produce research papers of at least twenty-five pages, disallowing our alternative, mixed-media web projects with much shorter (if no less rigorous) writing assignments. At the UCF, where I have been teaching digital history and public history courses since 2011, infrastructural support for collaborative, classroom-based digital research was negligible until a recent investment in full-time staff and student workstations for UCF's Center for Humanities and Digital Research. While UVA and UCF could not be more different as institutional hosts for DH coursework, each in its own way has reinforced my flexible, opportunistic approach to teaching and learning with digital tools. (See fig. 17.1.)

My experience with digital humanities tools dates to the early 1990s—the dawn of desktop computing and the World Wide Web—when I had the good fortune to work as a graduate research assistant on Edward L. Ayers's pioneering DH project, The Valley of the Shadow: Two Communities in the American Civil War, at the UVA. Ayers envisioned an expansive digital archive of primary sources that would serve as the basis for his next book while providing students, teachers, and the general public with a valuable teaching and learning resource. There was no precedent for this kind of digital humanities project, no model on which to elaborate; every interface had to be imagined, every object/text digitized and curated for public display. Ayers invited his graduate research assistants and project staff to participate fully in the iterative design process, and he generously credited each of us, by name, with contributions to the award-winning archive that resulted.[2]

As a learning space, the Valley project resembled a research lab or art design studio far more than a traditional graduate seminar. Like Disney animators, we added light, shadow, and motion to Ayers's big picture. I had some basic knowledge of HTML, having designed my own interactive course websites, but, as a Valley team member, I focused primarily on historical content/context and information design and left the advanced technology to others. While the Valley provided me with valuable on-the-job DH skills training, far more lasting—from my perspective as a prospective teacher—was the project's modeling of (to quote Lisa Spiro) core DH "values": collaboration, experimentation, and open access. The Valley project embraced and exemplified these values, which inform and inspire my work to this day.[3]

To extend their successful model of collaborative humanities research to other start-up projects, Ayers and founding Valley project director William

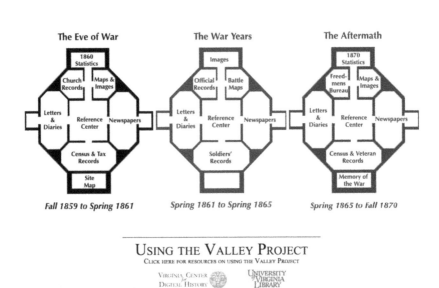

Figure 17.1. Screenshot of web portal for The Valley of the Shadow: Two Communities in the American Civil War. Courtesy of the University of Virginia Library, Virginia Center for Digital History (VCDH), and Institute for Advanced Technology in the Humanities (IATH), http://valley.lib.virginia.edu/VoS /choosepart.html.

G. Thomas III established the Virginia Center for Digital History (VCDH) in 1998. Located in UVA's Alderman Library, next door to the Institute for Advanced Technology in the Humanities, VCDH hired full-time staff— a director, an assistant director, a programmer, a web developer, a director of outreach and education—to assist interested faculty in developing projects for K–12 classroom use and beyond. VCDH's roster expanded to nearly a dozen projects, including Crandall A. Shifflett's Virtual Jamestown, Holly Cowan Shulman's The Dolley Madison Project, and my own Race and Place: An African American Community in the Jim Crow South. As project directors we relied on VCDH staff for back-end programming and front-end web design, and VCDH servers for long-term storage and the backup of data. VCDH provided us, in short, with vital institutional support for the development of faculty-driven DH projects prior to the emergence of free, open-access, DIY web-authoring tools nearly a decade later.

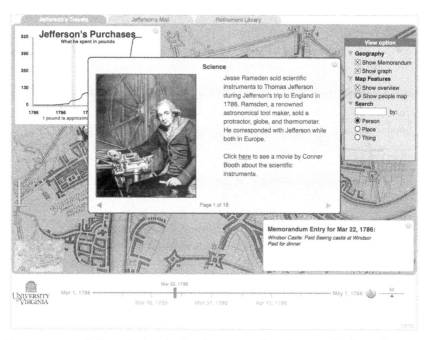

Figure 17.2. Our Jefferson's Travels visualization, with its dynamic displays of undergraduate student research, can be viewed here: http://www.viseyes.org /show/?base=jt.

By 2006, when I became director of VCDH, the landscape for center-based funding of new DH projects had changed. That year, the NEH launched the Digital Humanities Start-Up Grant Program, which encouraged scholars "to experiment with new methods and to make tools tailored to humanities problems." We quickly learned, from our discussions with NEH program officers, that projects advancing new methods and tools stood a far greater chance of being funded than those addressing compelling humanities questions or educational objectives alone.

Enter Bill Ferster, an interactive visualization specialist with experience building dynamic web-authoring tools for classroom teachers and students. Ferster joined VCDH as the director of technology in 2007 with a mandate to rethink traditional DH project development. He asked: What if we gave historians a customizable platform and tool kit to build their own interactive websites? And what if we engaged undergraduate history students in the R&D process just as Ayers had involved his graduate research assistants in building the Valley? (See fig. 17.2.)

Out of our discussions emerged a successful 2007 NEH Start-Up Grant proposal entitled "Jefferson's Travels: A Digital Journey Using the History-Browser." The grant abstract highlights our strategic focus on DH tool development, with humanities content relegated to secondary importance:

> The Jefferson's Travels Project is a joint undertaking of the Virginia Center for Digital History and the Thomas Jefferson Foundation to develop a highly interactive web-based tool that uses Thomas Jefferson's travels as initial content. A specially constructed interactive browser (the HistoryBrowser) provides for fast and easy navigation along the time and place dimensions. The HistoryBrowser encourages primary source documents to speak more directly to the audience by providing visualizations of the relationships, chronologies, and causal events. They will often contain word-based narrative, in written or oral forms to help connect the resources, but the browser allows for a new form of storytelling, using guided visualizations. These visualizations use new methods of interpreting and presenting historic inquiry, such as animation over time, charts, maps, data, and interactive timelines to graphically show the relationships between multiple kinds of information.[4]

A radically new teaching model, merging traditional archival research with training in DH methods, undergirded development of the HistoryBrowser. Before submitting the NEH Start-Up Grant proposal, Ferster and I had already prototyped the tool in a team-taught history capstone seminar called, simply, Jefferson's Travels. Here is the course description:

> HIUS 401 provides a unique opportunity to study Thomas Jefferson's 1786 journey to England and develop a state-of-the-art interactive website working closely with the Thomas Jefferson Memorial Foundation (Monticello). In this class we will perform all the tasks involved in creating a highly interactive website containing images, documents, maps, diaries, and digital narratives pertaining to Jefferson's six-week journey to England. Each day will be mapped geographically and linked to visual resources on the activities he participated in, places he visited, items he purchased, and people he met.
>
> Students will read secondary sources about Mr. Jefferson's trip, identify primary sources from Monticello Digital Library and other archives, work with digital maps, digitize new resources, annotate information, and create a powerful relational database. Class discussions will investigate ways that the information can use the new digital tools being developed at the Virginia Center for Digital History to make historical understanding more transparent and promote dynamic inquiry. Complex visualizations will be built as a result of these discussions using resources identified in the class, and added to the website.

Each student will complete a 10-page research paper, a short (2–3 minute) digital documentary using primary sources reflecting some portion of their research that interested them, and a "visualization" to be developed in consultation with the instructors. Grading will be based on reading responses/class participation (25 percent), a 10-page research paper (25 percent), and public presentation of the digital documentary and visualization (50 percent). The result of the class will be a highly interactive website that will contribute to the digital historical literature base for scholars, historians and educators, and provide students with their first publication.[5]

Students in the Jefferson's Travels course researched topics of interest to them—Jefferson's transoceanic correspondence, his social calendar in England, his daily purchases, etc. —and produced data- and media-rich visualizations that were woven by Ferster into a dynamic VisualEyes display.[6] The original Flash-based version of the HistoryBrowser, renamed Visual-Eyes to emphasize its visual design elements, provided a customizable template for Jefferson's Travels and other classroom-based DH projects, as well as scholarly research projects created by faculty and independent scholars. Unfortunately, the burden of site design and data visualization fell primarily on Ferster, who struggled to find students and faculty with adequate design skills willing to master the authoring program. (See fig. 17.3.)

Ferster's decision to upgrade VisualEyes for access on mobile and tablet devices using HTML5 created an opportunity to reengage history students in user interface design. As described in the authoring guide, the new, simplified VisualEyes5 interface features three viewing panes: "To the right, a story panel contains text and narration. The left side has a dynamic map on top, with an interactive timeline below it. All three panes are linked together, so that clicking on one can easily cause changes to the others." My first test project using the new version, mapping the travels of an itinerant preacher, convinced me that graduate students could quickly master the new authoring tools and use VisualEyes5 (as the HTML5 version was dubbed) to present their own work.[7]

Three UCF graduate students—Holly Baker, Mark Barnes, and Sarah Schneider—accepted my invitation to test-drive a beta version of VisualEyes5 on mapping projects growing out of their coursework and research. Two were veterans of my Digital Tools for Historians seminar, the third my thesis advisee with an interest in digital museum curation. Baker used the VisualEyes5 platform to chart the song collecting journeys of the Federal Writers' Project in Depression-era Florida. Barnes used it to link Florida military veterans' biographies, written by UCF undergraduate students, to overseas burial sites in France's Epinal American Cemetery. Schneider traced the transatlantic

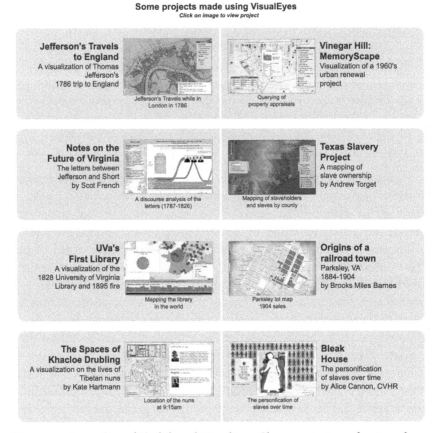

Figure 17.3. A sampling of Flash-based VisualEyes Classic projects can be viewed here: www.viseyes.org/viseyes.htm.

journeys of Jewish refugee children who fled Nazi Germany via France, ca. 1939–1942. The three shared web design tips with each other and reached out to Ferster, who welcomed the user feedback, for help with technical issues as they arose.

The students benefited in several important ways. First, they created working prototypes for digital projects linked to their own scholarly research. Second, they received validation and valuable feedback from peers at professional conferences, most notably Digitorium, the University of Alabama's Digital Humanities Conference. And, finally, their experience working with seasoned web developer Bill Ferster gave them insight into the interdisciplinary and intensely collaborative team design process that has come to define digital humanities. (See fig. 17.4.)

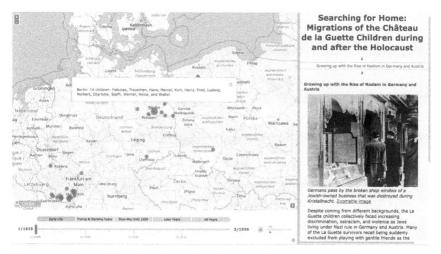

Figure 17.4. Sarah Schneider's "Searching for Home" exhibit, a public history component of her award-wining 2018 UCF History master's thesis, is accessible via the VisualEyes5 home page: www.viseyes.org/visualeyes. Photo credit: United States Holocaust Memorial Museum, courtesy of National Archives and Records Administration, College Park, Maryland.

Scholarly recognition of DH projects and the intellectual work involved in data visualization / web design is growing. Sarah Schneider's multimodal master's thesis ("Searching for Home: Migrations of the Château de la Guette Children during and after the Holocaust"), with its VisualEyes5 web project component, won the 2018 Outstanding Master's Thesis Award from UCF's College of Arts and Humanities. In addition to her 245-page academic research paper, based on extensive archival research, Schneider created an elegantly designed, richly illustrated, painstakingly footnoted VisualEyes5 exhibit for public audiences. Awards committee reviewers remarked on the excellence and potential "impact" of Schneider's VisualEyes5 web exhibit, which made her research accessible to audiences well beyond the academy.[8]

As infrastructural support for digital humanities scholarship grows, so does the potential for expanded classroom training in historical data visualization tools and web design. Cotaught courses, built around grant-funded projects like UCF's Veterans Legacy Program and UVA's Jefferson's Travels, offer a model. To quote Bill Ferster: "This kind of seminar combines the best of liberal arts and discipline-specific education with training in visual thinking and the application of new technologies. As importantly, it offers undergraduates [and graduates] an opportunity to present original research for peer review and online publication, adding value and purpose to their work."[9]

NOTES

1. For links to referenced VisualEyes projects, see Jefferson's Travels, http://www.viseyes.org/show/?base=jt (accessed February 14, 2020); UCF-NCA Veterans Legacy Program, K–12 Instructional Materials, https://vlp.cah.ucf.edu /k12.php (accessed February 14, 2020); and Sarah Schneider's Searching for Home: Migrations of the Château de la Guette Children during and after the Holocaust, http://www.viseyes.org/visualeyes/?848 (accessed February 14, 2020).

2. The Valley of the Shadow: Two Communities in the American Civil War, http://valley.lib.virginia.edu (accessed February 14, 2020).

For Ayers's autobiographical account of the Valley project's origins and development, see "A Digital Civil War," in Edward L. Ayers, *What Caused the Civil War? Reflections on the South and Southern History* (New York: W.W. Norton, 2006), 65–93.

3. Lisa Spiro, "'This Is Why We Fight': Defining the Values of the Digital Humanities," in *Debates in the Digital Humanities*, ed. Matthew K. Gold (Minneapolis: University of Minnesota Press, 2012), 16–34, http://dhdebates.gc .cuny.edu/debates/text/13 (accessed February 14, 2020).

4. NEH Grant Details: "Jefferson's Travels: A Digital Journey Using the HistoryBrowser" (2008). https://securegrants.neh.gov/publicquery/main .aspx?f=1&gn=HD-50291-08 (accessed February 14, 2020).

5. Scot French and Bill Ferster, "HIUS 401-F: Digital History Seminar /Jefferson's Travels," (University of Virginia, Fall 2007), http://www.vcdh .virginia.edu/courses/fall07/hius401-f/ (accessed February 14, 2020).

6. To view these student projects, see Jefferson's Travels to England: A Visualization of Thomas Jefferson's 1786 Trip to England, http://www.viseyes .org/show/?base=jt (accessed February 14, 2020).

7. Bill Ferster, "VisualEyes5 Authoring Guide," https://docs.google.com /document/d/1TBCCFo3Wc5NpkG4EVJdxYuhUdauV1b_KICUOhNZQhEI /edit?usp=sharing (accessed February 14, 2020).

8. Sarah Schneider's award-winning master's thesis, "Searching for Home at Château de la Guette and Beyond: Social and Spatial Dimensions of Jewish German and Austrian Children's Journey to Flee Nazi Persecution via Children's Homes in France" (Summer 2018), is accessible via the STARS repository of Electronic Theses and Dissertations, https://stars.library.ucf.edu/etd/6001 (accessed February 14, 2020). Her VisualEyes5 companion exhibit, Searching for Home: Migrations of the Château de la Guette Children during and after the Holocaust, is accessible here: http://www.viseyes.org/visualeyes/?848 (accessed February 14, 2020).

9. Anne E. Bromley, "With Digital Tools, Students Take Learning into Their Own Hands," *UVA Today*, December 13, 2017, https://news.virginia.edu/content /digital-tools-students-take-learning-their-own-hands (accessed February 14, 2020).

PART III

MAPPING AND AUGMENTED REALITIES

EIGHTEEN

—◊◊◊—

The Digital Flâneur

Mapping Twentieth-Century Berlin

CLIFFORD B. ANDERSON
Vanderbilt University

JOY H. CALICO
Vanderbilt University

ACCORDING TO WALTER BENJAMIN, THE flâneur strolls through the city apparently without purpose, taking note of features fellow pedestrians overlook. Benjamin compared the flâneur to a detective: "He only *seems* to be indolent, for behind this indolence there is the watchfulness of an observer who does not take his eyes off a miscreant."[1] Why draw on the figure of the flâneur when teaching digital humanities? In "Digital Flânerie: Illustrative Seeing in the Digital Age," Murray Skees calls on the concept of the flâneur when articulating the relevance of the computer hacker to the internet age. "The digitization of the modern mediascape, like the physiology of the crowds for the flâneur, turns the hacker into a detective."[2] Skees argues that the hacker observes and manipulates, uncovering crimes and solving them, so to speak. In our graduate seminar at Vanderbilt University, titled "The Digital Flâneur: Mapping Twentieth-Century Berlin," we aspired to train students both to see the technologies at play in the course and to intervene critically while learning the history of Berlin from numerous disciplinary perspectives.

ORIGINS OF THE COURSE

In 2014, Joy read *HyperCities: Thick Mapping in the Digital Humanities*[3] and was inspired to use the book and its website as the basis for an experimental one-hour course for the European Studies program she directed. Todd Samuel Presner had written elsewhere about teaching a general education course on the cultural and urban history of Berlin,[4] and Joy adopted *HyperCities* to acculturate first-year students to high-level, cutting-edge scholarship in a relatively low-stakes environment (one credit hour) while introducing them to digital tools and a major European city. She and coinstructor Peggy Setje-Eilers (Assistant Professor Emerita of German) scheduled the course for spring 2015. However, after fourteen students had enrolled and it was time to finalize the syllabus, the website became increasingly unpredictable. Google had stopped supporting the Google Earth plug-in on which the entire project was based, and the site was doomed. It looked like the class would have to be canceled until they contacted two colleagues in the library: Lindsey Fox, coordinator of geographic information systems, and Clifford Anderson, then director of scholarly communications. They became coinstructors and quickly adapted a digital mapping tool they had been developing so that the class could be offered. The undergraduate version ran for three years before Joy and Cliff redesigned it as a graduate seminar in German Studies with a focus on the *digital flâneur*, a term ripe for exploration and interrogation at the graduate level.[5]

The undergraduate version proceeded in reverse chronological order, enacting Presner, Shepard, and Kawano's notion of thick mapping and excavating layers of the city as we moved backward in time. In the graduate course, we moved in chronological order, accruing georeferenced maps, primary sources, scholarship, and technologies; the new transparency function for the maps on the website allowed us to follow developments more clearly. The *HyperCities* approach, alternating theoretical and philosophical discussions of thick mapping with technological sections written by different authors in distinctive fonts, also influenced our approach to coteaching.

Our interdisciplinary approach was meant to counter overreliance on the metaphor of reading the city as a [literary] text.[6] There is, of course, no single best scholarly vantage point from which to study a city per se. The metaphor of seeing guided our selection of readings (after all, Christopher Isherwood began *Goodbye to Berlin* with "I am a camera with its shutter open"[7]), but we also attended to listening. The literature of flânerie inspired our reading list because of its connections to Benjamin and his roots in Berlin. Many other authors thematized the city accordingly.[8]

Given the wide array of scholarship triggered by reunification of the city after 1989, we saw an opportunity to marry the literary, theoretical, and technological in a way that would be unique to Berlin. Studying the ways in which people navigated different iterations of its urban spaces since 1900 required moving spatially around the city and temporally through georeferenced maps representing different eras and regimes.

TOPICS AND TECHNOLOGIES

Our primary instructional tool was the mapping application that Cliff first developed with Lindsey for the undergraduate seminar and iteratively improved in the years since. Good alternatives for teaching with maps have emerged recently (e.g., Carto[9] and Esri Story Maps[10]), but we retained this platform so students could see how code, data, database, and tile server come together to form a functioning application. While commercial online mapping products hide components behind slick interfaces, our students could wander into the digital interstices.

We started with essential tooling for writing software, using git and Github for version control and the Atom editor for encoding data. We then commenced in earnest with the mapping technologies, beginning with JavaScript Object Notation (JSON)[11] to mark up geospatial points according to a standard called GeoJSON.[12] In another session, we explored sending and receiving data over HTTP, learning the rudiments of REST-style application programming interfaces (APIs). Students sent their points to an IBM Cloud-hosted database called Cloudant[13] (a derivative of the open-source CouchDB[14]) via an API tool called Postman.[15] As students gained skills with the tools, we became more ambitious, diving further into Cloudant by setting up individual databases. We had hoped to teach students to write simple map-reduce functions in Cloudant, but it became apparent that manipulating JavaScript required more knowledge than could be mastered in one or two class sessions. The same applied to georeferencing historic maps and loading them into Mapbox, a software-as-service GIS provider.[16] However, at midterm, students could encode and represent points on our course map, interacting directly with the underlying technologies to change the details and appearance on the fly. (See fig. 18.1.)

In the second half of the course, we covered a range of computational approaches for representing urban spaces. The analogy of strolling came to the fore as we promenaded from technology to technology, pausing only when code failed to perform or when we stumbled on unanticipated results. Given the speed of our tour, a better analogy would be to Franz Hessel, the quintessential flâneur of early twentieth-century Berlin. In the central section of *Walking in Berlin* (1929), Hessel jumps into a car with friends and drives kaleidoscopically through the city.[17]

Figure 18.1. Example of georeferencing historic maps.

We started our tour with CityGML, a modeling language for three-dimensional environments.[18] Students extracted features like buildings and viewed them in an application called Azul.[19] We also explored the underlying XML markup, discussing how adding a z-coordinate for depth enriches the representation of data but also makes them complicated to edit.

We then moved to Wikidata, a recent addition to the Wikimedia universe that extracts data from all language editions of Wikipedia (along with other data sets) and makes them searchable.[20] Students learned to log on to Wikidata, add facts to entries, and ask questions with the SPARQL query language. Students enjoyed exploring the visualization tools built into the Wikidata query interface,[21] creating maps, timelines, and other representations of information about Berlin.

Our next stop was Neo4j, a graph database with a simpler query language called Cypher.[22] Neo4j works very well for network analysis, and we used it to explore the U-Bahn network in Berlin. We extracted data from Wikidata (including latitude and longitude coordinates for the stations along with the connections between them), then transformed that data into lists of nodes and edges, which we loaded into Neo4j. We analyzed the network, locating the central-most nodes and the least-connected ones. We also applied Edsger Dijkstra's Shortest Path First algorithm to find optimal routes between any given set of stations.

The last destination was the programming language R. Our goal was to show students how to mine literary texts for representations of Berlin. They learned to set up R and RStudio, then imported a number of packages to support text mining, including tidytext.[23] We downloaded books from Project Gutenberg then explored their contents in various ways, analyzing, for instance, the sentiment of sentences containing the word "Berlin" across this impromptu corpus.

This speedy tour of technologies was meant to exemplify the necessity of abstraction. A city cannot be fully represented in its manifold concreteness. Just as Hessel reported only a fraction of what he saw in his wild ride across Berlin, so too any digital project selects an abstraction, removing whole categories of detail to focus on specific elements.[24] Our intention was to train students to approach digital humanities projects with critical awareness of what technologies represent and omit.

ASSESSMENTS

Using Digital Humanities in the Classroom provided valuable guidance for designing in-class activities, short assignments, and larger projects.[25] We separated the successful use of technology in presentations from the successful use of technology in the overall project, provided an opportunity for students to reflect on the experience of integrating their humanistic research and digital skills in a single project, and encouraged contributions to the greater public good through class exercises in adding data to Wikidata, making projects available on GitHub, and contributing to our map project on the public website.

Most graduate seminars meet once a week, but we divided this class into two seventy-five-minute meetings so that the technology would not feel overwhelming in the context of a long seminar setting. The first meeting each week was devoted to the discussion of readings and other materials, and students took turns leading discussions based on questions they posted to Brightspace in advance; the second meeting each week was devoted to technology.

At midterm, students demonstrated mastery of technologies thus far in ten-minute presentations on topics of their choice (such as nightclubs, or exhibitions at the Berlin Zoo). This exercise required them to mark up their points in GeoJSON, add references to images and YouTube videos along with descriptive text, and use HTTP calls to send their points to our map. This way we established common baseline proficiencies that students could build on for their major projects in the second half of the semester. Students reported that this gave them confidence and facilitated group learning, since they could help one another with those common technologies.

The final set of assessments allowed students the freedom to develop topics and technologies of interest. They could elaborate on the materials and digital representation of their midterm projects or undertake new research. Since we knew that exploring with new technologies can lead to dead ends, we did not put too much weight on the digital projects themselves, assigning papers to accompany the digital exercise. Students demonstrated their projects in class presentations. Their papers articulated a humanistic research question, explained why they chose the technologies they used to investigate it, and presented their findings. They also wrote short reflection pieces in which they processed the experience of using the technologies. These forms of assessment performed reasonably well, though in certain cases students' digital ambitions exceeded their technical expertise—an experience with which all digital humanists will identify!

LIMITATIONS OF THE FLÂNEUR METAPHOR

We wanted students to recognize and critique the limitations of this metaphor - specifically the dynamics of race, gender, and class that make flânerie readily available to certain individuals and off limits to others. We began with de Certeau's classic "Walking in the City" to remind students of the political dimension of navigating planned urban spaces.[26] We incorporated class visits from colleagues whose digital scholarship challenges assumptions about who resides in Berlin and how they move through the city (Kira Thurman on Black Germany, Peter McMurray on Islam[27]), and assigned readings about the ways in which women's spaces,[28] queer spaces,[29] and immigrant neighborhoods[30] configure different experiences of that city.

The metaphor of the flâneur also runs up against limits in the digital humanities. We had hoped our digital map would serve both pedagogical and research purposes. In the undergraduate seminar, students contributed points on the digital map according to major periods in Berlin's twentieth-century history (Imperial, Weimar, National Socialist, Allied-Occupied, Cold War, Reunified). We retained these points over three iterations of the course, creating ever-richer sets of markers.

Despite some difficulties—students' descriptive texts were of uneven quality, and some points strayed significantly from their actual historical locations—we retained this aspiration until the graduate seminar, when we added more maps and no longer required students to connect points with specific maps. What we gained in expressivity—for instance, it is now possible to locate Weimar nightclubs on maps produced during the National Socialist regime—cost our project in coherence. Students in the graduate seminar also uploaded large quantities of data from Wikidata, significantly expanding our site beyond the "hand-curated" data from previous years. But does the proliferation of data on our map serve any research interests? Or does it expose the shortcoming of strolling among the data without a fixed purpose? As we continue with both the course and the digital mapping project, we must rethink how and whether to retain the link between pedagogy and research.

FUTURE PROSPECTS

Enhanced audio capability would allow users to listen to clips of sounds or music one might have heard at any given location during the years represented by the maps (1895, 1908, 1920, 1936, 1947, 1970). We are investigating the use of the Music Encoding Initiative for that purpose.[31]

Another possibility would be to apply the course framework to other cities. The idea of "franchising" the course came up naturally in conversations with fellow faculty. We could easily imagine analogous courses such as Mapping Paris, Mapping Buenos Aires, or Mapping Taipei. Selecting (and digitizing) historical maps representing different epochs could pose a challenge, as might identifying analogous data sets for the computational exercises. Finding equivalent data sets for major Western metropolitan areas like Paris could be straightforward, while locating comparable data sets for non-Western cities might prove more difficult.

Teaching in the digital humanities requires blending humanistic inquiry with technical exploration. In the end, the biggest challenge in developing different editions of this course might be re-creating the complementary expertise and pedagogical partnership that made it possible for us to teach "The Digital Flâneur" based in Berlin.

NOTES

1. Walter Benjamin, *Charles Baudelaire: A Lyric Poet in the Era of High Capitalism*, trans. Harry Zohn (London: Verso Books, 1997), 41.

2. Murray Skees, "Digital Flânerie: Illustrative Seeing in the Digital Age," *Critical Horizons* 11, no. 2 (May 2010): 283, doi:10.1558/crit.v11i2.265.

3. Todd Samuel Presner, David Shepard, and Yoh Kawano, *Hypercities: Thick Mapping in the Digital Humanities* (Cambridge, MA: Harvard University Press, 2014).

4. Todd Samuel Presner, "HyperCities: Building a Web 2.0 Learning Platform," in *Teaching Literature at a Distance: Open, Online and Blended Learning*, ed. Takis Kayalis and Anastasia Natsina (London: Continuum, 2010), 171–182.

5. Ibid., 71.

6. Lutz Koepnick, "Forget Berlin," *German Quarterly* 74, no. 4 (2001): 343–354, doi:10.2307/3072629.

7. Christopher Isherwood, *Goodbye to Berlin* (New York: New Directions, 2012).

8. Alfred Döblin, *Berlin Alexanderplatz*, trans. Michael Hoffmann (New York: New York Review Books, 2018); Franz Hessel, *Walking in Berlin: A Flaneur in the Capital*, trans. Amanda DeMarco (Cambridge, MA: MIT Press, 2017 [German original, 1929]); Pascale Hugues, *Hannah's Dress: Berlin 1904–2014*, trans. C. John Delogu (Cambridge, UK: Polity, 2017); Isherwood, *Goodbye to Berlin*; and Vladimir Nabokov, "A Guide to Berlin," in *Details of a Sunset and Other Stories*, trans. Dmitri Nabokov (London: Weidenfeld and Nicolson, 1994).

9. See https://carto.com/.

10. See https://storymaps.arcgis.com.

11. Douglas Crockford, "JSON: Javascript Object Notation," 2006, https://www.json.org/.

12. Internet Engineering Task Force (IETF), "The GeoJSON Format," 2016.

13. See https://www.ibm.com/cloud/cloudant.

14. See http://couchdb.apache.org.

15. See https://www.getpostman.com.

16. See https://www.mapbox.com.

17. Hessel, *Walking in Berlin*.

18. Filip Biljecki, Jantien Stoter, Hugo Ledoux, Sisi Zlatanova, and Arzu Çöltekin, "Applications of 3d City Models: State of the Art Review," *ISPRS International Journal of Geo-Information* 4, no. 4 (December 2015): 2842–2889, doi:10.3390/ijgi4042842.

19. See https://github.com/tudelft3d/azul.

20. Denny Vrandečić and Markus Krötzsch, "Wikidata: A Free Collaborative Knowledgebase," *Communications of the ACM* 57, no. 10 (September 2014): 78–85, doi:10.1145/2629489.

21. See https://query.wikidata.org.

22. Ian Robinson, Jim Webber, and Emil Eifrem, *Graph Databases* (Sebastopol, CA: O'Reilly Media, 2013).

23. Julia Silge and David Robinson, "Tidytext: Text Mining and Analysis Using Tidy Data Principles in R," *Journal of Open Source Software* 1, no. 3 (2016), doi:10.21105/joss.00037.

24. Skees notes that computational abstraction (or "hacking") is "somewhat similar to Benjamin's constructions of dialectical images." See Skees, "Digital Flânerie," 284.

25. Claire Battershill and Shawna Ross, *Using Digital Humanities in the Classroom: A Practical Introduction for Teachers, Lecturers, and Students* (London: Bloomsbury, 2017).

26. Michel de Certeau, "Walking in the City," in *The Practice of Everyday Life*, trans. Steve Rendall, 3rd ed. (Berkeley: University of California Press, 2011), 91–110.

27. Kira Thurman is contributor and advisor at blackcentraleurope.com. Peter McMurray, "Pathways to God: The Islamic Acoustics of Turkish Berlin." PhD diss., Harvard University, 2014), https://dash.harvard.edu/handle/1/13064989.

28. Barbara Hahn, "Encounters at the Margins: Jewish Salons Around 1900," in *Berlin Metropolis: Jews and the New Culture, 1890–1918*, ed. Emily D. Bilski (Berkeley: University of California Press, 1999), 189–207; Despina Stratigakos, *A Women's Berlin: Building the Modern City* (Minneapolis: University of Minnesota Press, 2008).

29. Mel Gordon, *Voluptuous Panic: The Erotic World of Weimar Berlin* (Los Angeles: Feral House, 2000).

30. Annika Marlen Hinze, *Turkish Berlin: Integration Policy and Urban Space* (Minneapolis: University of Minnesota Press, 2013).

31. See http://music-encoding.org.

NINETEEN

—⁓—

Digital Maps as Content and Pedagogy

Alternative Cartographic Practices in the Humanities Classroom

STEPHEN BUTTES

Purdue University Fort Wayne

ONE OF THE GOALS OF pedagogy is to provide students with an appropriate map of the discipline so that they can navigate new disciplinary territories effectively and also create new relationships with the world that surrounds them. Our goal is for students not only to learn the discipline but also to intervene and modify it through the creation of new knowledge and the application of existing knowledge to new contexts to make sense of new phenomena. In this essay, I review three computer-mediated projects that enable students to do precisely that. In this sense, these final projects—three types of digital maps—are deeply connected to the content of the course. But they also serve a pedagogical function. They help students recognize the stakes of their final projects and focus on relating the knowledge created in their research projects to the discipline and their academic work more broadly. These projects make it clear that the function of our courses—and the promise of the digital humanities in their best form—is to make the meaningful *meaningful* to students by making it evident to them "what [they as] learners are doing."[1] In short, the digital humanities and, in particular, its mapping technologies can make it easier to frame the discipline, or, to "shape . . . [the] intentions and expectations" we have for students as they engage in learning.[2]

For many scholars, an attention to form is essential for constructing solid pedagogy. As with a "script for a stage play" that enables an individualized production night after night, the desired result in the classroom, consistent student learning semester after semester, "arises as a result of—not in spite of—the defining constraints."[3] However, as some scholars note, the constraints of traditional pedagogical approaches are often too rigid, drawing our attention to "technocratic competencies [such] as lesson planning, classroom manage-ment and outcome evaluation" instead of "responsive attunement to learn-ers."[4] These are not necessarily mutually exclusive, but the focus on the end product can obscure the processes that make its realization possible. For this reason, some argue for an "inventiveness of form": "inventive pedagogies must include interruptions to the familiar. Students will be most inventive when they are engaged in tasks that ask them to think freshly about forms that they already know well."[5] As I suggest in what follows, the traditional undergraduate research essay can often be rigid and rote with the essay as the end goal rather than the learning (the claims and the arguments) that the essay enabled. And yet as with lesson planning or assessment, the undergraduate research essay has an essential role to play in student learning. The key to inventiveness of form is "liberating constraints," that is, innovating the frame and engaging in new ways the constraints we put around our presentation of the discipline so that we can engage students more in learning and "liberate their thinking."[6] Innovations in mapping technologies and their availability to the digital humanities make them a useful tool for "liberating constraints" and making students aware of the knowledge they created in the research essay.

During the past three decades, advances in technological development have transformed both the practice of mapping and the practice of creating new knowledge in humanities research. The digital humanities have emerged as an umbrella term to describe these transformations and the way mapping and humanities research intersect with each other. A key example of this is network analysis, which has emerged as a standard practice in the digital humanities.[7] By making use of software tools, scholars can render visible the connections between concepts that they are attempting to demonstrate, such as the fre-quency of particular structures, terms, authors, or words. In this way, network analysis and the software tools it uses creates new knowledge through new forms of mapping that can be linked to the well-known and much older peda-gogical tool of "concept mapping."

A more recent literature, however, has innovated on the linear, networked concept map through the model of "mind maps," which are "visual, non-linear representations of ideas and their relationships."[8] The possibilities presented by new software for mapping make these new representations via colors, line thickness, images, hyperlinks, and other visual markers more easily available to students, and they have the potential to "liberate constraints" and make the "inventiveness of form" possible. For this reason, Biktimirov and Nilson, using Mind Manager 2002, suggest that the mind map can replace the essay: "Having students show their understanding in a mind map rather than an essay is not only more creative but also easier to grade."[9] But as I demonstrate in my survey of the three digital mapping projects below, students' use of software to create mind maps in combination with their final essays leads to learning that would not be available with either the essay or the mind map alone. More importantly, for the context here, this learning also would not be possible without the software platform the students utilized in creating their final projects.

MIND MAPPING, BLOGGING, AND TOPIC DISCOVERY

For mind maps, keywords are central to creating the visual and spatial relationships that comprise the representation of information presented in the class. In traditional mind maps, a predetermined central concept is placed at the center of a page, and secondary and tertiary concepts are related to the central concept through branches of additional keywords.[10] The characteristics of the mind map—brief, sharp keywords and the use of sized, bolded text—are easily related to blog writing and its tagging system. However, while the traditional mind map focuses on summarizing predetermined textbook content, the tagging system on blogs using Google's Blogger platform produces a word cloud that maps the central concepts and keywords of the course as they emerge with student writing. (See fig. 19.1.)

In 300-level courses in writing practice, cultural survey, and grammar review in Spanish, I assign cultural topics to provide an opportunity for practicing writing with the central grammatical structures we are reviewing in class. Early in the semester, I either have a conversation about keywords or invite our library liaison to discuss with the class the idea and function of keywords in using databases. During peer review of the written assignments, students have a conversation about the best keywords. After writing two blog posts on assigned topics, the students use the keywords in the mind maps to develop a third post of their own, which is aimed at expanding core course topics and allowing free practice with the grammatical forms studied in class. By pairing central keywords with secondary and tertiary terms, students discover topics that are related to course content but are oriented toward their own interests. Thus, while there are constraints on this assignment, students design the specific parameters of

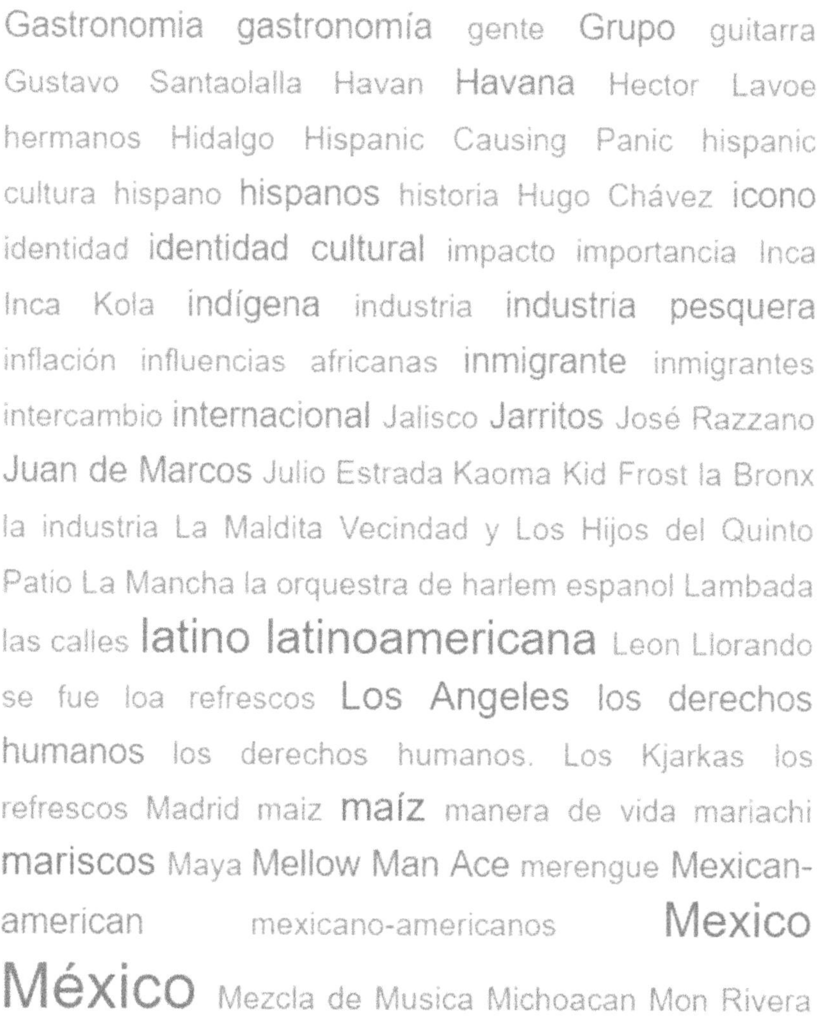

Gastronomia gastronomía gente Grupo guitarra Gustavo Santaolalla Havan Havana Hector Lavoe hermanos Hidalgo Hispanic Causing Panic hispanic cultura hispano hispanos historia Hugo Chávez icono identidad identidad cultural impacto importancia Inca Inca Kola indígena industria industria pesquera inflación influencias africanas inmigrante inmigrantes intercambio internacional Jalisco Jarritos José Razzano Juan de Marcos Julio Estrada Kaoma Kid Frost la Bronx la industria La Maldita Vecindad y Los Hijos del Quinto Patio La Mancha la orquestra de harlem espanol Lambada las calles latino latinoamericana Leon Llorando se fue loa refrescos Los Angeles los derechos humanos los derechos humanos. Los Kjarkas los refrescos Madrid maiz maíz manera de vida mariachi mariscos Maya Mellow Man Ace merengue Mexican-american mexicano-americanos Mexico México Mezcla de Musica Michoacan Mon Rivera

Figure 19.1. Selection from the word cloud–mind map from a level three hundred Spanish grammar and culture class (fall 2017), www.mapping.berlin.

their exploration of the culture and grammar of the Spanish-speaking world. They often write on pertinent cultural topics I would not have assigned, and they engage in exploring a wide range of grammatical forms in the process.

While I use the word cloud–mind map as a tool for topic discovery, it could easily be utilized for other purposes. For example, Scholarship of Teaching and Learning scholars acknowledge that past research demonstrates that "students

like it" when professors share their notes or PowerPoint slides, but they cau-
tion against this practice because it has the tendency to decrease "engagement
with the material."[11] Recent research has demonstrated that note reconstruction assignments can significantly improve student achievement.[12] The word
cloud–mind map can be deployed as a note reconstruction assignment.

GOOGLE EARTH AS PRESENTATION PLATFORM

In an advanced survey course of Latin American literature from the colonial
period through the beginning of the twentieth century, I gave the course a topical
focus to orient student research papers: Latin American landscape novels, or novels in which the description of a natural space (e.g., mountains, jungle, pampas)
plays a major role. In this class, I asked students to plot the textual evidence from
researched novels into the space of GIS maps made available by Google Earth.
More importantly, I broke the final paper up into five procedural stages with the
map as the end goal rather than only the research essay. In order to guide students
toward communicating their research about these literary works in a digital map,
I needed to structure their output in such a way that they would process and take
stock of unfamiliar aspects of the research process. While the two stages of the
writing process immediately preceding the map were a rough draft (on which I
gave them feedback for revision) and a final draft, I placed significant emphasis on
the first stage of the writing process. This was a "slanted" plot summary of their
selected novel along with twelve annotated passages of textual evidence from the
novel. In the plot summary, not only did students give a basic account of events
and characters but they also explained how the landscape they were assigned
played a crucial role in those events. Then students documented what they wrote
in the plot summary by selecting twelve passages from the novel. Before students
engaged in the writing, I gave them a rubric that outlined my expectations, and
we explicitly discussed these in class. More importantly, these twelve passages,
which the students would analyze in the research paper, would be the items plotted into the space of the map. It made clear to students that what they were communicating both in the research paper and in the presentation of those findings
was an analysis of textual evidence. This tangible connection between evidence
and argument made the focus of the assignment clearer: they understood that
they were putting forward a reading of particular aspects of the text rather than
simply "writing a paper." It kept the point of the assignment in focus. The most
important aspect of student learning in this redesign, however, was that in making the map, they analyzed their evidence again: this time from a visual point of
view. In discussion of the project after the public presentations of their research,
various students noted that they understood their arguments better after making

the map. Some even wished we made the map before writing the paper, but we engaged in discussion about why the paper needed to come before the map: the map is a form of communicating the full analysis that took place in the essay.

ROLAND BARTHES'S *PUNCTUM* AS A NOTE RECONSTRUCTION ASSIGNMENT

The most recent mapping technology I used in my classroom is digital photography as the basis of a note reconstruction assignment. As noted above, both "liberated constraints" and student engagement with course content through mind mapping and note reconstruction are key to better learning with the digital humanities. For years, I gave students the slides from my PowerPoint presentations after each class, believing that it would help students master the information. Research suggests otherwise.[13]

Driven by multiple student requests to take photographs of notes on the board and the fact that one of the last readings of the semester is Roland Barthes's *Camera Lucida*, which theorizes photography, I decided to utilize digital photographs to enable students to make "textual photographs" of the class session through a note reconstruction assignment. These textual photographs underscore the same ideas central to the "non-linear visual-spatial representation" of course information at the heart of the mind map. At the center of this idea is the content students would be seeing at the end of the semester. Barthes develops two terms that define the specificity of photography: the *studium* (a description of what's "in" the photograph, the "interesting" content the photographer wanted to capture) and the *punctum* (the viewer's experience of a particular detail in a photograph that connects at a personal level and makes the photograph memorable). The more powerful and important of the two for Barthes is the *punctum*, but it is also the one that students have a difficult time completely understanding. To that end, I incorporated the idea of the *punctum* as an implicit part of the note reconstruction assignment, which students posted on a class blog. Students took photographs of notes on the whiteboard and slides projected on the screen while also taking notes. Once during the semester, students posted note reconstructions on a class blog after engaging in a three-step process:

1. Post a photograph they took during class and explain how a specific detail in that photograph connected with them on a personal level (the *punctum*);
2. Explain how that point connected to the most important information covered that day (the *studium*); and
3. Provide a glossary of the most important terms developed in the session.

Students had difficulty with this assignment given that it was not typical and I had no models to show them, so there was some resistance to the assignment. It also may have drawn focus away from the final essay, which also was structured by "liberated constraints" modeled on the Google Earth essay project. Now that I have models to show students what I am hoping they can produce, the project can be more effective. It might be best, however, to choose one map to use in each class rather than both. But what is important to emphasize is that students did better on exams when they did not have access to my PowerPoint slides and they completed the note reconstruction assignment. The takeaway here is that simply using digital technologies does not improve student learning. Using digital technologies to interrupt the focus on the end goal and refocus students' attention on the learning process is what can improve learning.

NOTES

1. Brent Davis, Dennis Sumara, and Rebecca Luce-Kapler, *Engaging Minds: Learning and Teaching in a Complex World* (Mahwah, NJ: Lawrence Erlbaum, 2000), 24.

2. Ibid., 38.

3. Ibid., 88.

4. Ibid., 144.

5. Ibid., 198.

6. Ibid., 88, 89.

7. Dennis Tenen, "Visual-quantitative Approaches to an Intellectual History of the Field: A Close Reading," *Futures of Comparative Literature*, ed. Ursula K. Heise (London: Routledge, 2017).

8. Ernest N. Biktimirov and Linda B. Nilson, "Show Them the Money: Using Mind Mapping in the Introductory Finance Course," *Journal of Financial Education* 32 (2006): 3.

9. Ibid., 8–9.

10. Genevieve Zipp and Catherine Maher, "Prevalence of Mind Mapping as a Teaching and Learning Strategy in Physical Therapy Curricula," *Journal of the Scholarship of Teaching and Learning* 13.5 (2013): 23; Biktimirov and Nilson, "Show Them the Money," 8–9.

11. April Savoy, Robert Proctor, and Gavriel Salvendy, "Information Retention from PowerPoint and Traditional Lectures," *Computers and Education* 52 (2009): 858–867.

12. Dov Cohen, Emily Kim, Jacinth Tan, and Mary-Ann Winkelmes, "A Note-Restructuring Intervention Increases Students' Exam Scores," *College Teaching* 61 (2013): 95–99.

13. Ibid.

TWENTY

—⚏—

Fieldtrips and Classrooms in Second Life

A Few Realities of Teaching in a Virtual Environment

JACQUELINE H. FEWKES

Florida Atlantic University

I'm in a small classroom, surrounded with glowing screens on the walls. As I wait, my students—a young woman, a small rabbit, an even smaller mouse, a bear in a sailor suit, a snail-like creature, and a stalk of celery with arms and legs—return from our fieldtrip to archaeological sites. One by one, they pop into the room, some standing, while others simply float in the air around me.

This is not a nightmare just before the start of a new semester but rather an actual meeting of my Digital Ethnography class in our virtual classroom in Second Life. While my students' appearances may seem capricious and bizarre, our discussion on the relationship between images and identity had prompted them to choose their avatars with care and—in some cases—theoretical acumen. The "fieldtrips" were visits to three-dimensional (3-D) reproductions of sites hosted by a variety of organizations, meant to spark further inquiry on the subject of digital culture. (See fig. 20.1.)

When the digital entertainment company Linden Labs launched Second Life in 2003, it was touted as a cutting-edge virtual reality platform that could be used for many purposes. In contrast to other virtual environments that are largely game based (e.g., *World of Warcraft*), Second Life is a virtual world that acts as a platform for user interests. Second Life subscribers can purchase

Figure 20.1. The author's avatar stands in front of a classroom in Second Life.

virtual land and create their own unique content within that space. Thus, soon after Second Life opened, varied types of users flocked to the platform. Automobile manufacturers created advertisements where you could test drive their cars, politicians had campaign offices, fashion designers sold virtual outfits, and a few countries even established embassies within Second Life. Academic institutions were relatively quick to join in, and by 2007 more than 100 higher education institutions were listed as having educational sites on Second Life's directory; this number rose to 153 by 2012. During its first decade of use, Second Life hosted popular university programs in fields as diverse as nursing, language learning, archaeology, and accounting; a number of academics held classes and even full courses in this environment. Interest in the use of the Second Life platform for educational purposes has waned since that time, however, and, although Second Life continues to exist in 2018, most of the virtual campuses and classroom spaces are empty.

The role of educational sites in the virtual world of Second Life provides an interesting case study for exploring the potential and problems of teaching in multimedia digital forums. My goal here is not so much to chart the "rise and fall" of these institutional spaces but rather to highlight some crucial insights on teaching in digital spaces gained from experiencing and observing that process.

CREATING AND USING VIRTUAL SPACES

There is a clear necessity for specialized technical support for creating any digital learning environment, and, in spite of the user-friendly nature of Second Life, the platform is no exception to this rule. In discussions with educators interested in Second Life teaching, I have found that the development of user spaces has been a problem for those at universities that initially invested in virtual real estate but left the development of those spaces up to individual educators. Many of the professors interested in using Second Life lacked both the technical skill and the time to develop robust interactive sites. In contrast, universities that invested in larger organizationally supported site development projects—such as Stanford University's Libraries and Academic Information Resources (SULAIR) virtual library—had broader success and at least temporarily became thriving learning environments that offered meaningful learning spaces beyond virtual classrooms. The Stanford site, for example, housed virtual archives and student project exhibits that drew researchers, artists, and members of other communities to the university site.

Individual instructors need not despair, however, if they want to use Second Life without extensive institutional support. Some of the most successful classes I have led on Second Life started in a simple virtual class meeting but then drew up the resources of successful educational sites in "fieldtrips." Many of these are developed by organizations that had focused on digitizing and modeling specific sets of information, such as the digital re-creation of Çatalhöyük, a Neolithic tell site located in Turkey, by the Open Knowledge and Public Interest research group (OKAPI).[1] Other similar sites we have visited for archaeological education include the University of San Martín de Porres's Virtual Machu Picchu Project (where, just like in real life, students always end up getting delayed in the gift shop when we are supposed to "leave") and the Roma archaeology simulation, which allows students to interact with excavation tools and learn about techniques. Sites like these can be found throughout Second Life and are still available for general use. (See fig. 20.2.)

CHALLENGES

While fascinating to visit, the presence of many programmed objects, scripts, animations, and other details in such sites can be the cause of another set of serious educational concerns—unequal student access due to equipment needs. The Second Life platform is accessed online through 3-D browsing software called the "Second Life Viewer," which users need to download into their

Figure 20.2. The class visits the Roma archaeology site in Second Life to learn more about archaeological methods.

computers. While the program itself may not be too large for most computers, once on the platform users must constantly download data as the 3-D world's details fill in around their avatar. Teleporting to each new destination—the way that avatars move between sites in Second Life—requires the downloading of more data, making fast Internet connections necessary for an uninterrupted experience. Education on Second Life can, therefore, discriminate against those students who cannot afford the newest systems and fastest bandwidth.

Another challenge associated with teaching on Second Life is the online culture associated with the site. Maggi Savin-Baden succinctly states in her manual on using Second Life for higher education that "it is a very dangerous place and is full of pornography."[2] This warning, while perhaps extreme in its claim—Second Life hazards and content as varied as the rest of the Internet—has some basis and is worth considering. Since the "collapse" of Second Life for most educational and commercial purposes, many areas of the site have indeed become focused on fantasy role-playing and pornography. Educators bringing their students to Second Life should consider the ways that they want to address this, which, depending on the class, may involve: carefully curating sites for visiting, openly discussing the role of sexual content on the site, establishing a code of conduct with their students, ensuring that all members of the class are over eighteen years of age, and/or helping students navigate areas.

While access is generally free in Second Life, individual instructors interested in using Second Life may want to consider purchasing a subscription so that they can establish a building to act as a private classroom space.

A final challenge to using Second Life for educational purposes is establishing a clear benefit of interacting on the site. While Second Life has been compared to MMORGs (massively multiplayer online role-playing games), participants do not have to "play" a game with specific goals or objectives. Thus, while Second Life offers a rich multimedia experience, users may not seem to experience the gamification of learning that is frequently touted as a multimedia motivational tool for students. However, this narrow definition of a game, as well as the envisioning of its educational benefits, has been challenged in many works.[3] The strength of Second Life as an educational platform lies in its flexibility, as is evident in the platform's ability to accommodate varied user goals. The freedom of interaction in Second Life—as well as the possibilities for creating personalized content, such as buildings, images, objects, animations, and skins—makes it more than a glorified chat room. A few quick examples of how I have used Second Life in past courses can demonstrate some of these possibilities inherent in the site.

BENEFITS

Class meetings in the virtual world can help ground theoretical discussions. In a class on language and space, I have taken students to visit Second Life areas inspired by Islamic sites such as the Mecca complex and the Chebi mosque (a replica of a historical mosque in Cordoba). We used these trips as the basis for discussion about the concept of sacred spaces, considering whether it is possible to have such a thing as a virtual sacred space. Class discussion drew from Krystina Derrickson's article "Second Life and the Sacred: Islamic Space in a Virtual World,"[4] which links the experience of an interactive and mediated Mecca to Baudrillard's notion of simulacra.

Theory can also be acted on in Second Life, giving students the chance to apply ideas in ways that would be impossible in the physical world. Having read *Coming of Age in Second Life: An Anthropologist Explores the Virtually Human*[5] and *Human No More: Digital Subjectivities, Unhuman Subjects, and the End of Anthropology*, my digital ethnography class discussed what it meant to be human and the limits of self-representation.[6] We tried interacting with others, and among ourselves, in different forms, using "skins," which are purchased or created programs that change the appearance of Second Life avatars. We then reflected on the intricacies of self-representation in the contemporary world— hence, the celery stalk that showed up for our next class.

FINAL REFLECTIONS

In these cases, and many others, the high degree of options for personalization with settings, animations, and avatars in Second Life makes possible the creation of a robust virtual learning environment. Since Second Life is not a gaming platform with its own specific goals or objectives, to make it useful for teaching, faculty should think carefully about the types of objectives they want to create for their students. The strength of Second Life for teaching is that the goals can be varied and changing: as in my case, a professor may at first bring a class into the environment to gain appreciation of a particular site through a tour of its reproduction, then meet again to explore digital issues of interest that arose in that initial expedition. The relatively easy access and ability for individuals to join without institutional accounts or other support means that a class can enter into Second Life very quickly—even at a moment's notice if discussion in a physical classroom suddenly touches on a related topic—and leave just as quickly if the platform is not meeting class needs. Although many educational institutions no longer prioritize the further development of their Second Life sites, the high-quality interactive experiences they have created in the past remain and can be used by intrepid instructors. Second Life remains a rich and nuanced digital environment that can foster new learning possibilities and critically engage students with crucial concepts in the digital humanities.

NOTES

1. Colleen L. Morgan, "(Re)Building Çatalhöyük: Changing Virtual Reality in Archaeology," *Archaeologies* 5 (2009): 468.

2. Maggi Savin-Baden, *A Practical Guide to Using Second Life in Higher Education* (Maidenhead: Open University Press, 2010), 168.

3. Jane McGonigal, *Reality Is Broken: Why Games Make Us Better and How They Can Change the World* (New York: Penguin, 2011).

4. Krystina Derrickson, "Second Life and the Sacred: Islamic Space in a Virtual World," in *Digital Islam* (2008).

5. Tom Boellstorff, *Coming of Age in Second Life: An Anthropologist Explores the Virtually Human* (Princeton, NJ: Princeton University Press, 2015).

6. Neil L. Whitehead and Michael Wesch, *Human No More: Digital Subjectivities, Unhuman Subjects, and the End of Anthropology* (Boulder: University Press of Colorado, 2012).

TWENTY-ONE

—ᴡᴠ—

Narrative Maps for World Language Learning

SOFIYA ASHER
Indiana University

THERESA QUILL
Indiana University

THIS CHAPTER PRESENTS A SUCCESSFUL model for instructor-librarian partnerships and explores the use of digital humanities mapping in language-learning environments. The case study involved a collaboration between a geographic information system (GIS) librarian and a language instructor in an undergraduate intermediate Russian language course and an elementary Polish language course. The mapping project was jointly designed by the instructor and the GIS librarian to encourage a geographic understanding of Russia and Poland while challenging the students' listening, speaking, reading, and writing skills in a global language. Assignments for the two classes differed slightly to take into account the size of the class and the level of language ability. Both class assignments used the mapping program Esri Story Maps, which allows for narrative mapping by the inclusion of text and multimedia in a beginner-friendly web map.

PROJECT GOALS AND LEARNING OUTCOMES

Learning outcomes for these projects were slightly different for each class but followed the same general goals of increasing geographic awareness of countries where the language of study is spoken and searching for information in the target language in an authentic language environment. Learning outcomes for the Russian language class were measured by students' ability to locate major cities in Russia on a map and to find information by searching Russian language materials. The resulting collaborative digital map allowed students to interact with their classmates' work, and to visually comprehend the geographic scope and diversity of Russia.

Learning outcomes for the Polish language class were measured by students' ability to locate place names mentioned in a Polish song, demonstrate knowledge of areas of Poland outside of major cities, and practice case declension using city names.

A goal for both of these classes was to introduce a new tool that would engage students with the target language in a novel way outside of traditional textbook vocabulary and methods. Additionally, students gained basic familiarity with a popular digital humanities mapping tool and explored geographic regions where the language of study is widely spoken. By creating their own maps, students begin to think about the ways in which representations of space are constructed, and they are challenged to write for a digital medium in the target language.

THE STORY MAPS TOOL

Esri Story Maps is a free, open source web-mapping program created by Esri, the company that created ArcGIS, a GIS software that is one of the most popular in the world. While Story Maps is a free-to-use program, Indiana University's enterprise license with Esri includes increased access and the ability for students to sign into Story Maps with their university ID and passphrase, eliminating the need for students to create an individual account. This streamlined process for logging on decreases the amount of class time needed for setting up the tool and does not require students to remember an individual log-on and password.

Story Maps includes several app templates that are structured around different types of layouts and storytelling. These apps allow for varying amounts of text, images, and maps. The Map Tour, for example, is best for displaying a series of photos on a map. The Swipe Map is intended for comparing two layers or maps of the same geographic area, while the Map Journal is more text based, with integration between the textual narrative and a geographic map. The Map Journal and Map Series apps were used for this case study.

Each app includes a brief tutorial and a step-by-step wizard that walks the user through the beginning steps of creating a Story Map, making this tool a lightweight introduction to digital humanities mapping tools.

THE ASSIGNMENTS

Intermediate Russian

The class worked on a single collaborative map with each student responsible for an individual city. (See fig. 21.1.) Students created a narrative text about the city, added images and videos, and ensured their content was correctly displayed on the map. (See fig. 21.2.) Each student chose a city from a list of the eighteen largest cities in Russia. Students briefly browsed through information about the city before deciding which location to use for the assignment and made their choices for a variety of personal reasons: one student chose a city because they had already visited it, some students liked or found a city's name strange, while others chose a city they had never heard about. The GIS librarian created the structure for the collaborative map and instructed students to edit the map with their individual content over two in-class instruction sessions. The resulting map not only serves as a semester-long digital humanities project for the current students but also will function as an instruction tool for future classes to learn from and build on.

Intermediate Russian Assignment Steps
In step 1, the GIS librarian set up a Story Map "Map Series" and created a group within the university's ArcGIS Online organizational account. The librarian added each of the students' usernames to this group and gave them editing privileges for the Story Map. The structure of each institution's ArcGIS Online organizational account may differ, and the administrator of an institution's account may be required to assist in setting up a collaborative group for the project.

In step 2, the librarian set the general parameters for the Story Map and added a point layer of cities in Russia that had been selected by the instructor. This layer was created in Story Maps by uploading a CSV file of city names and coordinates, a process that does not require specialized GIS skills. At the beginning of the assignment, students were presented with a basic map with points representing each city. By starting with an existing map, students were able to interact with the map and the software without immediately being required to make edits.

In step 3, the class met in a computer lab with the GIS librarian for an initial introduction to the Story Map assignment. The librarian gave an overview of the software, including showing several examples of different uses for Story Maps. Each student signed into the software and ensured they had access to the group project. The librarian walked the class through the steps for adding a tab to the map and connecting their tab to the correct point on the map, so that

Figure 21.1. Map overview.

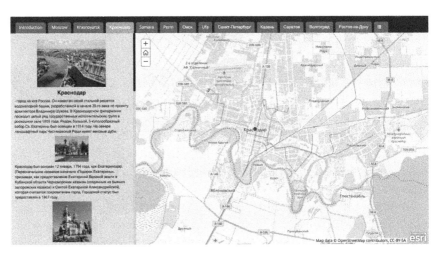

Figure 21.2. Students created content for their assigned cities, including photos and information from the official city websites.

when a user clicks on the tab for a city, the map will zoom to the corresponding city on the map. At the end of the initial instruction session with the librarian, each student created a tab on the map that corresponded with their assigned city. (See fig. 21.3.)

In step 4, students were responsible for adding information from official city websites to their assigned city tab on the map. Students were required to search the internet in Russian to find this information, read through official

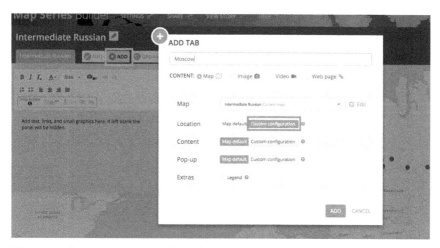

Figure 21.3. Students created a tab for their city.

government sites, and write an original paragraph describing the city in the target language. Students initially created the texts in a word processor and then copied and pasted them into the program in order to ensure that data would not be lost in the event of a software crash. Students did experience significant technical issues when multiple users edited the map simultaneously. In many cases, the software did not save every user's edits, requiring several students to repeat steps.

In step 5, the librarian and instructor met with the students for an additional class session in the computer lab prior to the assignment deadline. This session was intended to address any software concerns or questions about the assignment. The final product was a collaborative Story Map of eighteen cities in Russia, with a narrative paragraph accompanying each city. The map served as the final project for this class. At the end of the project, students were asked to record a five-minute speech convincing the whole class to visit their assigned city. Due to time constraints, unfortunately, students did not have a chance to present their cities in person to the class. This was a missed opportunity, and one that will be corrected if this project is implemented in future courses.

Elementary Polish

Rather than the entire class contributing to a single map, in this assignment, students were asked to create their own Story Map Journal of a Polish song. This format eliminated the technology issues experienced previously and did not require initial setup by the instructor or the GIS librarian. The song,

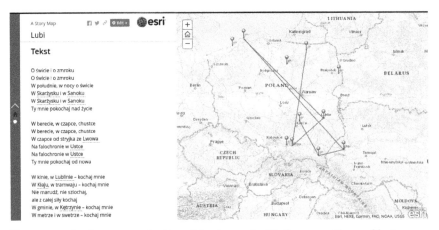

Figure 21.4. Students created a Story Map Journal with the song video and lyrics.

W kinie w Lublinie (In the Cinema, in Lublin), written in 2001, is very popular and includes place names in almost every line of the lyrics: a total of eleven unique places, one in genitive case and ten in locative case. Students were asked to map locations mentioned in the song to create a chronological map of places that connected the place names with official websites and/or media. To do this, students had to convert the geographic name from locative case into nominative case, look the place up using a Polish-language search engine (e.g., google.pl), and locate a website. It is a rather easy task for a major city like Kraków, but the song also mentions less well-known locations, such as Skarżysko-Kamienna or Sanok.

The resulting map led to a discussion about possible reasons why most of the cities were in central and eastern Poland, which encouraged a closer look at the geography of Poland.

Elementary Polish Assignment Steps
In step 1, the GIS librarian met with the class in a computer lab and introduced Story Maps as a tool, showing students several examples of successful maps. Each student logged on to Story Maps with their institutional log-on information and created a blank Story Map Journal.

In step 2, students embedded a video of the song and the text of the song lyrics. (See fig. 21.4.) They then connected place names mentioned in the song to the geographic location on the map by using the "map actions" option in Story Maps. Map actions create links between text and an action on the map. (See fig. 21.5.) In this case, when a user clicks on a city name in the lyrics text,

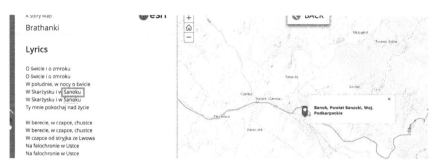

Figure 21.5. When users click on a city name, the map zooms to the geographic location.

the map will zoom to the corresponding location. Locating places on the map required students to draw on their knowledge about Polish geography and history to correctly identify the locations. In addition, students had to convert the geographic name in locative case into nominative case and look the place up using a Polish-language search engine, reinforcing skills covered in the class outside of the textbook environment.

ASSESSMENT/CONCLUSIONS

Overall, projects were received positively by the students in both classes. In their feedback, students repeatedly mentioned exposure to new vocabulary, the use of Runet (Russian-language internet), or, as one student put it, "weaving through some Polish based websites" and exposure to "outside the [text] book" language, as a positive experience. Students repeatedly responded with "I learned a lot." They learned new and interesting facts about their cities, and even about transportation in Russia. Interestingly, some students in the Russian language class referred to the city they never visited as "my city." Many students reported that the mapping activity increased their geographic understanding of the country and region, particularly in regard to areas outside of major cities. However, not surprisingly, heritage speakers found the activity less useful than nonheritage speakers in terms of learning more about the geography of the region.

Students appreciated the innovative nature of the assignment but easily became frustrated when the software did not perform as they expected. In particular, for the Russian class, students experienced issues when multiple users attempted to edit the collaborative map at once. While students were able to edit the collaborative map simultaneously, edits in Story Maps are not continuously saved. A user must press the "save" button for edits to be committed. The issue students experienced was that each time a user pressed "save," the Story Map would save that one user's edits but remove edits made by all other users. It is recommended to stagger edits to the map to ensure each edit is properly saved. A better workflow would have been for students to create content in an external word processor, then paste and save their edits into the Story Map one at a time. Instructors should be prepared to teach to varying levels of computer skills and to provide ample class time in the computer lab for students to explore the software.

TWENTY-TWO

—ᴟ—

Digitally Mapping Space and Time in History General Education Surveys

Google Maps and TimelineJS

JULIA M. GOSSARD

Utah State University

ON A STUDENT'S END-OF-TERM EVALUATION for my Modern Western Civilization course, they wrote that the class "taught [them] important skills about reading, research, writing and the internet." This statement encapsulated some of the course's most important learning objectives. Although gaining content knowledge in history is important, general education courses also offer students essential analytical, critical thinking, and research competencies that they can apply to their future lives as twenty-first-century citizens. These skills are scaffolded in my courses, culminating in a digital project to build students' digital literacy.

Over the past four years, I have designed and assigned two digital projects—"Mapping the Early Modern World" and "Food in the West: A Timeline"—for my general education surveys. Both assignments teach in-depth research skills and respond to Stanford University's History Education Group's (SHEG) 2016 study "Evaluating Information: The Cornerstone of Civic Reasoning." SHEG's research concluded that students displayed a "stunning and dismaying consistency" in their inability to evaluate the credibility and bias of online sources. The study suggests that this poses a serious "threat to democracy" if future citizens are unable to decipher bias and source legitimacy.[1] Students must have the expertise to assess a wide variety of sources that are available to them online. The digital projects that I assign start with SHEG's study in mind. They emphasize the historical thinking skills necessary to prepare citizens for the slew of misinformation they encounter on a daily basis. In doing so, students both implement twenty-first-century methods, such as employing digital technologies to visualize historical data across both space and time, and corroborate, criticize, and evaluate primary and secondary source materials.

PREPARING FOR DIGITAL RESEARCH PROJECTS

In these projects, students must negotiate a range of online sources, using at least one vetted digital primary or secondary source, such as an archival database or a public history magazine. Each assignment also requires students to use at least one peer-reviewed secondary source such as a book, a journal article, or a scientific research paper. To facilitate students' use of these sources, I spend a considerable amount of class time discussing the differences between primary and secondary sources and source reliability. I have students attend a library instruction day as well. This practice, though common on many college campuses, is important to introduce students to the library's physical and online holdings. Once they learn how to locate sources either through the library catalog directly or through a browser using smart searching strategies, students complete a five-point evaluation of every secondary source. I created a detailed "Source Evaluation Worksheet" that students turn in as part of their assignment. In the worksheet, students assess the source's authority, objectivity, accuracy, currency, and quality. If the source is found to be overly biased, out of date, unreliable, or otherwise insufficient, students must find another source to use. This process greatly enhances their ability to assess information for its credibility and usefulness.

With this process, "Mapping the Early Modern World" and "Food in the West: A Timeline" manage to reproduce the same components of a research paper, particularly finding reliable and credible evidence. But both the timeline and the map make students think that they are doing a different *kind* of research. They see their final projects as collaborative exhibits that present information to each other in a way that was accessible, student-centric, content-driven, and precise.

In the following sections, I introduce you to the basics of each of these assignments, concentrating on the learning objectives that they achieve. By mapping time and space digitally, students gain content knowledge while also building their digital literacy as well as project management skills that they can apply to a wide variety of future classes and careers.

MAPPING THE EARLY MODERN WORLD
WITH GOOGLE MAPS

The idea to assign a digital mapping project came to me when I decided to name a survey course, "Global Early Modern Europe." Throughout this course, I emphasized that Europe in the years between 1500 and 1800 was not an isolated continent. Instead, it was economically, politically, religiously, and ideologically connected to the wider early modern world. In particular, we studied the ways in which European states and people not only influenced the wider world but also how indigenous populations in the Americas, rulers in Asia and Southeast Asia, slave traders in Africa, and merchants in the Middle East influenced Europe. To provide a visual representation of this, students plotted the transmission of goods, people, ideologies, and cultural inventions across the early modern globe on a Google Map.

Over the course of the semester, students were responsible for four entries to the class's Google Map. (See fig. 22.1.) Each entry was approximately 200–250 words and could be about a person, place, idea, commodity, or thing (such as a piece of art or a battle). Much like an identification term on an exam, these entries defined the subject, gave dates, and provided historical significance. Students were encouraged to draw lines between the entries that were related, showing the larger connections of their topics. Now complete, the map is a striking visual of how intertwined Europe was with the rest of the world during the early modern period.

In addition to its benefits as a visualization to counter the myth of an isolated early modern Europe, the entries, deliberately spaced out over the course of the semester, scaffolded students' learning. Students were required to write on specific time periods for each entry, applying knowledge they gleaned from recent readings, discussions, and lectures. The individual entries helped them practice defining terms and providing clear historical significance. Most excitingly, the students also used this as a way to intelligently and quickly crowdsource information in preparation for their midterm and final exams. The assignment was not only a representation of their knowledge and work but a student-created tool for success.

A mapping project such as this can address a number of learning objectives as well as challenges instructors face when teaching a general education history course. The first and probably the most basic challenge this assignment helped me overcome was students' lack of geographic knowledge. With geography courses on the decline in many public schools in the United States, some of my students did not know how to read or interpret a map.[2] Students generally knew where Europe was, but they were not certain they knew where Italy was

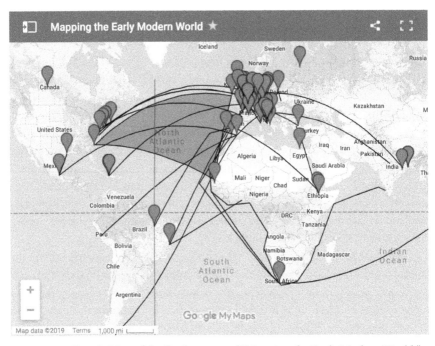

Figure 22.1. Google Map of the final version of "Mapping the Early Modern World," fall 2015.

in relationship to England. Nor were they exactly sure where the Holy Roman Empire or the Ottoman Empire were in relationship to the rest of Europe. This lack of geographic knowledge can be extremely hard to overcome for students who may not grasp the massive amount of travel that was involved in the trade of goods, ideas, and people in the early modern era. Although the Google Maps platform uses modern-day political boundaries, you can easily change the default setting to a topography map. Although none of my students did it, in future mapping projects I will encourage them to draw in the changing political boundaries of various kingdoms and empires to further emphasize the ebb and flow of geographic power.

The Google Map also helped my students recognize how the environment played a causal factor in social, economic, and political developments. For instance, they recognized the important roles that waterways played both as conduits of exchange and as barriers. For many students, the enormity and danger of a voyage like Magellan's took on a whole new meaning because they were able to chart it for themselves. They began to understand just how fundamental, difficult, and wide early exchange was. Using "Street View" and images, students could physically place themselves along travelers' routes. Although the

"Street View" setting places students in modern environments, it still allowed them to travel to Spain or Turkey where they could see the landscape, terrain, and space that generations have inhabited and changed. Going through deserts, scaling mountain passes, or avoiding harsh terrain were all factors that people in the past dealt with, giving context to voyages and routes.

In addition to providing a better geographic understanding, this mapping project afforded students a number of digital competencies including mastering the Google Suite of services. I had naively ascribed to the assumption that my students were "digital natives," more technologically savvy and adept than me.[3] Although this generation of students had effectively grown up on the internet, that did not necessarily mean that they possessed more knowledge of certain applications or internet practices than I did. In fact, very few of my students knew how to use the Google Suite beyond Gmail. This project required that students become familiar with Google Maps, Google Docs, and Google Sheets. Additionally, students learned how to effectively and efficiently use Google as a search engine. Although these seem like small learning objectives, students who now have these proficiencies in their digital toolboxes will be ready to use them for the rest of their college years and eventual careers.

This suite of applications and services is one reason I chose to use Google Maps over other geographic information system (GIS) and mapping platforms available for classroom use. Google Maps is still one of the most accessible. Many advanced GIS platforms require an expensive institutional subscription and can sometimes be limited to just Natural Resources or Engineering Departments. Google Maps, on the other hand, is free to sign up for and use. Chances are, too, most students already have a Gmail account that can serve as their log-on for the class Google Map. Sharing the map is simple and requires only a URL. Teachers can also customize privacy settings—allowing the map to be private or public—based on their preferences.

For instructors who are nervous about assigning a digital project, as I was when I started, this is a great place to begin. Google Maps is very user friendly and is easy to navigate. Google offers many articles and videos (support.google.com/maps/) to help you set up your own map. As with any digital project, the instructor should set aside a good amount of time to play with the tool themselves before assigning it. Additionally, instructors should think carefully about how this will work with their enrollment numbers. I used this assignment in a class with a smaller enrollment—40 students. I realized that it would not work well in my large 120-person class simply because the visualization would become jumbled. Instead, I took inspiration from this project to design a different kind of mapping assignment—one that charts the history of food across the modern era.

MAPPING TIME WITH TIMELINEJS: FOOD IN THE WEST

Tasked with teaching a large general education history survey like Western Civilizations or World History, instructors must decide how they will teach nearly a millennium's worth of knowledge. For over two decades, teacher educators and pedagogues have recommended the Understanding by Design framework that suggests instructors center these types of courses around a number of targeted questions or themes.[4] This allows instructors to successfully teach content knowledge while also focusing on skills-based learning. For my section of Modern Western Civilization, I chose to have students examine the history of the modern West through the lens of food. In particular, I felt students' knowledge of modern Western history and their digital literacy could be greatly enhanced with a digital group project, "Food in the West: A Timeline."

For the past five semesters, students in my Modern Western Civilization classes have used Knight Lab's TimelineJS to create a digital timeline on the history of food in the West from roughly 1700 to 2001. Whether the bread riots of the 1790s in France, the "Hungry 1840s," or the starvation of Russian citizens after the conclusion of World War II, food (and access to it) has been and continues to be a mobilizing factor for many in history. By examining what people ate and how they ate at different points in time, we can tell both what food was "in style" and much about economic conditions, social mores, political conflicts, religious issues, and nutrition.

Borrowing from the instructions and steps from "Mapping the Early Modern World," this timeline group project replicates a traditional research project. For example, students learn how to assess primary and secondary sources using the same "Source Evaluation Worksheet" I created for the previous project. Additionally, students tune their digital skills since TimelineJS runs on the Google Sheets platform.

Students worked in groups of no more than four to research and write timeline entries. Each group or individual was responsible for three entries to the digital assessment over the course of the semester. To ensure that we considered the entire period from 1700 to 2001, groups had to write one entry for each of these distinct periods:

1. The Enlightenment to the First Industrial Revolution
2. The First Industrial Revolution to 1914—the Start of World War I
3. World War I—2001

Entries were two to three paragraphs in length (300–350 words) and could discuss crops, meat, processed foods, recipes, utensils, rations, agricultural innovations, events related to food, or manufactured products from Europe.

Much like identification terms on exams, the entries were both descriptive and analytical. Students had to clearly explain how their entry represented the larger historical trends at the time, socially, economically, and/or politically. What resulted from these entries was a visually stunning, collaborative timeline of the history of food in the history of modern Western civilization.

I brought this timeline into class as much as possible, drawing attention to the students' work when it was relevant. This was a way not only to recognize students' hard work but also to further demonstrate how food reflected larger historical issues and events. For example, when we discussed the post-Stalin decade of the Soviet Union, we pulled up the timeline to examine a group's entry on "Khrushchev and Corn." The group's image, a cover of *Life Magazine*, shows an elated Khrushchev visiting a US farm, holding a huge ear of corn. A funny image, the other students in the class were immediately intrigued. The group explained that this photo was taken when Khrushchev visited the United States in 1959. The corn's size and abundance in the Midwest astounded Khrushchev. The students told us how Khrushchev was in the process of trying to build the Soviet Union's corn supply as a way to feed people and livestock, alike. Opening up the discussion to the larger class, we discussed how Khrushchev's corn experiments were indicative of a clear shift in Soviet priorities in the post-Stalin era, a clear example of scientific experiments, and a gradual thawing of the Cold War. Being able to bring the timeline into the classroom advanced in-class discussions significantly.

TimelineJS is an easy-to-use resource for instructors who want to implement a skills-heavy digital component into their course. Knight Lab provides detailed instructions and a template at timeline.knightlab.com/#make. All the instructor has to do is download the template to a publicly available Google Sheet, publish the sheet to the web, and then share the link with students who will input the information. Knight Lab does the rest, with the text automatically uploading to the visual timeline. Although it does take some checking and fixing on the instructor's part, it is not a time consuming or difficult process. TimelineJS can be used in a variety of courses, from high school history courses that want to prioritize chronology to college-level survey courses that want to emphasize change over time and even advanced graduate courses where the class works on a digital project together.[5]

MAPPING SPACE AND TIME: CONCLUSIONS

These digital projects have advanced students' content knowledge of early modern and modern European history with key attention to both chronology and geography. Equally important, my students have honed a number of transferable skills. My students are able to navigate multiple Google applications that allow them to collaborate with others. Perhaps most crucially, students walk away with better digital and media literacy. They carefully judge sources they encounter with a keen attention to author credibility, reliability, and bias. When applied to online sources, this helps students assess the nearly endless amount of information available to them. They will take these abilities not only into other college classrooms and their careers but into their lives as twenty-first-century citizens who must navigate the world of false and biased information.

NOTES

1. "Evaluating Information: The Cornerstone of Civic Online Reasoning," accessed November 20, 2016, https://sheg.stanford.edu/upload/V3LessonPlans /Executive%20Summary%2011.21.16.pdf.

2. Lauren Camera, "U.S. Students Are Really Bad at Geography," accessed November 20, 2016, *U.S. News and World Report*, https://www.usnews.com/news /articles/2015/10/16/us-students-are-terrible-at-geography.

3. Marc Prensky coined the term *digital natives* in 2001 to describe the new generation of students who were "native speakers of the digital language of computers, video games, and the Internet." This term has since been hotly contested in pedagogical circles. See Marc Prensky, "Digital Natives, Digital Immigrants," *On the Horizon* 9, no. 5 (October 2001): 1–6.

4. For an overview of this pedagogical method, see Jay McTighe and Grant Wiggins, *The Understanding by Design Guide to Creating High-Quality Units* (Alexandria, VA: ASCD, 2011).

5. Chris Babits, "Digital Teaching: A Mid-Semester Timeline," accessed April 4, 2019, blog February 20, 2017, https://notevenpast.org/digital-teaching -a-mid-semester-timeline/.

TWENTY-THREE

—ᚱᚢ—

Charting Urban Change with Digital Mapping Tools

MOLLY TAYLOR-POLESKEY

Middle Tennessee State University

TECHNOLOGY IN THE CLASSROOM IS a scary proposition since electronic devices tempt students to "check out" of their immediate surroundings. The goal of this mapping exercise, instead, is to use technology to heighten students' awareness of physical surroundings and help them discern changes in the built environment. Using digital tools in a history class is not simply a reaction to the encroachment of devices into every aspect of our lives and our studies[1] but an acknowledgment of the benefits they can bring to historical analysis.[2]

My Doing Digital History class at Middle Tennessee State University took advantage of multiple media to engage with the past and the present of our most immediate urban environment: Nashville. The course had two goals: to use a spatial history approach to consider how human history is shaped by our built environments (i.e., to increase spatial literacy) and to develop analytical and technical skills to draw and communicate conclusions. Spatial history focuses on time and space and, done well, "should detail how landscapes are constructed by human action."[3] The mapping exercise (see Appendix: Mapping Assignment) asks students to identify development patterns with respect to topography and other historical influences.

Readings such as Grady Clay's *Close-Up: How to Read the American City*[4] and John Stilgoe's *Outside Lies Magic: Regaining History and Awareness in Everyday*

Places[5] drew students' attention to sensory clues about the urban planning that shape our habitats. As we delved into American urban history, I incorporated the model of Anne Spirn's The Once and Future City course, which focuses on the dynamism of cities.[6] One way to observe changes in the relationship between the built and the natural environment is through historical maps.

The digital components of humanities classes need to enhance the overall learning about a topic, not the other way around.[7] In the case of the Doing Digital History class, this mapping exercise deepened our understanding of American urban development through a comparison of maps over time. The advantages of using digital tools to do this were many. First, large-scale digitization initiatives enlarged our source base by enabling the students to access historical maps in libraries across the country while giving them the ability to compare different copies of the same map held in distant collections. Digitization of these maps also meant that we could zoom in and out and toggle between maps quickly to facilitate the human-eye observation. We were aware, however, of the limitation of not handling the physical maps and, therefore, of possibly overlooking some piece of information contained in them.

The free georectification tool, Mapwarper, from Harvard University and the New York Public Library enabled us to make differences between maps more obvious. Georectification presented some awkward results, however, especially when we uploaded the georectified maps as KML (Keyhole Markup Language) files into the virtual globe application, Google Earth. Essentially, we were taking imperfect 2-D renderings of a spherical surface and fitting them back onto a 3-D canvas. The advantage of using Google Earth, though, was that we could toggle between georectified maps and the modern satellite images easily or layer the maps at different levels of transparency. All of the sources and tools we used were free.

Students started this three-part assignment independently and then we workshopped parts in class. Spatial history is inherently experimental and collaborative.[8] The use of the cloud-based project communication platform, Slack, made it easy for students to reach out to one another when they got stuck. This meant we could capitalize on the students' different skill sets.

In his exegesis about his controversial classroom exercise of fake Wikipedia stories, T. Mills Kelly noted that when we harness and inspire students' creative impulses through digital tools, the results can be surprising.[9] Student reflections from comparing bird's-eye perspectives of the city opened new lines of inquiry into the on-the-ground experience in Nashville. For example, one student noticed that arterial roads constrict and confine neighborhoods and saw neighborhoods engulfed by interstate highways from the 1908, 1968, and 1997 maps. He triangulated that with information from a *Tennessean* newspaper article about the decline in African American residents in those parts of the city.

Many students echoed the statement of Richard White that spatial history is about movement.[10] Even though they were studying static maps, most of the changes students noticed involved transportation and road patterns. One student likened the current of the Cumberland River to the current of commuters moving in and out of the downtown and to and from the parking lots around the new Titans football stadium. The final benefit of this digital mapping exercise was that students gained a familiarity with Nashville before researching and writing historical narratives about a particular part of the city.

APPENDIX: MAPPING ASSIGNMENT

The following assignment is an example of how to integrate historical maps, georectification, close map comparison, and analysis to notice changes over time. What is written is particular to our Nashville case study but could easily be adapted for other places.

Part I: Class Map Exercise

Locate three historical maps that represent Nashville at different periods of its history (see suggested map sources below).

Georectify maps using MapWarper (https://mapwarper.net):

1. First, create a free account with the website. Next, check your email for the link to activate the account. Now you can log on and upload the map you wish to warp.

2. To "rectify" the map you need to create "control points," that is, points that indicate what pieces on your map connect to certain geographic locations. You need at least three control points but experiment to see how many control points makes the most accurate overlay.

3. Select a point on your map and then the corresponding point on the OpenStreetMap image and "Add Control Point." You can crop the image, which is useful if you want to only make use of part of a map image. When you are done, "Export" the image as a KML file, which you can then easily open up in Google Earth.

Suggested map sources:

- Nashville Metro archives
- Tennessee State Library and Archives
- Old Maps Online (http://www.oldmapsonline.org/)
- Sanborn Fire Insurance Maps (available through our university library's website)
- *Singleton's Nashville Business Directory for 1865* (Nashville: Singleton, 1865)
- Historical map collections at Middle Tennessee State University's Walker Library
- Library of Congress Maps (http://www.loc.gov/maps/?q=ashville)
- Nashville Public Library has a detailed map (sixty-two different records!) in color from 1908 (http://digital.library.nashville .org/cdm/search/searchterm/Hopkins!atlas/field/all!all /mode/all!all/conn/and!and/order/nosort/ad/asc)

Part II: Your Historical Map Layers in Google Earth[a]

This part of the mapping project brings the historical maps you located in Part I into the powerful mapping capabilities of Google Earth. This application allows you to easily toggle between different map views, or layers, to more quickly observe discrepancies and start to question where and why changes took place. (See fig. 23.1.)

Setting up Google Earth
1. Install Google Earth (http://www.google.com/earth/index.html)
2. Open Google Earth and play with the functions to familiarize yourself with the application. Use the menu to add and remove layers of information.

Note: under the "Layer" heading on the lower left side of the window margin, Google provides a number of ready-to-go layers that can be turned on by

---

[a] Adapted from Jim Clifford, Josh MacFadyen, and Daniel Macfarlane, "Intro to Google Maps and Google Earth," *Programming Historian* 2 (2013), https://programminghistorian.org/en /lessons/googlemaps-googleearth.

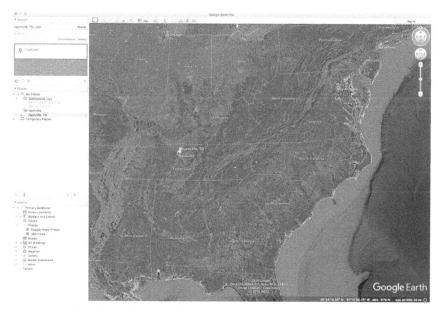

Figure 23.1. Google Earth screenshot centered on Tennessee.

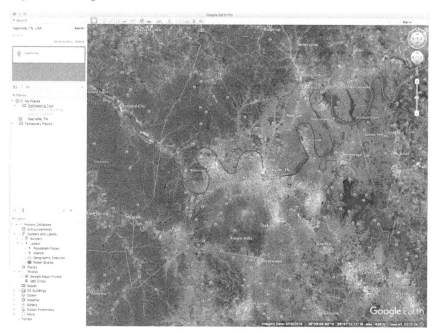

Figure 23.2. Google Earth screenshot centered on Nashville, Tennessee, with sightseeing layers removed and folder setup under "Temporary Places" for historic map overlay.

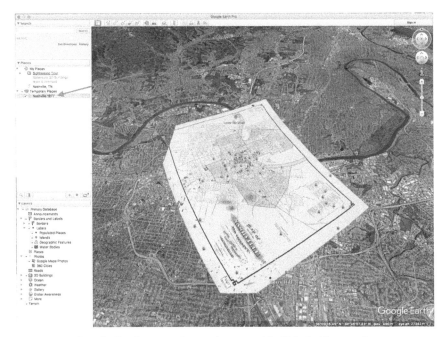

Figure 23.3. Google Earth screenshot with georectified Nashville map from 1877 overlaid.

selecting the corresponding checkbox. You may have to zoom in to see some of the features. (See fig. 23.2.)

Bringing Your KML File into Google Earth

- Download your map as a KML file from Mapwarper. KML is a file type that can be used with different geographic information systems software (like Quantum GIS or ArcGIS).
- Double click on the KML file in your Download folder.
- Find the data in the Temporary Folder in Google Earth. (See fig. 23.3.)
- Make a Nashville folder for yourself under the Places tab. (See fig. 23.4.)
- Move your historic map from the Temporary Files folder into your Nashville folder. Use the navigation buttons on the upper-right corner to adjust your perspective. (See fig. 23.5.)
- Save your work in Google Earth as another KML file (which will keep it as a Google Earth overlay) by going to File > Save > Save My Places.

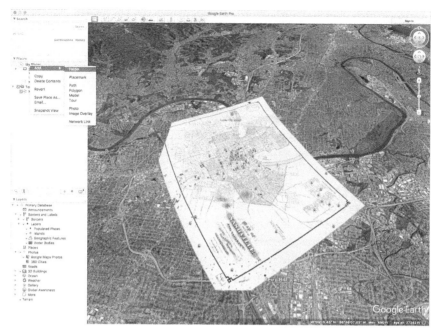

Figure 23.4. Google Earth screenshot demonstrating how to create a new folder for historic maps.

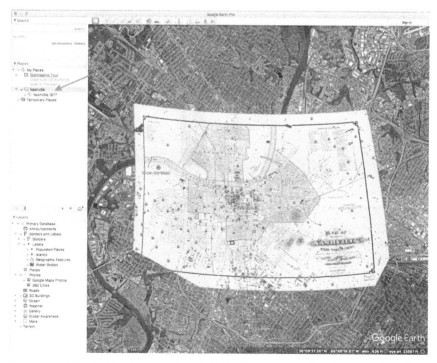

Figure 23.5. Google Earth screenshot depicting historic maps in a designated folder.

- Do this for each of the three historic maps you found and georectified.
- Upload these as KML files to Slack #exercises.

Part III: Tracing Change over Time

The objective of this final part of the mapping exercise is to give you a sense of how cities change over time, to prompt you to question why, and to search for answers.

Once you have found three digitized historical maps of Nashville, georectified them using Mapwarper, and uploaded them as KML files to Google Earth, toggle between the four different views (including the modern one) to complete the analysis outlined below.

Choose one specific site to focus on in Nashville. Locate that site on the different maps from different time periods. Note what changes you observe. Do some changes seem more meaningful than others? If you see something interesting in a neighboring area, you are welcome to shift or change your site.

As you describe the changes you see across time, are there any shifts that seem more sudden than others? Could these changes be related to one another? Do you note a pattern? What might explain these changes? For instance, were the changes the result of individual choice or part of larger shifts in the environment, society, politics, technology, or the economy? Review Kenneth Jackson's *Crabgrass Frontier* for material to test, substantiate, or revise your hunches.[11]

Describe what you have found, the causes you have identified, and your conclusions. Post your findings to #exercises in Slack.

NOTES

1. T. Mills Kelly, *Teaching History in the Digital Age* (Ann Arbor: University of Michigan Press, 2013).

2. William Cronon, "Who Reads Geography or History Anymore? The Challenge of Audience in a Digital Age" (Lecture in Geography, British Academy, July 7, 2015), accessed November 19, 2018, https://www .thebritishacademy.ac.uk/audio/who-reads-geography-or-history-anymore -challenge-audience-digital-age.

3. Ruth Mostern and Elana Gainor, "Traveling the Silk Road on a Virtual Globe: Pedagogy, Technology and Evaluation for Spatial History," *Digital Humanities Quarterly* 7, no. 2 (2013), http://www.digitalhumanities.org/dhq /vol/7/2/000116/000116.html; Richard White, "Spatial History Project," Spatial History Lab, 2010, https://web.stanford.edu/group/spatialhistory/cgi-bin/site /pub.php?id=29.

4. Grady Clay, *Close-Up: How to Read the American City* (New York: Praeger, 1973).

5. John Stilgoe, *Outside Lies Magic: Regaining History and Awareness in Everyday Places* (New York: Walker, 1999).

6. Anne Spirn, "The Once and Future City," February 5, 2018, accessed June 8, 2018, http://web.mit.edu/thecity/index.html.

7. Mostern and Gainer, "Traveling the Silk Road."

8. White, "Spatial History Project."

9. Kelly, *Teaching History*.

10. White, "Spatial History Project."

11. Kenneth Jackson. *Crabgrass Frontier. The Suburbanization of the United States* (Oxford: Oxford University Press, 1987).

TWENTY-FOUR

—ᴍ—

Shifting Frames of Interpretation

Place-Based Technologies and Virtual Augmentation in Art Education

JUSTIN B. MAKEMSON

University of New Mexico

PLACE-BASED AND PLACE-SPECIFIC TECHNOLOGIES OPEN up a new set of interpretative platforms for teachers and students interested in examining the relationship between the created object and its environment. For example, GIS (geographic information system) technologies make it possible to map information through the collection, analysis, and dissemination of multiple data sets within a single, layered geospatial representation, while GPS (global positioning system) technologies make it possible to support local seek-and-discover exploration through environmental interaction and ubiquitous information exchange, mobile learning, location awareness, and the incredible accuracy of satellite-based navigation.[1] MR/AR (mixed/augmented reality) technologies make it possible to create a sense of embodiment or presence within an enhanced, expanded, or modified local experience through links to embedded content and ubiquitous information services.[2] Still, not all new technologies work as viable options for student interpretative platforms. Today's art teachers have to be able to discern which technologies are appropriate for classroom use and when it would work better to reconfigure more familiar technologies to support virtual and local interactions with artwork. I am an art educator currently working in teacher preparation—this quick hit examines some of the ways that I have explored visual interpretation, technology, and location in my

172

Figure 24.1. Photograph of student accessing virtual tour stop using tablet and the augmented reality platform HP Reveal. Created by Justin Makemson (2015).

own classroom. Specifically, I recount two exercises: (1) encouraging students to reexamine initial, locally based interpretations of an artwork after interacting with the artwork in a virtual environment, and (2) briefly discussing the merits and drawbacks of digital interpretive platforms. Both exercises make use of readily available technologies.

In the first exercise, students worked in groups to research, design, and publish an MR/AR art and architecture tour of the university's historic campus (see fig. 24.1). The university where I was teaching is situated on the former estate of a wealthy southern matriarch whose property consisted of 170+ acres of Italianate gardens with a sizable collection of wrought iron gazebos, large stable facilities, greenhouses, a bowling alley, and a small zoological park. Students created a series of short documentary-style videos using iMovie and then linked the videos directly to selected campus locations using the HP Reveal (www.hpreveal.com). HP Reveal is an interpretative platform that connects and accesses creative content based on the recognition of geospatial patterns: users can trigger text, image, sound, and video files by positioning a mobile device to register a previously tagged location; content appears on the device screen superimposed on top of the trigger location, with the platform tracking and autoadjusting to slight fluctuations in alignment between device and location.

Project completed, tour participants began by picking up a small card printed with a tour explanation, technology requirements and instructions, and the geographic coordinates of five different tour "stops" from one of several campus locations; tour information was also published as a multistage geocache and available online at the Groundspeak-Geocaching website (www.geocaching.com) for off-campus participants to seek and discover. Participants navigated from geographic coordinate to geographic coordinate using a GPS-enabled device as a "GPS educational trail"—most participants defaulted to the location services application on their mobile phones.[3] Tour participants who successfully arrived at a designated stop used their tablet or phone to access video shorts. For example, participants triggered a video short on the former estate's Italianate gardens by holding their device up to the gazebo located at the first set of geographic coordinates (see fig. 24.1). My students decided to begin each video with a vintage photograph precisely superimposed over the present-day location: in the previous example, participants triggered a 1915 photograph of female seminary students, dressed in the long, dark skirts and white starched blouses and sitting in the gazebo on a sunny spring afternoon. Two project leaders monitored the overall design and cohesive packaging of video shorts, but every group of student designers developed their own distinct concentration and interpretive focus: the second group produced a video short that opened to a photograph of students painting at the base of the bell tower; this video then transitioned into a discussion of present-day studio spaces, programs of study, and course offerings. The third group produced a video short that opened to a vintage photograph of a women's basketball practice, players and coach dressed in full-length skirts and backboard attached to a nearby tree; this video then transitioned into a comparative review of past and present collegiate athletic programs. The fourth group produced a video short that opened to a photograph of a frozen fountain, something of a curiosity on a Southern campus; this video then transitioned into a synopsis of the estate's original water features, the renovation of the iconic water turned bell tower, and the university's endorsement of the bell tower as its identifying trademark. The fifth group produced a video short that opened to a photograph of the historic antebellum mansion; this video then transitioned to consider the university's ongoing preservation efforts and tour programs. Due to my relative unfamiliarity with projects of this kind, I initially presented the proposal for a mixed/augmented reality art and architecture tour to students in fairly open terms. The group then negotiated the tour's objectives, general approach, and procedure and scheduled benchmarks, delegated roles and responsibilities, and got to work—and by the end, the entire research-design-publish process had become practically autonomous.

In the second exercise, students combined visits to local art spaces with diagnostic work involving the digital imaging platforms Adobe Illustrator and Adobe Photoshop (see fig. 24.2). I introduced the project by drawing attention to some of the public art sites within walking distance of campus. Students then visited a site of their choosing: I required students to spend a minimum of thirty minutes on-site to photograph and sketch the site from multiple vantage points and to keep a written journal containing their initial interpretation of the artwork and impressions from the site.

Over the course of several semesters, I reworked this exercise to fit different teaching schedules and learning goals and to meet the learning needs of different student populations. In one version, I framed the exercise so that students had to use a specific tool or function to discover and document qualities of the object photographed during the site visit: students might use a combination of the pen and shape tools to create a record of design elements, linear convergence, shifting attention windows, golden ratio, and the rule of thirds, or they might apply filters to obscure details and look at color/value concentrations and figure-ground relationships or change to the image mode to reveal color and luminance orientations.

In the second version, I reworked the exercise so students would have an opportunity to figure out on their own how to virtually manipulate the photographs from their site visits to achieve a desired interpretative effect (see fig. 24.2). Specifically, I prompted students to: (a) change the original color exposure, contrast, saturation, and luminance of the created object; (b) redefine borders and reposition the object within the picture plane; (c) overlap or repeat design elements; (d) play around with the relative size of design elements; or (e) rework the level of detail/rendering in the photograph of the created object.

In the third version, I reframed the exercise to really concentrate on the relationship between and created object and the surrounding environment. Students first virtually manipulated the created object but left the environment intact; students then virtually manipulated the environment but left the created object intact; and students finally removed the created object from the original environment and replaced it with a completely different object. With each virtual manipulation, students compared interpretative conclusions to their photographs, sketches, and notes from the initial site visit. I found that

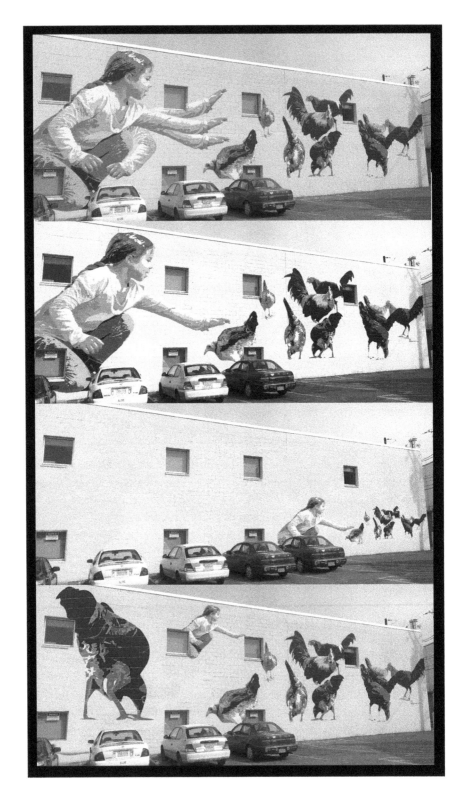

the virtual manipulations functioned similar to maps, cataloging the different qualities of the artwork and recording the creative decisions of the artist. These maps proved most interesting when layered on top of one another to create a multilevel representation of the various intentional and unintentional consequences of the artist's creative decisions.

In terms of theoretical support for my classroom practices, neuroaesthetics defines interpretative platforms as the operations and systems involved in the processing of visual information.[4] Semir Zeki explains the interrelationship between creative or artistic thinking and critical or interpretative thinking: "All visual art must obey the laws of the visual brain, whether in conception or in execution or in appreciation; that visual art has an overall function which is an extension of the function of the visual brain, to acquire knowledge; [and] that artists are, in a sense, neurologists who study the capacities of the visual brain with techniques that are unique to them."[5] More generally, interpretative platforms can be defined as self-other and self-environmental exchanges that support the development of constructs and beliefs relevant to the viewer's experience with an object, person, or space; exchanges involving new or additional platforms often bring something original, revealing, enriching, or thoroughly unanticipated to the interpretive experience.[6] From an educator's perspective, teaching interpretive platforms helps students understand how their audience generally perceives of and processes visual information, hone the use of formal design and artistic conventions including perspective, color theory, and figure-ground relationships, and more clearly communicate creative intent.

John Berger's *Ways of Seeing* is prescient in its discussion of technology as an interpretative platform: technologies such as television, print reproductions, and the camera offer unprecedented access to information about images and objects and open up the possibility for viewers to interpret artwork with a level of familiarity, authenticity, and expertise once reserved only for the culturally elite—technology demystifies and democratizes visual interpretation but at the price of separating the artwork from its intended setting and manner of presentation.[7] John Richardson's constructs of "territorialization" and "mobility" similarly demonstrate how technology can extend the influence of an object on a viewer beyond the initial encounter.[8] Unfortunately, interpretive platforms that overlook the importance of the created object's environment and presentation generate an incomplete representation of the created object's overall significance. While contemporary place-based technologies have the

Figure 24.2. Digital manipulations of photograph of Mark Horst's public mural "Reach," taken by a student during a site visit in Albuquerque, New Mexico. Created by Corey Smith (2019).

potential to reposition the viewer and reconnect local and virtual experiences, the interrelationship between technology and place can be complicated. Graham offers three "metaphors" to help explain different configurations of virtual and local participation:

1. Technology and place in a substitution-transcendence configuration operate as exclusive, parallel interpretive frameworks; virtual participation is prioritized over local participation or inversely local participation is prioritized over virtual participation.

2. Technology and place in a coevolution configuration operate as complementary but ordinal interpretative frameworks; prior virtual participation informs present local participation and prior local participation informs present virtual participation.

3. Technology and place in a recombination configuration operate as a concurrent and unified interpretative framework; virtual and local participation combine to create an interpretative experience that is more layered and nuanced than if the experience coevolved through successive virtual or local experiences.[9]

The interpretative exercises described earlier in the chapter roughly correspond to the configurations of recombination and coevolution.

In closing, today's teachers and students have the option to employ digital platforms and virtual augmentation to look deeper and more effectively critique/analyze artwork, to reveal implicit or previously unseen qualities of artwork, and to determine the viability of the artist's creative decisions. Digital platforms can be incredibly helpful in speeding up, slowing down, or resequencing interpretative processes. Digital platforms can be used to enhance the functionality and convenience of interpretative exercises and increase the number and variety of possible interpretative outcomes. More importantly, digital platforms can be used to disrupt the automaticity of exchanges between the student and the artwork. Based on my students' self-report and/or reflective examination of interpretative methods, I find that the diagnostic work within a digital platform (i.e., the projecting, mapping, marking, annotating, and comparing that shows up on the device's screen) roughly corresponds to the student's own meta-awareness of internal interpretative processes going on in the mind.

Even so, we as art teachers still need to consider when and how technology can enrich thoughtfully designed instruction instead of framing technology as the endgame of instruction. I believe that meaningful instruction is primarily driven by ideas and initiatives rather than developments in technology. The digital interpretative platforms and virtual augmentation techniques discussed in this chapter are similar in principle and practice to more traditional means of visual interpretation: I remember my undergraduate experiences mapping linear perspective with wax pencils and plastic transparencies and creating value studies out of graphite and grid paper—I even remember combining tracing paper and the copy ratio option on the Xerox machine to manipulate proportion and reposition objects within the picture plane. Digital interpretative platforms seem to be most effective when technologies are simultaneously ubiquitous and proactive and promote natural interactions—in other words, effective interpretative platforms create access to information when needed, support existing behaviors and open options for new behaviors, and operate in a nonintrusive manner.

NOTES

1. Herbert Broda and Ryan Baxter, "Using GIS and GPS Technology as an Instructional Tool," *Clearing House* 76, no. 1 (2002): 49; Maria Virvou and Eythimios Alepis, "Mobile Educational Features in Authoring Tools for Personalized Tutoring," *Computers and Education,* 44, no. 1 (2005): 53–68; Yueg-Min Huang, Tien-Chi Huang, and Meng-Yeh Hsieh, "Using Annotation Services in a Ubiquitous Jigsaw Cooperative Learning Environment," *Journal of Educational Technology and Society* 11, no. 2 (2008): 3–15; Kai-Yi Chin and Yen-Lin Chen, "A Mobile Learning Support System for Ubiquitous Learning Environments," *Procedia-Social and Behavioral Sciences* 73 (2013): 14–21.

2. Paul Milgram, Haruo Takemura, Akira Utsumi, and Fumio Kishino, "Augmented Reality: A Class of Displays on the Reality-Virtuality Continuum," in *Proceedings of the International Society for Optics and Photonics, Telemanipulator and Telepresence Technologies* 2351 (1995): 282–293; Elizabeth FitzGerald, Rebecca Ferguson, Anne Adams, Mark Gaved, Yishay Mor, and Rhodri Thomas, "Augmented Reality and Mobile Learning: The State of the Art," *International Journal of Mobile and Blended Learning* 5, no. 4 (2013): 43–58; Mario Lorenz, Marc Busch, Loukas Rentzos, Manfred Tscheligi, Philipp Klimant, and Peter Fröhlich, "I'm There! The Influence of Virtual Reality and Mixed Reality Environments Combined with Two Different Navigation Methods on Presence," conference paper, from *2015 IEEE Virtual Reality* (March 2015): 223–224.

3. Stefanie Zecha, "Outline of an Effective GPS Education Trail Methodology," accessed May 10, 2017, http://gispoint.de/fileadmin/user_upload/paper_gis_open/537545045.pdf.

4. Semir Zeki, *A Vision of the Brain* (Oxford: Blackwell Scientific, 1993); Robert Solso, *Cognition and the Visual Arts* (Cambridge, MA: MIT Press,

1996); Margaret Livingstone, *Vision and Art: The Biology of Seeing* (New York: Abrams Books, 2008); Irving Massey, *The Neural Imagination: Aesthetic and Neuroscientific Approaches to the Arts* (Austin: University of Texas Press, 2009).

5. Semir Zeki, "Statement of Neuroaesthetics," accessed May 5, 2009, http://www.neuroaesthetics.org.

6. Edmund Burke Feldman, *Art: Image and Idea* (Englewood Cliffs: Prentice Hall, 1967); Abigail Housen, "The Eye of the Beholder: Measuring Aesthetic Development" (EdD thesis, Harvard University Graduate School of Education, 1983); Michael Parsons, "The Place of a Cognitive Developmental Approach to Aesthetic Response," *Journal of Aesthetic Education* 20, no. 4 (1986): 107–111; Arthur Efland, "The City as Metaphor for Integrated Learning in the Arts," *Studies in Art Education* 41, no. 3 (2000): 276–295; Elliot Eisner, "Should We Create New Aims for Art Education?" *Art Education* 54, no. 5 (2001): 6–10; Paul Duncum, "A Case for an Art Education of Everyday Aesthetic Experiences," *Studies in Art Education* 40, no. 4 (1999): 295–311; Philip Yenawine, *Visual Thinking Strategies: Using Art to Deepen Learning Across School Disciplines* (Cambridge, MA: Harvard Education Press, 2013).

7. John Berger, *Ways of Seeing* (London: BBC and Penguin Books, 1972).

8. John Richardson, "The Materiality of Space," in *Matter Matters: Art Education and Material Culture Studies*, ed. Paul Bolin and Doug Blandy (Reston, VA: National Art Education Association, 2011), 36–46.

9. Stephen Graham, "The End of Geography or the Explosion of Place? Conceptualizing Space, Place and Information Technology," *Progress in Human Geography* 22, no. 2 (1998): 165–185.

TWENTY-FIVE

—⚋⚋—

Using Podcasts to Teach Short Stories

LISA SIEFKER BAILEY

Indiana University-Purdue University Columbus

I HAVE CREATED A SERIES of podcast assignments that I have used in teaching a sophomore-level Introduction to Fiction course. This methodology encourages close reading, attention to the sound and rhythm of language, a sense of ownership in one's reading, and confidence in development of interpretation. Using podcasts is a useful way to teach and learn. For many students, listening feels less like work than reading does, and hearing words read in a storytelling voice encourages listeners' empathy. Students often feel like they know the voices they listen to, and that connection reduces the solitary feeling of studying. In their review of recent studies on podcast applications in language learning, Masudul Hasan and Tan Bee Hoon found that some perceptions students had about podcasts "included the opportunity for students to learn at their own time, and to listen to specific materials that they miss or do not understand multiple times."[1] I like to encourage auditory learning, and I emphasize the import of honing one's listening skills. Podcasts are especially effective for auditory learners, and they expressly help English language learners. I encourage students to read the story at the same time they listen to the podcasts, and, for students who ask if it is okay to multitask, I tell them that it is fine, if it works for them. While referencing P. Snape and W. Fox-Turnbull's study of technology education in New Zealand, Tony Whitefield points out that today's students "need to be engaged in authentic, real world activities, must socially construct outcomes, make connections with others, and collaborate with a range of partners."[2] My podcast assignments create such authentic real-world activities by providing students with social opportunities to learn in an active learning environment as they share their work with their peers as well as with me.

I have taught this series of assignments in both hybrid and face-to-face classes. After assigning short stories to be read as homework, I ask students to reread them, explaining that the most successful reading of a text is usually a rereading of it—when you can approach the text without having to discern its characters and plot anew, and you can concentrate on the subtleties of language and rhythm. I emphasize how listening to recordings of stories can inspire readers to envision a story's elements in a different way than we might when we concentrate on the words alone. In the online portion of the class, this assignment works well because it incorporates web sources, and students know they can hit pause should they need to look up a word or take a break and come back to the podcast. In a face-to-face class, I host a listening party as a flipped classroom activity in which students listen together and experience communal reactions and a follow-up reflection discussion on the experience. Fernando Rosell-Aguilar writes that a "number of theories of learning can support the use of podcasting for language learning: constructivism; the use of authentic materials for language learning; informal and lifelong learning; theories on the use of learning objects for the provision of learning materials; mobile learning; as well as the practices of chunking and just in time teaching, among others"[3] While Rosell-Aguilar's point is made regarding language learning, I have found that his argument applies to learning the complexities of literary analysis, too.

"ARABY" PODCAST LISTENING AND LEARNING TOOL

Students listen to a podcast from LibriVox, which offers a reading of James Joyce's "Araby" by Julie VW,[4] and a podcast from *The Guardian*, which offers Richard Ford reading "The Student's Wife."[5] After listening to the podcasts, students take time to think about what they noticed, considering key ideas, new insights, or thoughts they would like to explore further, and post such ideas online in discussion boards in the learning management system. The next class discussion evolves from specific elements of language from both "The Student's Wife" and "Araby," which students write about.

Responses to the assignment vary greatly. Students are likely to express that they find "Araby" difficult to read. They are often taken aback by the language of a different era. It is hard for me to remember that the language in "Araby" is over a century out of style, as Joyce published this short story in his 1914 collection *Dubliners*. Some students enjoy listening to the podcast in an accent unlike their own. In fact, when I teach Shakespeare and texts from the medieval period, I often encourage students to read aloud imitating a British accent, as it helps them find both the rhythm of the language and a comfort zone for words with which they are not likely to be familiar. Students are also likely to report that they notice the narrator of "Araby" uses a dreamlike tone. Hearing that soft-spoken sound in the narrator's voice can help students realize that the narrator is recalling a memory. Listening to the story particularly benefits students who are used to reading for plot and not as good at realizing that the depth of literary fiction is found in character development. Students often emphasize that the podcast forces them to slow down and listen and that they enjoy hearing the words come to life, and their reflective discussion allows them time to develop further insight into the meaning of the story. "Araby" is a particularly good story to use for this exercise, as the plot is small, but the ideas and the epiphany in the story are intense and powerful.

Raymond Carver's "The Student's Wife," which appeared in his 1976 short story collection, *Will You Please Be Quiet, Please?* elicits responses from students that indicate they are far more comfortable with the ideas and language in this short story than they are with those of "Araby." Students write about ways they can relate to the relationship problems the couple appears to have and about their own experiences with insomnia and percolating problems with significant others. The online discussion forum opens the door to students finding ways to be confident about what they notice, and it helps them ferret out the interesting ideas. Once they start responding to each other, they build a community for analysis on the board. Online discussion forums help them build their reading and analytical skills, because the discussion is all theirs. I set up parameters for them to follow, but I do not respond to the postings; instead, I allow them to monitor themselves, and I grade them on following directions, not on literary interpretation. It is exciting to see how the postings quickly become deeper and more detailed, as they learn from one another what is interesting to read in their responses to peers as opposed to what is rather obvious. I have also been exceedingly impressed with how the online discussion demands that each student work in tangible ways. In-class discussion often leaves some shy or introverted students without as large a platform to share ideas as the online discussion forum. I have also been impressed with how often students write far more than the required posting word count, which illustrates their enthusiasm for the process. While I have used this assignment as social learning in a hybrid class, the method could be used in a face-to-face class as a flipped classroom activity, in which the students come to class having read the stories, spend a class period listening to the podcast and writing on the discussion board, and then follow up with a lively oral discussion based on reading responses, preparing for the next level of critical discussion shepherded by the instructor in the follow-up class later in the week.

"A&P" PODCAST CREATION LEARNING TOOL

A few weeks later in the semester, I ask students to make a podcast of themselves reading John Updike's "A&P" as they imagine Updike might read it. After students read the story expressively to make readers engage with the story and think about it, they write a brief commentary in which they examine how one or two specific lines from the story help it achieve its effects. I suggest that they note how they emphasize effect(s) in their reading, and I have them post that commentary along with their podcasts attached on the discussion board. I then require them to respond to two peer posts by examining the wording that surrounds one of the quotations a peer examines. I have them either build on the peer's ideas or demonstrate a contrasting way of thinking about the language. The point is for them to examine new ideas; in other words, notions not yet discussed on the board. I set a shorter word count on these peer responses, about 100–150 words each.

Creating their own podcasts generates a great deal of enthusiasm from my students. They love getting the chance to make the story their own by reading it their way. Reading the story aloud helps them get the humor in the narrator's choices of imagery, tone, and attitude. Sometimes students write about technological problems in their postings, and sometimes they write about how they must make time to get away from the busyness of their lives in order to concentrate on the story and to create a podcast that others can actually hear. Some of these discoveries have seemed so fundamental to me, that I have been quite taken aback. However, I have realized that some of my students do not value a quiet place for study; often, they discover such a space helps them focus on literary analysis. Postings and responses to peers thus create a fresh and enticing way for students to discuss the story on their own terms. By directing them to post about individual sentences in the work, students are guided to strong close readings and deep interpretations of specifics. The online discussion forum becomes a space in which students demonstrate agency and want to show off their great ideas, and it gives them the opportunity to take as much time as they want to think about what they might say before they post it. Such a technique for discussion is a far different animal than the celerity required to get ideas on the floor in a face-to-face class discussion. After the podcast creation assignment, I have responded with a lecture podcast to answer questions on the discussion board and to explain the import of Updike's allusion to the Greek myth of the judgment of Paris.

"A&P" is not too long, so the podcasts do not seem unwieldy. Moreover, a question comparing Updike's story to "Araby" works beautifully on the midterm or final exam. By focusing on the details of the aesthetics that the narrators in both stories appreciate and why, not only have I had successful large group discussions but also students demonstrate in their exams and essays how well they understand both the surface and the deeper meanings of each narrator's desires for a world he cannot be a part of.

TECHNOLOGY TIPS

I enable podcast feed on the discussion board, so students can use a computer with a camera, as well as a smartphone, MP3, or other digital recording device. In the past, I have had a few students who did not own recording devices use flip cameras they could check out from the library resource center for this assignment. There are plenty of apps students can download to create their podcasts, such as Anchor, Podcast Addict, iTunes, uStudio, Podcast Generator, Podbean, Buzzsprout, Transistor, Castos, or Blubrry. I have found it best to encourage students to use whatever device or application they are most comfortable with. The higher the student's level of confidence in using an app or device, the better their confidence in fulfilling the interpretive part of the assignment. Some of my students are more tech-savvy than I am, and it is a delight to learn from them how to use applications I am not familiar with. Sometimes, however, I have students who are not comfortable with technology. I offer a list of steps for the application I find most user friendly that works in-network on campus. That way, students who are less technologically experienced can follow through on the assignment with little additional help.

In conclusion, I want to reemphasize, as I do for my students, that most analysis comes from rereading. We read the first time through to discern plot, identify characters, and discover the themes and scope of a story. Multiple readings allow us to look for trends, find connections, and decipher details that can support our individual ways of reading a work of literature. Using the examples and details we discover to explain how and why our ideas work is the means for building a satisfying critical discussion and the groundwork for developing a cogent literary argument. By creating assignments that layer podcasts, online discussion boards with interactive responses from student peers, in-class discussion, and clarifying podcast lectures, students experiment with ideas and devote more time to each step of interpretation, which results in opportunities to learn more than they might without the help of multimodal learning and teaching techniques.

NOTES

1. Masudul Hasan and Tan Bee Hoon, "Podcast Applications in Language Learning: A Review of Recent Studies," *English Language Teaching* 6, no. 2 (2013): 133.

2. P. Snape and W. Fox-Turnbull, "Twenty-First Century Learning and Technology Education Nexus," *Problems of Education in the 21st Century* 34 (2011): 149–161; Tony Whitefield, "Pedagogy in the Evolving Tech Environment—What Has Changed?" *ICICTE 2012 Proceedings* (January 2012): 289. *EBSCOhost*, www.ulib.iupui.edu/cgi-bin/proxy.pl?url=https://search-ebscohost-com.proxy.ulib.uits.iu.edu/login.aspx?direct=true&db=eue&AN=85747944&site=eds-live. Accessed May 15, 2018.

3. Fernando Rosell-Aguilar, "Top of the Pods—In Search of a Podcasting 'Podagogy' for Language Learning," *Computer Assisted Language Learning* 20 (2007): 477.

4. James Joyce, "Araby" in *Dubliners*, read by Julie VW as a librovox recording, podcast, https://librivox.org/dubliners-by-james-joyce/. Accessed January 8, 2015.

5. Raymond Carver, "The Student's Wife," read by Richard Ford in the *Guardian UK: Culture Podcast*, produced by Tim Maby, podcast, https://www.theguardian.com/books/audio/2012/dec/23/richard-ford-raymond-carver-wife. Accessed January 8, 2015.

PART IV

PUBLIC SCHOLARSHIP AND COMMUNITY ENGAGEMENT

TWENTY-SIX

Building La Florida

Rethinking Colonial Florida History in the Digital Age

J. MICHAEL FRANCIS
University of South Florida, St. Petersburg

HANNAH TWEET
University of South Florida, St. Petersburg

RACHEL L. SANDERSON
University of South Florida, St. Petersburg

LA FLORIDA: A BRIEF INTRODUCTION

Leafing through the faded pages of a seventeenth-century book of baptisms from St. Augustine, Florida, a frustrated reader, likely an eighteenth-century Spanish priest, scribbled a brief comment on the book's opening page. It read: "My dear lord: Not even the Devil could read this; the handwriting is so terrible I cannot understand a single word in it."

Though certainly exaggerated, the anonymous note conveys a sense of frustration shared by many contemporary students of early modern history, namely, the inability to read original documents. Indeed, history students face a range of obstacles when it comes to working with primary sources: accessibility, time, the need for specialized training, and the challenge of deciphering centuries-old script. All create additional barriers that can limit student engagement, especially with sources written in languages other than English.

At its core, La Florida: The Interactive Digital Archive of the Americas (www.laflorida.org; see fig. 26.1) was designed to address these challenges and thereby provide undergraduate and graduate students with unique opportunities to engage in meaningful primary source research. The vision was to create a collaborative, interdisciplinary digital platform to present colonial Florida

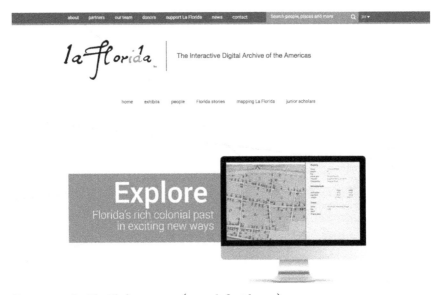

Figure 26.1. La Florida home page (www.laflorida.org).

history to a broad audience in a creative, engaging, and interactive manner. Although La Florida's content focuses on the history of colonial Florida, a period bound between 1513 and 1821, we hope the site will serve as a useful model for other digital history projects.

La Florida site formally launched in March 2018; however, the project's origins date back a decade earlier, with an initiative to train undergraduate- and master's-level students to read original sixteenth-century Spanish script. For students of early modern Spanish American history, including Spanish Florida, language training remains a serious obstacle to student engagement with primary documents. While there are some fine collections of primary sources in translation, the body of translated material for Spanish Florida pales by comparison to the hundreds of thousands of original digitized documents, drawings, paintings, and maps housed in dozens of archives, libraries, and museums around the globe. In Spain alone, eight different state archives, including Seville's Archivo General de Indias (AGI) contribute to a remarkable site called PARES, the portal for Spanish archives (http://pares.mcu.es). PARES hosts an expansive collection of open-access digital material, allowing users to consult thousands of digitized documents related to the history of Spain and its global empire. For scholars, open access to online resources such as those housed on PARES are critical for the advancement of research. Yet for students without specialized training, these collections remain of limited value.

Thus, in the fall of 2006, historian J. Michael Francis developed a two-semester program to teach students how to read sixteenth-century Spanish handwriting, or paleography. Though topics change each year, the assigned material focuses on the early decades of Spain's attempted colonization efforts in the southeast. Using digitized documents housed on PARES, students spend eight months learning how to decipher five-hundred-year-old texts, words, and abbreviations that "not even the Devil could read." Initially, the paleography program's primary goal was to prepare a select group of undergraduate- and master's-level students for advanced graduate studies and help them become more competitive candidates for admission into top-tier doctoral programs. Since 2007, more than one hundred students have participated in the program, more than a dozen of whom continued on to PhD programs in colonial Latin American history.

Each year, the paleography program is organized around a central theme, such as early colonial legal disputes, Spanish-Indian relations, sixteenth-century conquest expeditions, slavery, pirates and piracy, or daily life in St. Augustine. In addition to four exams and in-class group work, each student is assigned a unique set of unpublished original documents to transcribe. Students who successfully complete the program are then eligible to participate in an eight-week summer study abroad in Spain to conduct original archival research.

Certainly, the availability of PARES made the paleography program possible, and each year new initiatives contribute to the ever-expanding volume of digitized documents. In 2012, an exciting new opportunity introduced even more material to paleography students, providing further impetus for La Florida project. That year, Bishop Felipe J. Estévez authorized a team from the University of South Florida, St. Petersburg (USFSP) to digitize St. Augustine's parish archive, which houses the oldest extant parish records from any region of the continental United States. Over a ten-month period, USFSP graduate students Saber Gray and Arthur Tarratus digitized the archive's extensive marriage, baptism, confirmation, and death records—more than nine thousand pages of documents spanning the period between 1594–1840. By early 2013, St. Augustine's colonial parish records were digitized and, thanks to Vanderbilt University historian Jane Landers, housed online and made available to anyone with internet access (www.slavesocieties.org). Collectively, these invaluable documents provide a unique window into colonial St. Augustine society, chronicling the lives of the city's European, African, Native American, and mixed-race inhabitants. Figure 26.2, for example, is one of the few surviving sixteenth-century marriage records. The page's final entry, dated February 21, 1594, records the marriage between Antón Criado

Figure 26.2. Marriages, Box 1 fol. 89r (1594). Archive of the Catholic Diocese of St. Augustine. St. Augustine, Florida.

and a woman named Biolante [Violante], both Native Americans from Nombre de Dios, a Timucua Indian mission community located just outside of St. Augustine.

With the ever-expanding network of open-access digital databases, students and scholars alike have unprecedented access to original documentation. However, accessibility alone does not translate into student or public engagement. The inability to read the records remains the most common obstacle, and Spanish paleography requires advanced language training, a skill relatively few possess. The USFSP paleography program was designed to help overcome this obstacle, but the program also had its own limitations and frustrations, the most significant of which was the absence of a venue for students to share their research. After spending the entire academic year working with original documents, none of which have ever been published, exciting and innovative student research projects stalled. Semesters ended, students graduated, and ambitious long-term initiatives remained in various stages of completion. Soon it became clear that the paleography program was just an initial step; contributing to the world of digital research required a more comprehensive approach, one that extended beyond a two-semester course.

With that, the idea for La Florida was born. Its aim was twofold: to introduce digital humanities into the classroom and, in turn, provide a lasting platform for faculty-student research. Just one critical piece was missing: the technology.

A PARTNERSHIP FORMED

In early discussions about La Florida project, the long-term vision was to build a site equally supported by twin pillars: innovative historical content and cutting-edge technology. The paleography program and the widespread access to digital material provided a strong foundation for building content, but the project lacked a technology partner. That changed in 2016, with a serendipitous meeting with Francisco Guitard, chief innovation officer for Edriel Intelligence, a Madrid-based start-up company that specializes in creative technologies. A team began to form. At USFSP, Francis recruited two master's students, Rachel Sanderson and Hannah Tweet, to serve as associate directors. Both Sanderson and Tweet had participated in the two-semester paleography program, and both had conducted original archival work in Spain. Advanced paleography students were assigned to take the lead in a series of research projects, ranging from a prosopographical study of the 1539–1543 Hernando de Soto expedition to a survey of widows and orphans in eighteenth-century St. Augustine. For students, this was the first time they had an opportunity to define and develop a long-term research project, one rooted in a detailed survey of primary source material.

Francis, Guitard, Sanderson, and Tweet became the core team for La Florida's initial phases of development. Sanderson and Tweet immediately assumed important leadership roles while working with fellow students, scholars, and the community, often hosting collaborative work sessions as La Florida team continued to grow. Over the next two years, the Florida-based team worked closely with Guitard and his team in Spain to outline the site's organizational framework and design, and to develop the technology that would be used to present a wide range of research data.

Ultimately, the goal of La Florida was to reach as broad an audience as possible, to build a site that would appeal to academics, students, teachers, and the general public. Finally, on March 15, 2018, at an event hosted by the Organization of American States in Washington, DC, the team celebrated La Florida's formal launch.

LA FLORIDA: THE INTERACTIVE DIGITAL
ARCHIVE OF THE AMERICAS

La Florida: The Interactive Digital Archive of the Americas is divided into five distinct sections, each one designed to provide opportunities for long-term research projects, including senior, undergraduate, and master's theses, as well as assignments appropriate for students enrolled in semester-long courses.

Section One: People

Perhaps the most ambitious feature on the site is the People section, an interactive database that records biographical information about the thousands of
men and women who lived in Florida at any point between 1513 and 1821. At the
time of La Florida's launch, the database included information about more than
thirty-seven hundred individuals, with thousands more to be added in future
phases. This content was a sample of material drawn from nearly ten years of
Francis's archival research and the research of graduate students trained in
Spanish paleography. From the onset of the paleography program in 2006,
student projects and participation enriched the information now housed in
La Florida's database. Now, the database offers a clear sense of purpose and
direction for paleography students. In the two years leading up to La Florida's
launch, more than a dozen students, graduate and undergraduate alike, initiated projects that are still underway, with the purpose of creating, or contributing to, a comprehensive data set that will be added to the site. This collaborative
approach not only ensures that quality content will continue to be added to La
Florida; it also creates opportunities for students to publish and share their
research with the public.

Creating the platform for La Florida's People database took the combined
efforts of the USFSP team of researchers and Edriel's team of database designers. Under the leadership of Guitard, Edriel created a database software
specifically designed for historical data entry. Edriel's digital platform allows
scholars to record all types of complex biographical data, such as physical
descriptions, literacy rates, places of origin, occupations, family connections, personal affiliations, or to track an individual's movement over time.
The platform is dynamic and flexible. It is designed to capture the complexity
and nuance of historical information, whether it is the lies that people tell
or the intricate networks they build. All data points have a primary source
citation, guiding users directly to the original document. Moreover, information is searchable and interactive; users can apply filters, design personal
inquiries, and create advanced infographics. In the process, visitors to the
site can track individual and collective histories across time and place, contributing significantly to genealogical research. The database also accom-
modates other types of data for which there are detailed archival records,
such as ship manifests, food supplies, hospital inventories, and trade goods.

La Florida project would not be possible without the commitment and
tireless research of student scholars. Under the leadership of Associate Directors Hannah Tweet and Rachel Sanderson, students participated in monthly
"data meetings," four-hour sessions designed to address potential problems

their data could pose and to discuss the disparate needs their data sets presented. Students contributed to solutions, offering new perspectives and helping craft recommendations for the implementation of the technological solutions. Then, the USFSP team communicated their concerns and insights with Edriel's team. This process was repeated throughout the two years it took to build the database platform.

While professional scholars will surely find this kind of database valuable, the site was designed in part by students, with students in mind. Presenting historical content in a dynamic digital framework is not in itself a novel idea. However, the current emphasis on STEM-based studies is encouraging a fresh wave of historical interpretation, using technology to examine historical questions and convey findings. For example, students at any level can use the information in the People section to create detailed heat maps, highlighting the diverse backgrounds of the men and women who colonized Florida. Advanced students might combine data from the People and Mapping sections to explore the nature of property ownership in 1764 St. Augustine, highlighting the many properties owned by women and free blacks. With the available dynamic tools and the abundance of rich historical documentation, La Florida's People section has limitless potential for faculty-student research, both short and long term.

Section Two: Exhibits

The aim of La Florida's Exhibits section is to offer users a museum-quality experience, with curated thematic digital content. The site launched with an exhibit titled *Life and Death in Colonial St. Augustine*, which houses the digitized parish records from St. Augustine's Diocesan archive. Visitors can view high-resolution images and access transcriptions by scrolling over the original script. Over time, all nine thousand pages will be transcribed and translated, providing unprecedented access to some of the country's earliest colonial documents. Transcribing and translating the documents currently housed in Exhibits is a long-term project designed for advanced paleography students. Many of the pages are badly damaged and accurate transcriptions require advanced paleography. Several students who have completed the eight-month program participate in developing this part of the site. Students work in teams before submitting their work to scholars to complete the rigorous vetting process.

To create the interactive transcription, La Florida utilizes a program specifically designed for this process, where each word is carefully outlined to produce a digital imprint. Edriel Intelligence will apply this data to create a specialized optical character recognition (OCR) program, part of a broader initiative to develop technology that will digitize and automatically generate transcriptions of original Spanish documents. Students who participate in this project, therefore, not only are developing transcription and translation skills but also are introduced to the challenges and advantages of international collaboration and communication.

Life and Death in Colonial St. Augustine is the first of many exhibitions to be housed at La Florida. Future projects will include interactive visual and audio elements, covering a broad range of thematic topics such as Black Society in Spanish Florida, Health and Healing, Piracy, and Florida Missions.

Section Three: Mapping La Florida

Mapping La Florida presents historical maps on a creative, interactive digital platform, making old maps accessible and allowing users to explore colonial Florida's changing landscape. Each layered map allows scholars to add multimedia content, including text, audio, video, and 3-D animation, providing users with opportunities to interact with colonial maps rather than simply to view them. The site launched with two maps, one of which is a detailed plan of eighteenth-century St. Augustine. They were both grounded in student research projects and both required extensive paleography training and archival work. For example, the 1544 Alonso de la Cruz map, based on information gathered after the 1539–1543 Hernando de Soto expedition, plots more than one hundred Native American settlements scattered across the southeast. Our first step was to transcribe all the text, creating a key that Edriel could use to create the digital map. However, it is worth noting that this is just the first phase in a number of projects that will use the map as a platform to display content related to the Hernando de Soto expedition. The next phase will involve identifying all known archaeological sites associated with the expedition, a project that allows nonpaleography students to participate in the research. Digital artifacts will be plotted on the map, which will include even more text, images, and animations.

The 1764 Juan Joseph Eligio de la Puente map builds on a two-year project conducted by USFSP master's student Trevor Bryant. As an undergraduate student, Bryant enrolled in the paleography program and he spent three summers conducting archival research in Spain, most of it focused on gathering information about the men and women who lived in St. Augustine during the eighteenth century. Bryant's extensive research formed the core of the data currently available to site visitors. However, like the Alonso de la Cruz map, future phases will transform the map even further. Edriel has initiated a project to create a 3-D virtual St. Augustine, based largely on Bryant's findings. Moreover, a new team of master's students continues to work on refining the data and preparing the material for its online platform. As a result, users can now hover over an individual property and a detailed overview of the property and its owner emerges, providing information that would otherwise be lost to viewers. The biographical data represented on the map links to individual profiles in La Florida's People section, allowing users to move seamlessly throughout the site.

The Mapping La Florida section provides valuable opportunities for a wide range of students to engage in research. Students who do not possess the pale-ography skills can engage with the more technical aspects of the section, which will include 3-D imaging and GIS.

Section Four: Florida Stories

Florida Stories is a platform for original video content, featuring dramatic tales of the forgotten people and events that shaped Florida's colonial past. These animated videos, each three to five minutes in length, include a creative blend of historical illustrations, original musical scores, and contemporary artistic renderings. Creating Florida Stories offers opportunities for faculty-student collaboration across a wide range of disciplines, including art and music. Perhaps more than any other section, the Florida Stories feature has generated a great deal of student interest. Fascinating stories of forgotten figures fill the archives, and student scholars often uncover dramatic tales of triumph and tragedy. Indeed, two of the three videos currently on the site were not only written and developed by students working in conjunction with Edriel but the product of student archival research. Such a project also brings interdisciplin-ary elements into the history classroom. For example, in a newly developed course entitled History and Myth in Spanish Florida, Francis assigned students to draft a script and produce a five-minute Florida story, based on a semester-long research project (a strategy that can be adapted in any number of courses across disciplines). Students were required to create a detailed storyboard, including images and accompanying music. The exercise required that students search for copyright information, a task that few students had ever considered. Indeed, the assignment is designed to introduce students to a broad range of skills, from historical research to video production. University technology ser-vices provide necessary equipment, allowing students to construct and narrate their production. High-quality submissions are considered for publication on La Florida site. (See fig. 26.3.)

Section Five: Junior Scholars

The Junior Scholars section is designed to engage a new generation of stu-dents with the humanities. The site launched with a messaging feature with

Figure 26.3. Florida Stories video: "Luisa de Abrego: Marriage, Bigamy, and the Spanish Inquisition."

historic fonts and secret codes, allowing users to draft and send email messages written in scripts from the sixteenth, seventeenth, and eighteenth centuries. The letters in each font were taken directly from original documents. Using Adobe's graphic design programs, students trace individual letters, numbers, and symbols and convert them into functioning fonts. The assignment allows students to enhance language training and improve their paleography while also developing graphic design skills useful in any career. In time, the Junior Scholars section will feature educational games, videos, and web-based activities for people of all ages, providing additional opportunities for faculty-student research collaboration.

MOVING FORWARD

La Florida's long-term success will require a multidisciplinary and collaborative approach, supported by enduring institutional partnerships and academic ties between scholars, students, and experts in technological innovation. To reach a broad audience and engage the public, the content must be accessible and multidisciplinary, appealing to audiences outside the humanities. For example, an ongoing project will explore the topic of health and healing in colonial Florida. Spanish archives contain rich details about the medicines used to treat illness and disease, including detailed hospital inventories that date back to the late sixteenth century. This project, and others like it, is designed to invite faculty and students with interests in STEM-related fields to participate in La Florida.

Over time, a long-term approach to faculty-student research collaboration will provide unprecedented access to the remarkably rich, though much forgotten, history of colonial Florida. At the same time, La Florida project will give scholars and students a unique and creative outlet to present their work in digital format. Indeed, faculty-student collaboration remains La Florida's core principle and will continue to guide its future development. Challenges remain, including finding long-term funding solutions, but there is reason for optimism. In the first three months since launch, the site attracted more than twenty thousand visitors and received international media attention. In 2020, La Florida received a $250,000 major initiatives grant from the National Archives. New academic partners continue to join the project and what began in 2006 as a two-semester course in Spanish paleography is now an international initiative involving students, scholars, and technology experts from institutions across Spain and the United States.

(Dis)Placed Urban Histories

Combining Digital Humanities Pedagogy and Community Engagement

ZACH COBLE

New York University

REBECCA AMATO

New York University

THE COURSE "(DIS)PLACED URBAN HISTORIES" has been offered each spring since 2015 at New York University's Gallatin School of Individualized Study and brings a historian's perspective to investigating the impacts of gentrification and urban planning strategies in rapidly changing communities in New York City. During the 2016 and 2017 course iterations, Professor Rebecca Amato, collaborated with librarian, Zach Coble, to create online digital exhibits to showcase the students' fieldwork and to create a resource for participating community partners. While the faculty-library partnership was successful in creating a digital humanities pedagogy that helped students build methodological and technical skills, the process also revealed shortcomings about working with communities with low access to computers or with aging populations with few technical skills.

COURSE OVERVIEW

Neighborhood change comes in many varieties. Mid-twentieth-century urban renewal in US cities brought bulldozers and tower-in-the-park housing developments to dozens of poor neighborhoods considered ripe for revision. Twenty-first-century gentrification, meanwhile, has brought

LOSING SOUL

A CALL FOR CULTURAL
CENTERS

Charlotte St. c. 1975

With ruin comes abandonment, and with abandonment, comes ruin. In *GovPilot's* article discussing the fall and rise of the South Bronx, writer "alannah" argues that the stereotypical image that is associated with the South Bronx -- of burning buildings, the subsequent rubble, and the poor people who used to inhabit said buildings -- is the, "physical manifestation of improperly applied data, economic depression and the snowballing issue of property blight." She says that as "[droves] of residents left the South Bronx for more suburban areas and [as] property values plummeted ... [r]emaining residents watched their living conditions begin to deteriorate. After all, post-WWII rent control policies provided building owners little incentive to maintain their properties." Furthermore, alannah talks specifically about the mishandling by then-Mayor Lindsay of data regarding the fire departments' budgets and other similarly city-run benefits, that were either downsized, eliminated, or misused in the area.

Also, the property developers and owners were quick to allow their buildings to fall into disarray, as the residents were all low-income, and therefore the upkeep was often more expensive than their return. Red-lining and zoning plans implemented by real estate agencies were also vital players in the fall of the area.

Why does the South Bronx
need cultural centers?

Losing Soul

Disconnected Borough

The BDC

Moving Forward: Music Hall and
more

Sources Used

Figure 27.1. Exhibit about Jay Sanchez, resident of Los Sures.

high-end commerce and affluence to areas once occupied by low-income and working-class communities. In both the South Williamsburg neighborhood of Brooklyn and the Melrose neighborhood of the South Bronx, a series of changes has influenced the streetscapes and lives of residents. Deindustrialization, arson, landlord abandonment, and a mid-1970s city policy of "planned shrinkage" made large areas of both neighborhoods dangerous or unlivable, while migrants from Puerto Rico and the American Black Belt and immigrants from the Dominican Republic, Mexico, and Ecuador, among other places, struggled to survive in what remained of their communities. Today, massive reinvestment in these neighborhoods, as well as large-scale rezonings, have resulted in new middle-income and luxury housing and business development that has increased displacement pressures on these still predominantly low-income communities of color. (See fig. 27.1.)

This course, offered in partnership with the Brooklyn-based community organization Southside United HDFC in 2015 and 2016 and the Bronx-based community organization WHEDCo (Women's Housing and Economic Development Corporation) in 2017 and 2018, invites students to become activist historians whose objective is to collaboratively interpret the impact of neighborhood change on long-time residents and workers in South Williamsburg and Melrose. Students conduct oral history interviews and archival and secondary research, meet with activists and residents who are working to protect the interests of the current communities of these neighborhoods, and produce collaborative digital projects that are intended to be accessible to community organizations and residents for the long term. Oral history training takes place in the classroom through readings, practice interviews, and listening sessions. Students read chapters from classics in the field such as Alessandro Portelli's "What Makes Oral History Different" and, Thomas L. Charlton, Lois E. Myers, and Rebecca Sharpless's *History of Oral History*.[1] They work collectively with the instructor to determine potential interview questions, and they review both the ethical guidelines for Research on Human Subjects (via NYU's Institutional Review Board) and the process of working with release forms. Students are matched with neighborhood residents and workers who volunteer to be interviewed. Some interviews last the requisite one hour, while others go on much longer or are followed by additional interviews. In at least two cases, students have maintained friendships with their subjects. Even when the course has shifted away from oral history toward deep, place-based research, students have developed affinities for the neighborhoods they study in surprising ways. As one student from the Bronx who participated in the spring of 2018 iteration writes, "Through the research that I conducted within this course, I now have greater respect for my community, gaining a greater understanding of its historical significance within New York City." When combined with the existing scholarship on these neighborhoods and their histories, the oral histories and archives of personal items the students produce offer a glimpse into the lives of ordinary New Yorkers whose sense of place in the city is increasingly at risk. Students become both historians and coproducers of primary documents.

In each iteration of the course, the culminating project has been both a digital presentation and a public program through which the results of research are shared with the community. From 2015 to 2017, the public program was a free, museum-quality exhibit temporarily installed in the community under study. In 2018, the students produced historical narratives for the history-based app Clio, all of which will inform WHEDco's project to create historical markers and walking tours in Melrose and nearby Morrisania within the next year.

DIGITAL HUMANITIES PEDAGOGY

In 2016 and 2017, the library supported the course by providing online hosting space and technical support for digital exhibits. The support was offered by the Digital Scholarship Services (DSS) Department at NYU Libraries, which helps faculty and students incorporate digital humanities tools and methods into their research and teaching, including help with project management,

WHOSE SWEAT REAPS THE 'EQUITY' OF 'SWEAT EQUITY' ORGANIZATIONS? - A CONCLUSION.

Greywolf and Uku Littlehawk's reclamatory success is laudable for a myriad of reasons - the physical labour which they put into creating a home that would not disintegrate, being in "constant communication" with the city workers who managed the T.I.L program and in the leadership roles they took on in order to ensure a home for themselves and their fellow tenants. Greywolf described other tenants as relatively "lackadaisical" (or maybe afraid of what was to transpire) regarding their desire or ability to give their time to the responsibilites which followed the training through the Urban Homesteading Assisting Board (UHAB) that readies tenants to manage and maintain their buildings (5).

"A lot of the people... wanted the apartment, they were comfortable in the apartment and that's pretty much as far as it goes. But, you know, we look at it a little differently. We look at it as, if something happened, then we failed. And, we look at it as 'we can not fail', because if we fail where are we going to go? We have nowhere to go. And that was our message after the first meeting, we were telling the rest of the people in the building, we said... 'okay, we all think this building is going to get abandoned why don't we just pack up and go move into other buildings?' And, people looked at me like I'm stupid, they said 'what do you mean? With what?', and I said, **'that's right. With what? We don't have nothing. We can't go nowhere. So we have to, you know, protect this as much as we can'. And um, yea that's pretty much what we did"** (4).

Nvwoti Utana, "Big Medicine", an enrolled North East Band Cherokee landscaper, contractor and friend of Greywolf's helping repaint the building's interior.

The Urban Reservation's red and Golden entrance.

Uku Littlehawk, president of the Associated Cooperative Board, in a tenant association meeting.

Figure 27.2. Omeka exhibit on "Whose Sweat Reaps the 'Equity' of 'Sweat Equity' Organizations?" from the 2017 (Dis)Placed Urban Histories course.

data analysis and visualization, and digital storage and publishing. To streamline this suite of services, DSS began offering the Web Hosting service in 2016. Web Hosting uses Reclaim Hosting's Domain of One's Own service to provide flexible, shared-hosting web publishing environments, including one-click installation for popular content management systems such as WordPress and Omeka. The "(Dis)Placed Urban Histories" course used this service to build two Omeka sites, one for the South Williamsburg community and another for the Melrose neighborhood of the South Bronx.[2] Moreover, this type of collaboration represents an ideal partnership for the library, by providing easy-to-use technical infrastructure and light instructional training in support of NYU's digital humanities pedagogy.[3] (See fig. 27.2.)

To ensure that their work would be preserved, shared, and legible to a broad audience just as would be any public archive or museum exhibit, students also learned how to translate their academic work into publicly accessible written and visual products. The students were trained in digital humanities methods, specifically in how to use the Omeka digital exhibit platform to transform their coproduced primary documents into a narrative-based online exhibit and archive.[4] Coble visited the course to give an Omeka workshop in which students learned about Omeka as a tool for archiving, curation, and exhibit-building as well as practical skills, such as how to add items and create exhibits in Omeka. While the workshop seemed like a simple introduction to Omeka, this approach is useful when introducing a new tool and especially when working with students with diverse technical backgrounds.[5]

Prior to each workshop, Coble and Amato would meet to review the website's technical details to ensure they meshed with the course goals and also to establish training goals for the workshop. These brainstorming and planning meetings were helpful for creating a more personalized training session and identifying areas for improvement. For example, during the second year, we included a section on audio editing basics, based on feedback from the previous year's students who had requested more support for creating audio clips of their oral history interviews.

LESSONS LEARNED

Collaboration at all levels of the course development is key to its success. The course changed from year to year based on feedback from and the evolving needs of both community partners and students. As those changes were identified, it was essential to collaboratively brainstorm the ways in which the digital component of the course could be adapted for different outputs. Adaptations included not only introducing different technologies but also serving students at a mix of academic levels with a range of technical knowledge. This meant structuring the training to include everything from the very basics of engaging with the digital tool (e.g., logging on and navigation) to more advanced skills (e.g., effectively using Dublin Core fields in the archive and applying techniques of "good design" to the exhibits). Coble also made himself available to students for one-on-one consultation and technical assistance.

For the purposes of a classroom course, the objectives of training students in historical methods and digital technologies were met quite well. Again, the availability of relatively easy-to-use digital tools, excellent training and support from the library, a skilled classroom instructor, and open communication between all of the participants proved a recipe for a success.

Limitations occur, most dramatically, in meeting the objective of creating a resource that was accessible to community partners and residents. Many of the community members with whom the class worked were older and did not actively use digital technologies. Some participants did not have computers or email addresses, and, even when they did, neither was used regularly.

Delivering a web-based archive and exhibit, then, was interesting, but impractical. Indeed, most of the community members the class interviewed preferred to have their oral histories transcribed and delivered to them in hard copy. If any were interested in hearing their audio files or accessing the web-based project, they would ask Professor Amato and her students to share those pieces with their children or grandchildren instead. For community partners, the web-based projects were more useful but still limited. Since the sites were built and supported by NYU, partners did not have control over them and only had access via clunky, hard-to-remember URLs (e.g., starting with http://hosting .nyu.edu). Bronx-based WHEDco, in particular, made use of the collected oral histories for research and advocacy, and, in May 2019, NYU was able to transfer the site to WHEDco for management at a new, easier to recall URL (www.melrosestories.org).

The course offered all of its stakeholders—that is, the instructor, librarian, students, community partners, and community participants—important lessons about the pedagogical potentials of digital humanities technologies. Perhaps the most illuminating was this: it is important to think critically about how a digital platform will be used and by whom. Through careful planning and collaboration, a digital humanities pedagogy was developed to support course goals and enrich student learning *in the classroom*. Training in tools like Omeka offered students invaluable experience in creating, cataloging, and interpreting source material, which developed their ability to critically and productively analyze historiographical processes. Challenges emerged when trying to engage broader communities with an equally broad range of relationships with technology. While there can be many good reasons to introduce digital humanities tools and methods in a course, there might also be less obvious reasons why such an approach requires support outside the scope of the traditional university classroom, and it is important to carefully consider the larger goals and context of the course before and during the process.

NOTES

1. Alessandro Portelli, "What Makes Oral History Different," in *Oral History, Oral Culture, and Italian Americans*, Italian and Italian American Studies, ed. L. D. Giudice (Palgrave Macmillan: New York, 2009); Thomas L. Carlton, Lois E. Myers, and Rebecca Sharpless, eds. *History of Oral History: Foundations and Methodology* (Lanham, MD: AltaMira, 2007); Thomas L. Carlton, Lois E. Myers, and Rebecca Sharpless, eds. *Thinking about Oral History: Theories and Applications* (Lanham, MD: AltaMira, 2007).

2. "Displaced Histories 2016," NYU Gallatin, 2016, accessed February 13, 2020, http://displacedhistories.hosting.nyu.edu/courses/spring2016/; "(Dis) Placed Urban Histories: Melrose," NYU Gallatin, 2017, accessed February 13, 2020, http://www.melrosestories.org/.

3. Yasmeen Shorish, "Data Information Literacy and Undergraduates: A Critical Competency," *College and Undergraduate Libraries* 22, no. 1 (January 2015): 97–106, doi:10.1080/10691316.2015.1001246.

4. Brett D. Hirsch, ed., *Digital Humanities Pedagogy: Practices, Principles and Politics* (Cambridge, UK: Open Book, 2012), https://doi.org/10.11647/OBP.0024; Jake Carlson and Lisa Johnston, eds., *Data Information Literacy: Librarians, Data, and the Education of a New Generation of Researchers*, Purdue Information Literacy Handbooks (West Lafayette, IN: Purdue University Press, 2015).

5. Brandon T. Locke, "Digital Humanities Pedagogy as Essential Liberal Education: A Framework for Curriculum Development," *Digital Humanities Quarterly* 11, no. 3 (2017), http://www.digitalhumanities.org/dhq/vol/11/3/000303/000303.html.

TWENTY-EIGHT

—ᗰ—

Digital Exhibitions

Engaging in Public Scholarship with
Primary Source Materials

RHONDA J. MARKER

Rutgers University

THE SEABROOK FARMS COLLECTION OF photographs contributed by the
Seabrook Educational and Cultural Center in the New Jersey Digital Highway (NJDH) was one of the first collections included in the statewide online
cultural heritage site and remains the largest single collection with more than
three thousand resources. For the most part, it has not enjoyed the use that
would be commensurate with its size when compared with other NJDH collections. In the fall of 2015, a course at Rutgers University-New Brunswick on
"Public Histories of Detention and Mass Incarceration" proposed using the collection of photographs from Seabrook Farms along with other primary source
and archival materials in their study of the subject.

Among the outcomes for the course, students would address "the possibilities and challenges that come with producing and disseminating histories for
consumption outside of the classroom" (from the course syllabus). The teaching and learning of historical events often sparks in-depth study and investigation of events from multiple perspectives. This results in enlightenment and
a greater understanding of both past and current events. The production of
histories for external consumption, such as the exhibitions that the class prepared, added complexity to the work. Public statements about photographs,
documents, and other artifacts had to be supported by evidence from multiple

sources and buttressed by an understanding of multiple historical contexts. The students were expected to consult multiple information sources when they composed interpretative narratives for any single artifact. Intellectual property issues, beyond those of basic attribution, had to be evaluated for their effect in a global online environment, especially for the class's open access digital exhibition and website. The students were expected to understand and apply basic US copyright and the fair use factors. Learning about digital objects, metadata, and user search behavior was integral to the digital exhibition component of the course. Students were expected to select, digitally prepare, and describe photographs, videos, and documents using standards that would allow public users to find and view them.

Students in the class engaged with primary materials, both online and in print archives, to produce exhibit panels. Students brought their insights, informed by readings and discussion on the subject, to critical interpretations of photographs and documents from a variety of sources. They also grappled with the challenges of sharing documents, photographs, videos, and other works while balancing the interests of copyright, social advocacy, and technological capabilities. The class produced two main projects. Students curated an exhibition panel that is included in the Humanities Action Lab's traveling exhibition, "States of Incarceration."[1] The exhibition opened at the New School in New York City in April 2016 and will exhibit through August 2019 in the United States. Students also curated a complete online exhibition hosted by NJDH.[2] These projects provided a platform for developing exhibition and event planning skills, exploring issues around copyright, and—through applying metadata and historical interpretation to works that are not intrinsically self-described—discovering the depth of information that is present in original materials. (See fig. 28.1.)

The students engaged with the Seabrook Educational and Cultural Center Records in the NJDH statewide digital repository, the Records of the War Relocation Authority (National Archives, Washington, DC), the Records of the War Manpower Commission (National Archives, Philadelphia), the Office of War Information Photography Collection, Farm Security Administration (online at Yale University), videos in the Densho Digital Repository, and Consumers League of New Jersey Records (Special Collections and University Archives, Rutgers University). Their understanding was enriched through instructor-assigned readings, discussion, and writing about the subjects of the primary documents. Most of the students were upper-level undergraduates, along with a few graduate students. They applied both a broad knowledge and their own subject expertise, gained through the course readings and exercises, to interpret the original documents.

Figure 28.1. Main page of Invisible Restraints: Life and Labor at Seabrook Farms, with a simple image collage and introductory text.

In addition to applying rich interpretation to the materials, the students gained an understanding of how to use primary sources in their research and scholarship. Beginning immediately upon enrollment at Rutgers University, students are required to take and complete an academic integrity tutorial before the first month of classes. Library instruction at Rutgers University Libraries emphasizes information literacy and appropriate citation. This class, with its use of primary source materials in a public exhibition, allowed the students to delve more deeply into questions of copyright and public domain, reproduction of copyrighted materials, permissions, and citation requirements beyond those used in an academic research paper. Preparing the panel for the national traveling exhibition and putting together the digital exhibition challenged the students to consider the consequences of providing open access to research resources along with considerations of the protection of copyright for creators.

The students first examined the digital photograph collection of Seabrook Farms. Because the collection does not have a finding aid, the students spent time searching and browsing the thousands of photographs. In order to help the students narrow their focus, not to mention keep to the subject of the course, they were asked to choose one of the thirty-nine first person narratives from the "I Remember" project.[3] Individually and in small groups, the students wrote reflections on the narratives. They considered the people, places, and things that shaped a Seabrook Farms resident's memories and questions such as how perspectives affect formed memories, and what the students could learn from the resident's perspective.[4] In another classroom assignment, the students selected three images from among the Seabrook Farms photographs that depict one of the topics studied in the class. The students were reminded that the photographs and descriptions were created by the Seabrook Farms Company and asked to decipher and question what company officials intended to portray in the images. What emerged were essays around themes of community; company town; life, labor, and wartime legacies; and race, gender, and ethnicity.[5] These two interpretative exercises yielded such rich content that they were added to the online exhibition website. (See fig. 28.2.)

The creation of the digital exhibition provided the most opportunity for librarian involvement with the class. Four class sessions included specific library instruction. A librarian provided an overview of copyright, fair use, and license issues. The students would be handling mostly copyrighted materials, and they would be using them in a public display. Because this is a different use case from the conventional classroom research paper, the students needed to be able to understand and apply fair use factors, especially the first one (purpose and character of the use). When the students began to select the items for the online exhibition, they would also follow specific directions for obtaining permission and applying appropriate citations to the digital items. The librarian used the copyright education opportunity to examine the students' own author rights with respect to their individual and collective creations that were destined to be made openly available on the internet.

Figure 28.2. In her visual essay, a student references a published memoir and a 1946 newspaper article—and points out the bare shelves that belie the photograph's intent. Image from "Seabrook Farms," a digital collection of the New Jersey Digital Highway.

In another library session, the students learned about digital exhibition preparation. This section presented an overview of the steps that are common for both a physical exhibition and a digital exhibition and included examples of digital exhibitions. Some of the common processes are the selection, identification, organization, and description of items in the exhibition. Instruction emphasized the need to determine the rights for the items beyond those of obtaining permission to include them in the exhibition. Because a digital exhibition is the equivalent of publication, the standard exhibition loan agreement is not sufficient for inclusion. The students had to put to use the previous instruction on copyright.

Metadata instruction gave the students insight into the power of a data-driven information infrastructure. The digital exhibition framework draws both its content and its organization from the metadata in the records for the exhibition items. This includes the "case" descriptions, item descriptions, and even the order in which all of them are displayed. The metadata instruction was tailored to the specific outcomes of the course but also included explanations of the principles behind key requirements. Required metadata elements—and there are few that apply across the board to all digital collections—gave insight into the infrastructure for a repository that supports multiple collections of many types of resources. For example, the students learned that what might seem apparent within the context of a single type of object, such as a still image, needs to be made explicit in an environment that also included videos, sound recordings, and text documents. The students learned about some of the metadata value standards that are in widespread use such as the ISO 8601 date and time format.[6] The librarian provided information forms and a spreadsheet template to record metadata for selected items. Invariably, the research assistants who worked to compile the online exhibition itself had to return to individual items to retrieve additional information. (See fig. 28.3.)

A librarian spoke with the class about digitization standards and processes for reformatting the nondigital resources that would be included in the online exhibition. However, it became clear that the time required to scan or reformat these items was beyond the scope of the course. As a result, the in-class instruction was limited to an overview of the most common digital formats for still images, text documents, videos, and sound recordings. The class also learned about the components of a digital package including the metadata, the digital file, searchable text, and secondary files such as a thumbnail image. The librarian and course instructor determined that it would be necessary to provide additional training and oversight for this component of the project. In the months following the completion of the course, two of the students

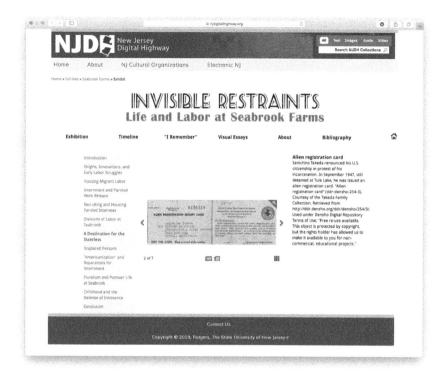

Figure 28.3. Metadata meets intellectual property rights: attribution and terms of use are displayed prominently in this exhibition panel. Image of an item from Invisible Restraints: Life and Labor at Seabrook Farms, a digital exhibition of the New Jersey Digital Highway.

continued as research assistants to complete the online exhibition and website and received specific instruction on digital formatting.

The course instructor identified additional collections that augmented the Seabrook Farms collection in NJDH. Students combed through finding aids, indexes, and online files to identify resources that brought a deeper understanding of the themes of mass incarceration through the lens of the Seabrook Farms experiences. The cumulative effect of delving into a variety of print and video archives allowed the students to find deeper interpretations than are possible when an individual document or a single collection of documents is viewed on its own. The process of selecting and organizing the exhibition sharpened the students' narrative voice.

At several points, concepts that seemed obvious to the expert (whether a copyright expert, a metadata librarian, or a digital file curator) needed to be reintroduced to the students. Copyright issues were difficult to understand. This project included special citations in the metadata for items from some sources. The exhibition pieces had to convey citation information along with notices that use of the items was in line with the policy of the organization that made the items available. Some organizations did not have public notices of their policy, or the policy was not clear, and the research assistants or instructor contacted the organization directly.

With regard to metadata, the initial compilation of information was invariably sparse. The students learned that they would have to supplement the metadata contained in the individual object with information obtained from other sources. A website, for example, might have information about a creator that was not repeated in individual item descriptions on that website.

For the most part, students began the class unaware of the variety of digital file formats. Although they are frequent digital content users, they generally are not sophisticated digital creators. The creation of the digital exhibition required them to understand the purposes and benefits of different formats (e.g., TIFF image files) and pay attention to digital file resolution. Some of the early scans had to be repeated in order to comply with the NJDH digital standards. (See fig. 28.4.)

One area that did not receive attention is that of accessibility of the website, the exhibition, and the digital objects in them. The exhibition and its panels as well as still images in the exhibition have alt text tags. The text documents have a readable text layer and most of the documents have quality, legible text. The photographs featured in the Visual Essays have text captions. The videos, however, do not have captioning or transcripts. Accessibility features were in place due to the library's standards at the time of the course. The students could have benefited from exposure to digital- and web-accessibility standards, and especially the resources of the Web Accessibility Initiative at W3C.[7] Consideration of public use of the exhibition by people with physical disabilities would have been relevant in a class that was studying people who were physically and politically constrained.

It was a privilege to observe students engage with the NJDH resources and other original material. Through this course, students participated in the fundamental activities of a public historian: original research, historical interpretation, and exhibition and event planning. In addition to their personal growth, the students brought the Seabrook Farms photographs to life. This collection of mostly black-and-white photographs of midcentury South Jersey is, well, fairly colorless. Through the topic of incarceration and detention—which we realize is woven into the fabric of life chronicled by these photographs—the

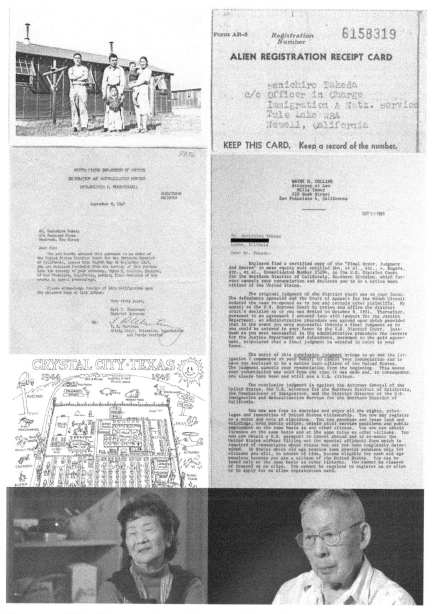

Figure 28.4. Digital formats in the exhibition included still images, text documents, and videos. Image of a panel from Invisible Restraints: Life and Labor at Seabrook Farms, a digital exhibition of the New Jersey Digital Highway.

students uncovered meaning and nuance that was lurking behind placid scenes of packing asparagus, lunch at the park, and filling out citizenship forms. This experience demonstrated the potential of library digital collections to involve students in their discovery, interpretation, and understanding.

ACKNOWLEDGMENTS

The author thanks Professor Andy Urban for his vision and generous invitation to the Rutgers University Libraries to participate in this course; Kayo Denda, Women's, Gender and Sexuality Studies Librarian; the many RUL professionals who lent their expertise; and the students who brought enthusiasm and diversity of insight to the project.

NOTES

1. "States of Incarceration," Humanities Action Lab, accessed May 29, 2018, https://www.humanitiesactionlab.org/statesofincarceration.

2. "Invisible Restraints: Life and Labor at Seabrook Farms," New Jersey Digital Highway, accessed May 29, 2018, https://njdigitalhighway.org/exhibits /seabrook_farms.

3. "I Remember Project: Table of Contents," RUcore: Rutgers University Community Repository, Seabrook Educational and Cultural Center, accessed May 29, 2018, https://doi.org/doi:10.7282/T3GX494S.

4. "I Remember," New Jersey Digital Highway, accessed May 29, 2018, https://njdigitalhighway.org/exhibits/seabrook_farms/i_remember.

5. "Visual Essays," New Jersey Digital Highway, accessed May 29, 2018, https://njdigitalhighway.org/exhibits/seabrook_farms/visual_essays.

6. "ISO 8601 Date and Time Format," International Organization for Standardization, Organisation Internationale de Normalisation, accessed May 29, 2018, https://www.iso.org/iso-8601-date-and-time-format.html.

7. "Making the Web Accessible," Web Accessibility Initiative (WAI): W3C, World Wide Web Consortium, accessed November 9, 2018, https://www.w3.org /WAI/.

TWENTY-NINE

—✳︎—

Oral History in the Digital Age

The Krueger-Scott Collection

SAMANTHA J. BOARDMAN

Boardman Consulting

www.samanthajboardman.com

JUST OVER A DECADE AGO, while researching for a documentary on Newark, New Jersey's historic Krueger-Scott mansion, I made a serendipitous discovery. Tucked away in a drawer in the Newark Public Library (NPL) lay a collection of over one hundred Great Migration oral history narratives, still in their original audiocassette format, unheard for over a decade. Only a few of the interviews had been transcribed but those that were hinted at the depth and breadth of the collection. Over the next ten years of working with the preservation and development of the collection—first as a graduate student and later as a freelance public historian—I gained a comprehensive view of the potential for digital humanities to make accessible previously underutilized resources, recover lost voices, and engage students and the larger community with historically rich, emotionally resonant content.

Assembled in the mid-1990s, the collection was an initiative of the Krueger-Scott Mansion Cultural Center.[1] The project brought in esteemed scholars of New Jersey's African American history to capture the experiences of Newarkers who had arrived in the city during the Great Migration as well as lifelong residents. Working from a ten-page questionnaire, trained citizen volunteers gathered narratives from their peers in relaxed, informal, data-rich conversations.

Topics ranged from family networks and travel conditions to neighborhood recollections, leisure activities, foodways, customs, and politics.

Rutgers University-Newark's American Studies Graduate Program partnered with the NPL to digitally preserve and index the collection for inclusion in a prototype cross comparative database of immigration and migration oral histories it was assembling. This partnership further cemented Rutgers's ties with another Newark anchor institution and affirmed the university's commitment to the local community. As an American Studies graduate student with a background in digital audio, I assisted with the digitization and indexing of the narratives, working with the team and digital humanities librarian, Krista White, to preserve the analog audiocassettes to archival specifications while collecting and entering metadata into the RUCore digital repository using the Library of Congress MARC schema. For a budding scholar of public humanities this was invaluable hands-on experience in both the protocols of digital preservation and potential multimedia applications of the collection.

The Newest Americans collaborative multimedia project on post-1965 migration, codirected by Rutgers professor Tim Raphael and documentary filmmaker Julie Winokur, found fertile subject matter in the collection's migration narratives, now available as MP3 files and accessible via the web portal hosted by Rutgers Libraries.[2] The digitization of the oral histories enabled multiple simultaneous uses with the collection employed concurrently in a variety of courses and projects, with each application teasing out new layers of meaning and discovering new ways to use and present these life stories and their insights.

Interviews in the collection frequently recounted the effects of midcentury urban renewal projects on Newark's African American community. I worked with photojournalist Ashley Gilbertson to pair historic images from the NPL archive with contemporary photographs, resulting in "Slide Through Time," a photo-essay of then-and-now portraits starkly illustrating the neighborhood destruction many narrators pinpointed as a precipitating cause of the 1967 riots.[3] In another project, fellow American Studies graduate student Katie Singer embedded archival photos and MP3 audio clips in a multimedia essay on oral history narrator Louise Epperson, a local activist who battled the development's incursion.[4] The digital formats of these materials enabled them to coalesce on the web for a rich multimedia 360-degree view of this moment in Newark's history. (See fig. 29.1.)

Singer's work digitally indexing and analyzing the narratives, much of which she incorporated into her dissertation, yielded another discovery when she found that one of the interviews belonged to Coyt Jones, the grandfather of current Newark mayor Ras Baraka and father of poet Amiri Baraka.

Figure 29.1. Krueger-Scott African-American Oral History in Newark.

Further exploration of Jones's narrative, detailing his journey from South Carolina to Newark in 1929, yielded an anecdote about a local department store that would not hire him due to the color of his skin. The poignancy of a family's trajectory from enduring flagrant racial discrimination to sitting in the mayor's office served as the inaugural subject for Newest Americans' media creation partner Talking Eyes Media's digital video short "We Came and Stayed: Coyt Jones/Ras Baraka."[5] The digital short screened at film festivals across the region, further introducing new constituencies to the fruits of the oral history collection.

Nick Kline, Rutgers professor and originator of the GlassBooks project, saw the potential of the migration narratives to resonate with the students in his undergraduate Book Arts class, many of whom were first- or second-generation immigrants. He worked with Artist-in-Residence Adrienne Wheeler, herself the daughter of a Great Migration arrival, to design a course that taught the city's history through selected narratives from the collection. I assisted in curating narratives from different eras in Newark's history from which students worked to create artist books made of glass addressing themes they found especially resonant. The resulting collection, *Provisions*, was exhibited to the public free of charge.[6] The creation of the exhibit and the students' responses to the oral histories was captured in the short digital documentary, "A Place of Entry."[7] The books they created brought the digital narratives into the physical world as works of art, with public exhibition providing an opportunity for the university to demonstrate its commitment to local community history.

Due to the accessible and reproducible nature of the "Slide Through Time" photo-essay and the two short digital documentaries, these projects gained traction with undergraduate and secondary school instructors who used them in curricula. Journalism professors used the example of "Slide Through Time" to teach students to analyze changes in the built environment with comparative photography. An Introduction to Multimedia course took the then/now concept and expanded its application to neighborhoods throughout the city, with students creating short multimedia pieces based on original historical and contemporary research.

The Krueger-Scott collection served as the centerpiece for the NPL's 2016 Black History Celebration in an exhibit I guest-curated titled *We Found Our Way': Newark Portraits from the Great Migration.*[8] The exhibition, its title inspired by a line from the narrative of Isaac Thomas Jr., featured the *Provisions* collection, Newest Americans short digital documentaries, MP3 players loaded with clips from the oral histories themselves, and visual materials including photographic portraits of the narrators, historical photographs, and selections from the library's extensive fine prints collection.[9] Displaying these digital and physical artifacts together created an opportunity for public education just as they had contributed to student learning on campus. The digitization of these materials and the digital products created from them made this trove of Newark's history accessible to the exhibit's visitors and the exhibit served as a showcase for Rutgers and the Newark Public Library to demonstrate their commitment to preserving and telling the stories of the local community.

Using digitized archival visual materials from *We Found Our Way*, I curated two subsequent exhibits for the library, organized and printed onto Sintra board to enable them to travel and/or be displayed in different environments. The first, a two-dimensional reproduction of sections from the original exhibit, included the MP3 player displays and was installed in the NPL's James Brown African American Reading Room. The second exhibit focused on Zaundria Mapson, a narrator who had migrated to Newark with her family as a baby and spent her childhood in the city with frequent trips to see relatives in the South. This exhibit, featuring photos of the narrator as a child growing up in Newark, toured Essex County elementary schools as an age-appropriate, firsthand educational resource for exploring themes of the Great Migration and segregation.

In 2018, I became the principal investigator for a grant project funded by the New Jersey Historical Commission that enabled full transcription of the Krueger-Scott collection and the creation of a prototype digital map to track addresses referenced by the narrators in their interviews. Plotting migration journeys of narrators to and through Newark in this way would create opportunities to compare and contrast these experiences with other historical and contemporary migrations and illustrate the effects of displacement in the city. Our project demonstrated the potential of this data presented in an interactive, web-based form, and provided copies of the digital transcripts both to the NPL and Rutgers University Libraries.

The Krueger-Scott Oral History Collection presents an opportunity to apply digital humanities technologies and techniques to an otherwise underutilized local history resource. The digital preservation and indexing of the collection offer valuable experience to graduate students to learn skills valuable to emerging public scholars. This preservation likewise leverages the assets of Rutgers University to create an accessible digital archive of local history and reinforce partnership with anchor institutions to freely disseminate these stories.

The development of the narratives into photo-essays, short digital documentaries, and web-based maps provides collaborative opportunities for graduate students and postdoctoral fellows to work with media professionals to research and produce multimedia materials. These become curricular resources for undergraduate and graduate courses, with their reach extending beyond campus for public and elementary education. Public exhibits combining digital materials and physical artifacts offer another way to encounter these histories and couple the emotional resonance of oral histories with the embodied experience. Combining digital audio, web content, photojournalism, video production, and fine art, projects like these realize the potential of oral history collections to educate and enlighten in the classroom and in the community.

NOTES

1. Rutgers University Libraries, "About the Collection," on the Rutgers University Libraries' The Krueger-Scott Oral History Collection, https://kruegerscott.libraries.rutgers.edu/about-the-collection, accessed June 8, 2019.

2. Rutgers University Libraries, The Krueger-Scott Oral History Collection, https://kruegerscott.libraries.rutgers.edu/, accessed June 8, 2019.

3. Tim Raphael, Ashley Gilbertson, and Samantha J. Boardman, "Slide through Time," Newest Americans website, http://newestamericans.com/issues /issue-02-newark-then-now/, accessed June 8, 2019.

4. Katie Singer, "Over My Dead Body!" Newest Americans website, http:// newestamericans.com/over-my-dead-body/, accessed June 8, 2019.

5. Ashley Gilbertson, Ed Kashi, and Julie Winokur, "We Came and Stayed: Coyt Jones/Ras Baraka," Newest Americans website, http://newestamericans .com/wecameandstayed-baraka/, accessed June 8, 2019.

6. Samantha J. Boardman, Nyier Abdou, Rachel Dennis, and Nick Kline, "Glassbook Project: Provisions," Newest Americans website, http:// newestamericans.com/the-glass-book-project/, accessed June 8, 2019.

7. Nyier Abdou, Cinematographer, "A Place of Entry" (TRT: 5:53), Talking Eyes Media/Newest Americans, 2015, https://vimeo.com/127531269, accessed June 8, 2019.

8. Armand V. Cucciniello III, "Other Voices: NJ Art and Oral History at the Newark Public Library," Hip New Jersey, February 22, 2016, https:// hipnewjersey.com/tag/newark-public-library/, accessed June 8, 2019.

9. Katie Singer, "Voices of Newark's Past at 'We Found Our Way': Newark Portraits from the Great Migration," Brick City Live, February 5, 2016, https:// brickcitylive.com/art/katiesinger/voices-of-newarks-past-at-we-found-our-way -newark-portraits-from-the-great-migration/, accessed June 8, 2019.

THIRTY

—⟋⟍—

The Infusion of Digital Humanities in an Introductory Political Science Course at an HBCU

Lessons Learned

CARMEN WALKER
Bowie State University

THE CLASSROOM IS NEVER AN empty space. Among the many things it may hold are all the experiences that open possibilities for empowerment and connection. However, the classroom may also hold experiences that simply underscore existing patterns of inequality and passive consumption. Most important, it is clear that potentiality exists within the classroom. Borrowing energy from the nineteenth-century black female activist Anna Julia Cooper, it must always be understood that, "when and where we enter," the necessary tags for our belonging must come with us—the identities, histories, and voices that help us find and locate ourselves in this world and certainly the educational experience.[1] Until recently, I had not taken time to reflect on the baggage that I also brought into the room; baggage like pedagogical practices and assumptions that were taking up space and creating obstacles for my students' belonging and pursuit of an authentic learning experience.

The most memorable lessons usually begin with, "It all started with . . ." and yet, early in the fall semester it really did simply start with an idea to infuse digital humanities into my class. Having incorporated traditional humanities forms like art, biographies, films, music, and even poetry into other political science courses, I understood the value these items added to the statistics and data that shaped the objective world of politics and power. The addition of digitized resources would be a continuation of the ongoing quest to center the human experience and help students create meaning in our study of centuries'-old struggles for power. I would use digital resources to facilitate a lesson on the significance of the US Constitution in recognition of Constitution Day.

I AM AN AMERICAN DAY

From college campus lectures and virtual celebrations to elementary school speeches, today's recognition of the September 17, 1787, signing of the US Constitution has evolved from an annual presidential proclamation first announced in 1940. These early efforts encouraged the recognition of newly naturalized citizens and annually reinvigorated reminders about the responsibilities and privileges of American citizenship. Later, a 1952 House Resolution would establish the national observance of "Citizenship Day," and in 1956 congressional legislation would create "Constitution Week." By 1998, this public law had been amended and renamed "Constitution and Citizenship Day." In 2004, the law was further amended making the annual recognition of Constitution and Citizenship Day a requirement for any educational institution receiving federal funding.[2]

Considering the youthful age of this country, I have always been fascinated by the idea that ours is the longest-surviving single-written constitution in the world. My hope was to transfer this excitement and fascination to my students. Thus, the Constitution Day class assignment centered on two activities. The first activity involved a class discussion on the significance of the US Constitution. The second activity would be a public class reading of the entire US Constitution. The first aspect of this assignment would require several things: first, situating the historical, social, political, and economic context in which the Constitution would be written and debated; second, understanding key actors; and last, analyzing important eighteenth-century arguments both supporting and opposing this document. Certainly, this would be an excellent opportunity for students to reflect on the ways in which the US Constitution has evolved to embrace the growing and changing needs of this project we call American democracy.

There exists a working discussion on the definition of digital humanities. Over time, the ideas expressed in these conversations have shaped and reshaped my perspective. I initially limited my definition of digital humanities to that of a product; a computerized or digitally produced or reproduced cultural work, historical narrative, or artistic creation.

The National Archives, Smithsonian Institution, and Library of Congress are just a few examples of institutions now offering digitized collections of primary sources once only available to those fortunate enough to visit

Figure 30.1. Nineteenth-century suffragist Mrs. Suffern with her sign "Help us to win the vote."

their locations. We traveled through time examining photographs like that of nineteenth-century suffragist Mrs. Suffern with her sign, "Help us to win the vote," with the aid of classroom technology and students' laptops, smartphones, and iPads.[3] Digitized eighteenth-century diaries, newspapers, letters, and images could also help students visualize the significance of the constitution debates between the federalist and the antifederalist. (See fig. 30.1.)

WHAT DOES THE US CONSTITUTION MEAN TO YOU?

"What does the US Constitution mean to you?" Mine being a morning class, I was used to sometimes getting off to a slow start. This, however, would not be one of those mornings. For example, students were quick to acknowledge the importance of civil liberties, civil rights, and the concept of limited government. The responses were so fluid, they almost seemed rehearsed, I remember thinking. That they remembered high school social studies lessons meant they would surely appreciate a lesson that would build on their existing knowledge. However, my next lesson asking students to discuss the meaning of the US Constitution in their lives was met with comments such as "it has been something used to oppress," "it protects the rights of men, but not women," and "it seems to be an intangible dream for some." The comments slowly outlined a different path for this class discussion. These comments would also be expressed in several of the written reflections submitted. One student would share the following, "With many black lives being taken for granted, I believe at this point the Constitution is no longer considered to be as important to me, because it would appear that only a select few benefit from the many benefits that are associated with the Constitution."

My preparation for this activity had not made room for the critiques and stories offered by students who had made it very clear that they had to negotiate their dreams and understanding of the US Constitution in the face of sometimes open hostility to their race, age, economic status, religion, and sexuality. Their critiques were not so different from the nineteenth-century suffragists I asked them to connect with. However, their voices could not be found in my Constitution Day lesson. While I had asked students to walk in the footsteps of eighteenth-century farmers from Shays' Rebellion and many former patriots, who would expose the economic class interests of a nation under the Articles of Confederation, I failed to acknowledge the daily tightrope they walk.

Still, while the images were not beautiful, I was prepared to utilize my digital humanities resources to discuss the contradictions of a document created to protect freedom along with the importation of slaves until 1808 and the institution of slavery until 1865. For example, eighteenth- and nineteenth-century newspapers like *The Rights of Man*, provide opportunities for students to read how the constitutional protection of slavery created a precarious status for all African Americans.[4] These digitized sources provide an opportunity to discuss how technology has shaped the way we communicate political discontent in a society.

Through access to online audio recordings of Supreme Court oral arguments, students could imagine themselves in the court room as Supreme Court Justices listened to lawyers argue whether or not the Article I congressional powers could be used to uphold the Civil Rights Act. (See fig. 30.2.)

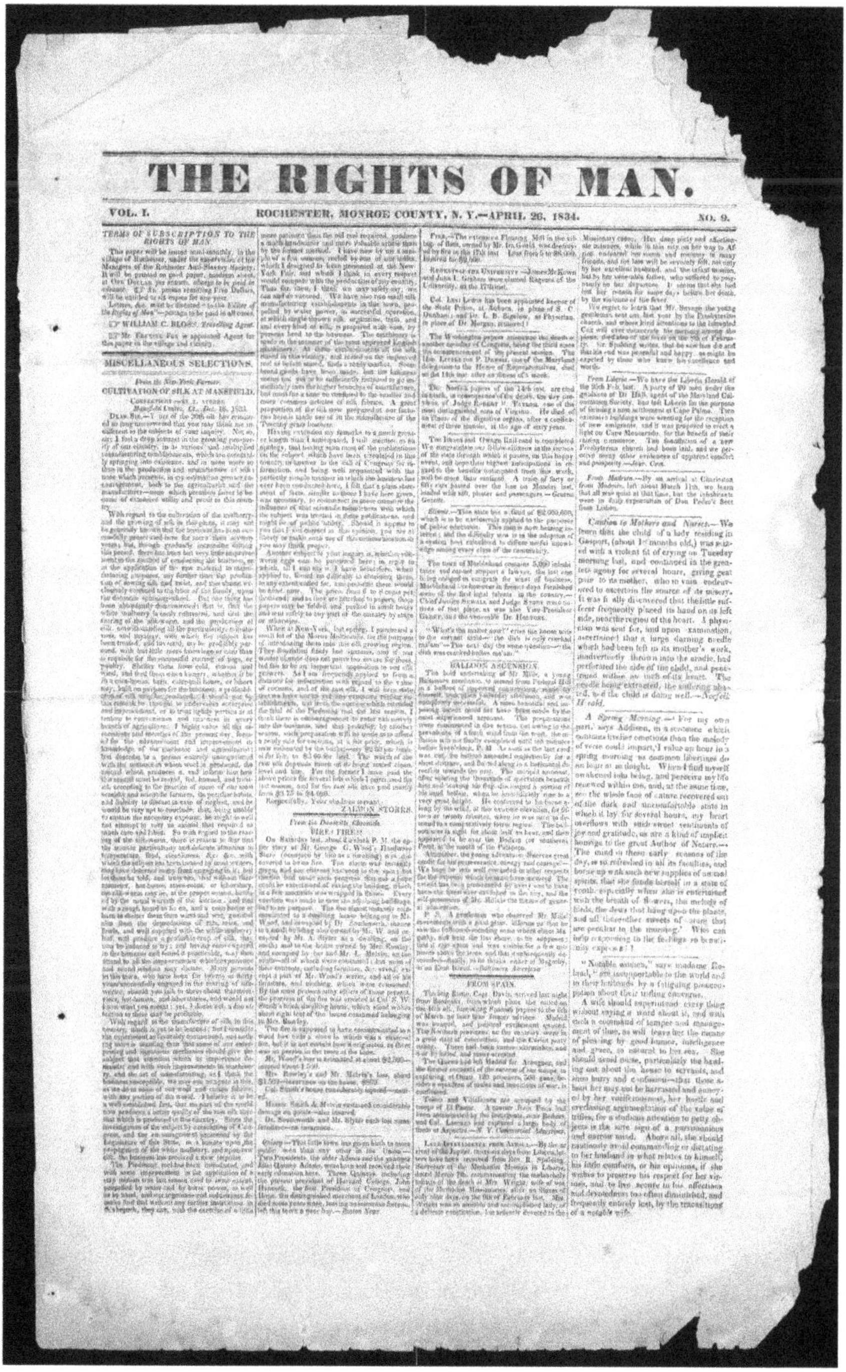

THE RIGHTS OF MAN.

VOL. I. ROCHESTER, MONROE COUNTY, N. Y.—APRIL 26, 1834. NO. 9.

TERMS OF SUBSCRIPTION TO THE RIGHTS OF MAN.

MISCELLANEOUS SELECTIONS.

CULTIVATION OF SILK AT MANSFIELD.

FIRE! FIRE!!

BALLOON ASCENSION.

FROM SPAIN.

Figure 30.2. Screenshot of *The Rights of Man*, page 1, April 26, 1834.

Figure 30.3. March in the fight against racism.

While I came prepared, the students also came prepared to tell their stories and I needed to listen. They explained the relationship of the Thirteenth
Amendment to twenty-first-century mass incarceration. The students asked
me to consider being in the shoes of Sandra Bland or those of Tamir Rice's
mother. (See fig. 30.3.[5]) They understood that Article I allowed states to deny
individuals with felonies the right to vote. Some asked me why the holder of
Article II executive authority was empowered based on an electoral college that
dismissed the will of the majority in the 2016 presidential election. Finally, a
student athlete in the class had no problem informing me that the Constitution
did not seem to protect the free speech of the NFL football players kneeling
to protest inequality in the country. It was the first week of the NFL season
and I had forgotten about the ongoing national anthem protests. With all of
this, I left the class feeling that I failed at my initial digital humanities activity.
However, I had only failed at proselytizing. This was one of the longest classes
I'd had in a long time.

RESPONDING TO THE "CLAP BACK"

There was a lot to unpack from that class. I needed to step outside my feelings
to reflect on my goals for the assignment. The first question I asked myself was
why it seemed as if the students rejected this activity? Was this rejection, or was
this something else? In his 1990 work, *Scholarship Reconsidered: Priorities of the*

Professoriate, Ernest Boyer reminds us that scholarly questions surrounding the teaching and learning experience should always be present for faculty who are intellectually committed to continued growth in the pursuit of moving beyond simply passing on lessons to "transforming and extending" knowledge.[6] Like my experience, these moments within the classroom when things do not go as planned may provide research questions that, left uninterrogated, hinder our growth as faculty and our commitment to the growth of those we are dedicated to educating.

The Constitution Day discussion was supposed to be an opportunity to incorporate digital humanities in the classroom, and it built on my definition of digital humanities. In retrospect, I am more convinced that what looked like rejection was more of a dialectical process of students thinking critically about the way in which we tell the story of this country and the US Constitution. Whose voices and experiences are captured and used in this digital humanities movement? There are many questions that must be answered. The students used their voices as tools to resist the marginalization of their experience in the classroom. For the students, the US Constitution needed twenty-first-century interpretations and critical reflection; something not provided by my activity.

While I had not yet figured out what to do with my digital humanities resources, reflection gave me the opportunity to reconsider my commitment to making the classroom a space for the practice of freedom and visibility. Consequently, I decided that I would not dismiss that day as a fluke. Rather, I would intentionally build on their truths shared in class. I decided that I would ask students to create original artwork or take original photographs representing their critiques and their hopes for what the Constitution could mean. To accompany the images, students were also asked to contribute a personal story. The students welcomed the opportunity to share their creations with the class and others. This led to the creation of a collective visual representation and personal narrative of the US Constitution.

While I had only seen one dimension of my students on the first day of our discussion, this final project revealed the beautiful multidimensional realities that informed their understanding of the US Constitution. The images reflected the children of young mothers and new fathers committed to improving the Constitution's protections for the sake of their children. From generational photographs to drawings, they constructed their own images of what the Constitution meant to them. Students used this assignment to center their identity in the discussion on the US Constitution. A student of Palestinian descent contributed a beautiful photo of his mosque. A selection from his narrative accompanied his photo. His message expressed the sense of security

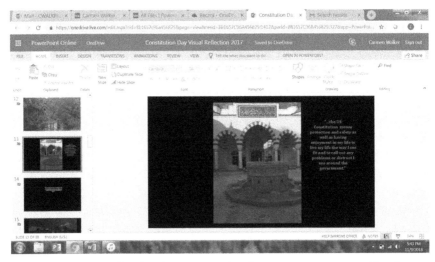

Figure 30.4. Picture of student's mosque with reflection on constitutional freedoms. Courtesy of Mohamad D. Ashkar.

the US Constitution gives him. This was digital humanities. It was more than hyperlinked resources and historical images. It was an act of collective work and recognition that everyone can shape the narrative of the human experience within any political, economic, historical, or social context. (See fig. 30.4.)

MY FRAMEWORK FOR UNDERSTANDING DIGITAL HUMANITIES IN THE CLASSROOM

On the surface, it seems as if digital humanities is simply about the inevitable nexus between technology and historical, literary, artistic, and other cultural products. But there must be more. As I learned, digital humanities encompasses more than finding and accessing digitized interpretations of the human experience. Matthew G. Kirschenbaum provides a brief historical and conceptual overview of digital humanities. What is clear from both his 2010 article, titled "What Is Digital Humanities and What's It Doing in English Departments," and his 2014 work, "What Is Digital Humanities, and Why Are They Saying Such Terrible Things About It," is that digital humanities is a house with many rooms.[7] It contains rooms that provide space for computational histories, differences in its definition, methodological outlooks, and interdisciplinary networks of people trying to make sense of the meaning in practice of digital humanities. Because of its social nature, collaborative outlook, project orientation, and reflective nature, digital humanities will always be an unsettled house.

This house will always shift because digital humanities is something to be worked with and a framework to be worked through; it represents the constantly changing products, ideas, and practices of the human experience. There is always room for renovations and improvements. The lesson for me is that working with digital humanities is a pedagogical practice committed to preserving, constantly exploring, and critically interrogating social life in its various cultural forms. As such, digital humanities class projects should be loud. They should make us uncomfortable. They should be capable of shifting silence and rote responses, while connecting and validating the fact that we all belong and have contributions and experiences worth remembering. These projects and activities should facilitate the creation of community sources of knowledge that open discussions about power, justice, and the good life. Digital humanities must allow students the opportunity to question what we ask them to consume. It must encourage both students and faculty to challenge, evaluate, and share their interpretations of the human experience.

NOTES

1. Anna Julia Cooper, *A Voice from the South* (New York: Oxford University Press, 1988).

2. For more information on Constitution Day, please see historical resources provided by the Library of Congress at https://www.loc.gov/law/help /commemorative-observations/constitution-day.php (accessed August 19, 2019).

3. See the George Grantham Bain digital photographic file collection, which is available online at the Library of Congress at https://www.loc.gov /item/2005684084/ (accessed August 19, 2019).

4. See the Rochester, New York, Public Library digitized collection *Many Roads to Freedom* at http://www.libraryweb.org/rochimag/roads/home.htm (accessed August 19, 2019).

5. Image used with permission of student.

6. Ernest L. Boyer, *Scholarship Reconsidered: Priorities of the Professoriate* (San Francisco: Jossey-Bass, 1990), 24.

7. Matthew G. Kirschenbaum provides two great discussions on digital humanities: "What Is Digital Humanities, and Why Are They Saying Such Terrible Things about It?" *Differences* (2014): 46–63, and "What Is Digital Humanities and What's It Doing in English Departments?" *ADE Bulletin* (2010): 1–7.

No More "Dusty Archive" Kitten Deaths

Discoverability, Incidental Learning, and Digital Humanities

JUILEE DECKER

Rochester Institute of Technology

THE TUMBLR SITE "DUSTY ARCHIVE Kitten Deaths" seeks to change perceptions through its threat that every time the term "dusty" or "musty" is used in reference to an archive, the ghost of foundational archives theorist Theodore Schellenberg (1903–1970) kills a kitten (see fig. 31.1). While an empty threat, the URL and its referent posts initiate laughter and remind us of the unwary language used in the discussion of archives—the very repositories without which much of our own work as scholars could not be completed. This chapter advocates for fewer kitten deaths by demonstrating how archives have potentiality as sites of digital scholarship and collaboration among undergraduate students in the explication of a project that is keyed to physical collections and their repositories as spaces for discoverability and incidental learning.[1]

Initiated by the archives staff at my institution in the fall of 2014 and expanded in 2015 to include students as collaborators and cocurators, *The Stories They Tell* engages students to assess, research, author, revise, and synthesize material for public-facing on-site and online deliverables. Moreover, the project is informed by the premise of museums—and, by extension, collections and repositories including library and archives—as sites of informal learning. Given this condition, then, such a project based in situ at an archive bears witness to

Figure 31.1. Screenshot of Dusty Archive Kitten Deaths blog. Dusty Archive Kitten Deaths, https://dustyarchivekittendeaths.tumblr.com.

a digital humanities practice that opens the students to broader audiences than such curricula and other undergraduate practices might traditionally yield.[2]

PART I: GROUNDED IN THEORY

My work as a collaborative scholar and researcher in digital humanities and museum studies informs project-based courses that I teach, which aim to demonstrate, through their own enactment, an understanding of what museums are and do. The focus on museums as a framework for examining digital humanities pedagogy is intentional here due to the context of the project deliverables, online and on-site exhibitions that highlight lesser-known archival collections. Further, the primary research and exhibit work enables students to shine a light on lesser-known collections for an on-site and online public, to make documents, photographs, objects, and realia more "discoverable" and to engage in incidental learning.[3]

This tethering to "museums" is intentional because museums are seen as sites of informal learning thanks to the work of scholars, enthusiasts, and practitioners—including John Cotton Dana (1856–1929), John Dewey (1859–1952), and George E. Hein (1932–)—each of whom arrived at this notion of the museum as a space for experience and engagement, even as their paths varied. Moving from the museum to the archive, theorist Theodore Schellenberg, though he did not use the term "experiential" per se, would seem to share these frameworks for use, as he emphasized the research use of archives—their capacity to serve as usable material for others. Thus, as museums and archives are repositories that offer convening spaces suitable for discoverability and incidental learning, they inform the construction of knowledge and exploration of identity akin to the modes of identity formation proffered in exhibition spaces.[4]

PART II: PRAXIS—RIT ARCHIVE COLLECTIONS

Rooted in the theoretical approaches outlined above, I teamed with our university archives staff to develop an annual project that involves the creation of an on-site exhibition with a mirror site online. Annually, the exhibit makes its debut in conjunction with the university's homecoming. Its beginning, however, takes its cues from the call of the Society of American Archivists' President Kathleen Roe's 2014 challenge to archivists to "live dangerously" by sharing examples from their collections that give voice to individuals who have a unique, surprising, or compelling story to tell. Answering this call, students work alongside archives staff and me to curate an exhibition that shifts attention and changes perceptions by presenting the archives as viable, active spaces for dangerous living, for scholars and seekers—as rescuers of kittens—through the exhibition titled *The Stories They Tell*. Over five weeks, we examine Rochester Institute of Technology (RIT) Archive collections, select items, image them, write exhibit labels, install works, and prepare the companion online exhibition. Through this project, students engage in the classroom as well as the library and archive, in both the actual and the virtual worlds, transitioning these spaces into platforms for assessing, researching, authoring, revising, and synthesizing material for the public. The classroom and archive (housed in our university library) serve as a crucible of activity where we, as students, faculty, and staff, contribute collectively and individually to a larger project—the activation of the archive where discoverability and incidental learning serve as chief outcomes of our practice.[5]

Working both on-site in the archives and in a computer lab, students are tasked with thinking about their collections in analog and digital terms and curating for both environments. On-site, what would capture attention? What would tell the story accurately online, without the aid of archives staff or the broader spatial layout of the exhibit? The project is clearly steeped in experiential learning practices proffered by museums writ large and, in particular, meets educational objectives of our digital humanities and social sciences program. In addition, *The Stories They Tell* fosters discoverability and incidental learning as outlined below.[6] (See figs. 31.2 and 31.3.)

Figure 31.2. Author Juilee Decker (at right) and student Brienna Johnson-Morris discuss findings on Hettie Shumway, who moved to Rochester in 1934 and fueled her passion for deaf education. Photo credit: Sara May.

Figure 31.3. Student Landyn Hatch drawing a mock-up of her exhibit on library benefactors Charles F. Wallace and Florence Murray Wallace.
Photo credit: Sara May.

DISCOVERABILITY

Discoverability refers to the ease with which something, such as an item or a file, can be found. Within the context of this project, the exploration of archives and examination of collections and related primary and secondary material (as well as the creation of new primary material) leads to the "presentation" of such materials for a public-facing audience. Such work engages multimodal literacies and interdisciplinary practices that blend "learning, doing, imagining, researching, creating, and partnering" in the production of on-site and online content for the library's broad visitorship. Discoverability thus occurs in three stages: first, as a result of being selected for exhibit, items chosen for exhibition become more visible by virtue of being on view in the university library and, therefore, accessible to thousands of patrons per day; second, through the preparation of the online exhibit on the RIT Archive Collections' website (including the précis, label copy for each item on view, and the application of metadata), the online discoverability of these materials is increased; third, the content prepared by the class becomes part of the archive collection's record of the materials, thus drawing connections between the immediate materials and broader contexts.[7]

INCIDENTAL LEARNING

Incidental learning is a by-product of some other activity. For this project, incidental learning takes two forms: collaboration skills as well as content-based learning. In terms of collaboration, students gain skill sets in teamwork and communication as the experiential practice of such a project encodes such skills as essential to the workflow. For example, peers vet one another's label text in order to see if the content "makes sense" to a reader other than the author. Students also share knowledge peer to peer as they work online and on-site (in Drupal, the primary content management system that we used from 2015–2017, and Omeka, which we have used since 2018) as well as construct physical exhibits. Thus, the entire class learns by doing (the experiential nature of this project), and, in turn, we collaborate in order to support the exhibition workflow.[8]

In the case of content knowledge, *The Stories They Tell* requires that students construct knowledge about their subject (the focus of the collection that each student is tasked with researching and exhibiting). For instance, if the subject was a student at the university in the 1900s, knowledge about the curriculum at that time would be useful as history but also as a method for weaving together the threads of a story to be crafted. Or, in the case of a themed, rather than biographical exhibit focus, incidental learning is required in order to construct a narrative that is gleaned from several sources—archival, primary, and secondary. Evidence of such awareness comes from the fall of 2017 instance of the project: students were asked to comment on what they have learned on their own, as part of the exhibition process. It simply would not be enough to toss a few items into an exhibit case or post a few images, attach metadata, and provide description online. As one of the students recounted:

> Given that my collection, the Bertha E. Butts collection, only contains her sewn dress, scrapbook, and obituary, I really had to expand my horizons in order to tell an engaging, interesting, and informative story. I turned my attention to the Rochester Athenaeum and Mechanics Institute (RAMI) Domestic Science Department records. Within this collection, I found a wide array of intriguing materials and information about the program. While looking through these records, it was as if I was learning about the domestic science program through the lens of the first female students enrolled at RAMI.... As I dug deeper into the records, I wanted to know why women were enrolling.... From my modern standpoint, I couldn't help but smirk at the idea behind advocating for a woman's independence in making her own clothes and cooking her own meals while still confined to the role of homemaker. However, this was probably a monumental step for women in the early 20th century and allowed them to be students and to become experts at their craft. Materials like this made me excited to learn more about the first female students at RAMI, like Bertha E. Butts, and to convey their story in the Domestic Science Department through my exhibition while allowing viewers to trace the evolution of female students in college, generally, and at RIT.[9]

The student tasked with researching the school colors of our institution over the years stated it this way:

> The archives had no information on the sweater other than the name of the woman who donated it, so I emailed her and she sent me a lot about the sweater's history, including who made it (a graduate student named Stevie), and a story about how I actually have a duplicate because the original was stolen the first night it was on the [tiger] statue.... Personally, I feel that the incidental learning involved with this project has been one of the best parts of it. I've learned a lot about RIT since starting research on my items, and a lot of that information has been things that relate, but aren't directly needed for my collection and exhibit. And if nothing else, I've now gained a nice trivia fact about the Pantone numbers for the official RIT colors from working on this.[10]

Students are fully aware that such an engagement in a prismatic approach is necessary in order to prepare an exhibit for an on-site and online public. In light of both facets—discoverability and incidental learning—this project's public dissemination through the website and the on-site exhibition served to activate the archive in new ways. Libraries, archives, and other collecting institutions, in both the actual and the virtual worlds, have the capacity to serve as the locus of community and knowledge making in the space of digital humanities courses.

CONCLUSION

Beyond the individual experience of each student, it is important to note how the project-based learning experiences described above are never static. The courses themselves, in addition to the projects embedded within, serve as iterative spaces that mirror the approaches adopted by museum and archive theorists a century ago who claimed for these entities the prospect of informal learning (Dana, Dewey, Hein, and Schellenberg). In addition, the experiences in the classroom, library, archive, and museum inform the construction of knowledge and exploration of identity akin to the modes of identity formation proffered in exhibition spaces as articulated by Hooper-Greenhill, Peers and Brown, Simon, and many others.

In terms of digital humanities learning outcomes *The Stories They Tell* engages students in the tangibles of primary documents and realia that, in turn, foster object-based learning and the integration of data where multiple sources yield new expression, creation, and engagement. This body of work also explores notions of production, reception, circulation, and preservation of digital scholarship. Moreover, practices based in archives and grounded in museum theory foster the kind of connections between informal learning and formalized education observed and fostered by Kelly Miller and Michelle Morton, who note that "twenty-first-century models for collaborative learning and teaching are emerging, especially in the digital humanities, where students study primary sources in digital formats and apply new technologies to pose and answer research questions."[11]

Thus, in conceiving of the university archive as an incubator for discoverability and incidental learning at the helm of digital humanities practice, I explicitly reject the notion of the dusty archive in favor of a model where the archive is a crucible of activity where we—as students, faculty, and staff—work with primary materials held in university archives. And so we save kittens everywhere from the ghost of Schellenberg.

ACKNOWLEDGMENTS

An earlier version of this paper was originally presented in March 2016 at the Digitorium Digital Humanities Conference at the University of Alabama, Tuscaloosa. Sincere thanks to Dr. Emma Wilson for giving me the opportunity to present my work at the conference and, further, to share my work through this publication. Thank you also to the RIT associate archivist, Jody Sidlauskas, who is an amazing collaborator and facilitator. Finally, thanks are due to students who have enrolled in Cultural Informatics since the fall of 2015. I have so enjoyed collaborating with each of you. Finally, regarding the title of this paper, I want to acknowledge that, as with so much of my work, it was an archivist (Jennifer Whitlock, of the Vignelli Center for Design Studies, http:// vignellicenter.rit.edu/) who turned me on to the Dusty Archive Kitten Deaths Tumblr page, which was initiated in 2014. Thank you, Jen. And thank you to all of us as we work in analog and digital means to prevent dusty archive kitten deaths.

NOTES

1. Dusty Archive Kitten Deaths, http://dustyarchivekittendeaths.tumblr .com/, accessed November 16, 2017.

2. For discussion of museums as sites of learning, see John Dewey, *The Essential Dewey*, ed. Larry Hickman and Thomas M. Alexander. Bloomington, IN: Indiana University Press, 1998; John Cotton Dana, "The Gloom of the Museum," part of *The New Museum Series* distributed by the Newark Museum, Newark, NJ, 1917; and George E. Hein, *Learning in the Museum*, London: Routledge, 1998.

3. Digital Humanities and Social Sciences Program Description, December 11, 2014.

4. See Theodore Schellenberg, *Modern Archives: Principles and Techniques* (Chicago: SAA, 1956, repr. 1975), 13–15; Theodore Schellenberg, *The Appraisal of Modern Public Records* (Bulletin No. 8 of the National Archives: 1956), 46; Jane F. Smith, "T. R. Schellenberg: Americanizer and Popularizer," *American Archivist* 44, no. 4 (Fall 1981): 316; Eilean Hooper-Greenhill, *Museums and the Interpretation of Visual Culture* (New York: Routledge, 2000); Laura Peers and Alison K. Brown, *Museums and Communities: A Routledge Reader* (New York: Routledge, 2003); Nina Simon, *The Participatory Museum* (Santa Cruz, CA: Museum 2.0, 2010), http://www.participatorymuseum.org/; and Juilee Decker, "Beyond Cul-de-Sac Pedagogy: Museum Studies as a Landscape of Practice," *Transformations: The Journal of Inclusive Scholarship and Pedagogy* 26, no. 2 (2017): 176–193.

5. Kathleen Roe, "A Year of Living Dangerously for Archives," Society of American Archivists, http://www2.archivists.org/living-dangerously/value-of -archives, accessed November 16, 2017.

6. See DHSS Educational Outcomes as outlined in DHSS Program Proposal, 2–3.

7. Ibid., 2; Lynn Wild et al., *Strengthening the Core: Renovation and Expansion of the Wallace Center (TWC) at RIT*, Rochester, NY: RIT, April 2017, 3. The Wallace Center was renamed Wallace Library in early 2018.

8. See Robert G. Crowder, *Principles of Learning and Memory* (New York: Psychology, 2015); Pat Crawford and Patricia Machemer, "Measuring Incidental Learning in a PBL Environment," *Journal of Faculty Development* 22, no. 2 (May 2008): 104–111. On the team-teaching approach to using Drupal, the content management system for our online exhibit, see Juilee Decker, "Beyond Cul-de-Sac Pedagogy: Museum Studies as a Landscape of Practice," 183–184.

9. Kate MacLaren, "Blog Post II: Incidental Learning," *RIT Museum Studies*, September 19, 2017, https://ritmuse.wordpress.com/2017/09/19/blog-post-ii -incidental-learning/, accessed November 16, 2017.

10. Lizzy Carr, "Incidental Learning," *RIT Museum Studies*, September 20, 2017, https://ritmuse.wordpress.com/2017/09/20/incidental-learning/, accessed November 16, 2017.

11. Kelly Miller and Michelle Morton, "Hidden Learning: Undergraduates at Work in the Archives," *Archive Journal* (September 2012), http://www.archive journal.net/notes/hidden-learning/, accessed November 16, 2017.

THIRTY-TWO

—ᴍᴍ—

Global Engagement and Digital Technology

MARY R. ANDERSON
University of Tampa

WILLIAM M. MYERS
University of Tampa

TO WHAT EXTENT DO EXPERIENCES outside the classroom broaden student engagement? While the course we describe in the following pages was developed by political scientists at a medium-sized comprehensive university with a tradition of liberal arts education, the structure, objectives, and lessons of the course can be applied to a variety of disciplines.

In the spring of 2017, we set out to develop a course to bring policy networking to life using digital technology. The course was unique in several respects. First, the course was designed as a team-taught course, with two faculty members working together to deliver the curriculum over the course of fourteen weeks. Second, the course relied heavily on digital technology and real-world application, which meant that unlike traditional university courses, a large portion of the material students were to use to complete the course requirements depended on information contained in the digital world and not in traditional textbooks. Thus, the faculty and students had to be flexible and have the ability to adjust when necessary. Third, the course included a ten-day travel experience to our nation's capital, Washington, DC, at the end of the semester.

EXPERIENTIAL EDUCATION AND GLOBAL ENGAGEMENT

Students like plans. Students like goals. Students like boxes they can check. Why? Students want tangible skills that will lead them to a career after graduation. This idea is at the heart of experiential education. As educators, one of our primary tasks is to help them connect the dots; help them understand that what they are studying in the classroom has real-world applicability. Proponents of such an active learning approach argue that student knowledge, engagement, teamwork skills, and openness to varying perspectives are engendered as a result.[1] This is precisely what John Dewey introduces in his groundbreaking work. Dewey[2] asserted that education coupled with doing has the greatest potential for achieving long-term learning. His pioneering work has paved the way for teacher-scholars who have heeded his call to develop courses that combine substantive academic content with out-of-classroom experiences.

According to the Association for Experiential Education, "experiential education is a philosophy that informs many methodologies in which educators purposefully engage with learners in direct experience and focused reflection in order to increase knowledge, develop skills, clarify values, and develop people's capacity to contribute to their communities."[3] This essay chronicles the development, implementation, and evaluation of a global engagement course with these tenets in mind.

COURSE DEVELOPMENT

Students who have a desire to work in Washington, DC, need to possess three essential skills: they need to be able to write effectively, understand data analysis, and communicate (network) with others. We developed a course that aimed to meet these objectives and then put the students in the field to apply what they had learned in a real-world setting.

Development of a course such as this one includes careful preparation and flexibility. While these may seem contrary to one another, any course that relies on digital real-time technology must meet these conditions. Further, a course that includes out-of-classroom experiences must be prepared for situations that require altering a carefully crafted plan at any point in time. This means that students enrolled in such a course need to be able to handle the stress that often accompanies these types of circumstances. Learning by doing began at the outset, prior to course registration. Our intention was to have this course mirror as closely as possible the experience students may encounter if they choose to seek a position in the policy field in Washington, DC.

Before the course even began, interested students submitted an application for acceptance to the course and provided a résumé highlighting their skills and a personal statement explaining how this experience would benefit their long-term career goals. Student applications were reviewed by the faculty, and select students were invited for an interview where they were asked a set of questions that would give the faculty a sense of the level of commitment each student had for the course. The design of the course required that students demonstrate individual initiative, the ability to collaborate in a team setting, and flexibility. Once interviews were complete, selected students were invited to the course and provided a registration clearance. Seats in the course were limited to fifteen students, and a spot was not secured until a deposit for the travel component of the course was deposited at the bursar's office (note: a separate account may need to be created for additional student fees collected for travel; it is important to work with financial partners at the university early in the development of the course to get these established).

COURSE IMPLEMENTATION 1: DELIVERY
AND DIGITAL TECHNOLOGY

The course was delivered over a fourteen-week semester by a team of two faculty members. The course had six objectives, which can translate to any course using digital technology. These included: (1) to communicate effectively to develop and convey ideas and information; (2) to examine issues rationally, logically, and coherently; (3) to understand the foundations of science, scientific methods, and the impact of science on society; (4) to be able to synthesize the knowledge of and understand issues emanating from a variety of disciplinary perspectives; (5) to identify personal values and the values of others and to defend personal positions; (6) to understand both the commonality and diversity of human social existence in an interdependent world. Two class meetings a week were devoted to class lecture, group activities, and discussion related to the assigned readings. The typical classroom meeting facilitated the development of learning and critically analyzing the literature, placing current issues in historical and comparative context, and developing an intellectual curiosity. One class meeting a week was devoted to lab, where students played the role of congressional staffer. Among the range of skills necessary to be a successful staffer is the ability to acquire information from diverse sources, think logically about complex material, approach and solve problems creatively, and tolerate ambiguity. In order to cultivate these skills (relevant to both classroom and lab settings), each student identified a particular piece of legislation and was tasked with tracking its progress and formulating a strategy that would ensure its ultimate passage.

We placed particular emphasis on the legislative information provided by Congress.gov as well as a range of other sources of digital technology including political party platforms,[4] major legislative enactments related to a particular policy area,[5] and interest group comparisons.[6] "Congress.gov is the official website for US federal legislative information. The site provides access to accurate, timely, and complete legislative information for Members of Congress, legislative agencies, and the public. It is presented by the Library of Congress (LOC) using data from the Office of the Clerk of the US House of Representatives, the Office of the Secretary of the Senate, the Government Publishing Office, Congressional Budget Office, and the LOC's Congressional Research Service. Congress.gov is usually updated the morning after a session adjourns."[7] This website provided a wealth of information about the legislative process, but our students paid particular attention to several key pieces of information, including amendments, cosponsors, and committees. Amendments reflect changes in the text and, therefore, the effect of the legislation. The number of cosponsors is important because the more members who sign on to support a bill the higher its chances of eventually being passed. Committee assignments and activities are characterized by hearings, modifications to the text, and, if successful, discharge to the full legislative body for a vote.

This website as well as the others were used to learn the status of particular bills and to strategize who the key players in the process would be—whether the goal was to pass or defeat a particular bill. These players could include interest groups, other members of Congress, think tanks, etc. These all led to the final product, a legislative strategy memo that students would use in their meetings with policy makers in Washington, DC.

COURSE IMPLEMENTATION 2: EXPERIENTIAL LEARNING AND GLOBAL ENGAGEMENT

This course included three engagement opportunities. First, students applied and interviewed for the position. Second, they played the role of congressional staffer: using digital technology, they tracked bills as they moved from introduction through committees and on to the next chamber, researched and identified the key policy actors also involved in the policy-making process, such as interest groups, think tanks, bureaucratic agencies, and any other stakeholders that could influence the outcome, and conducted in-depth research on these policy actors by accessing websites, digitized documents, and publicly available data. Third, the course culminated with a study away experience in Washington, DC, where students engaged with the various policy actors they had identified for many of their assignments. For example, students had the opportunity to meet with the legislative director for a large advocacy group, a member of Congress and her staffer, and an analyst from a world-renowned think tank. The use of digital technology coupled with face-to-face interactions with policy actors resulted in bringing the material to life in a way we could not have accomplished in the classroom alone.

COURSE EVALUATION 1: STUDENT REFLECTION

During the out-of-classroom experience to Washington, DC, students put into practice the skills they had acquired over the course of the semester. They practiced networking, communicating information, and writing and analysis. Each day of the ten-day experience students kept an electronic daily journal (we used Blackboard's capability for this exercise). The purpose of the electronic journal was to record their experiences and interactions and to begin to informally reflect on what they had learned. The informal reflections entered in the daily journal were used to create a final reflection paper. In this final paper, students reflected on the travel experience as a whole, how the experience outside the classroom compared to what they learned inside the classroom, how these experiences were related to each other, and how they complemented each other. Below is a sample of excerpts from these daily journals and reflections.

- "Hilary Shelton (Legislative Director NAACP Washington Bureau) spoke to us about his role and many of his stories. Not only was this man interesting, but he also related to most of our class examples regarding established interest groups, like how important coalitions and age are when becoming influential. He also provided us with NAACP memos for different issues that also mirrored the ones we learned in class."
- "Alec spoke to us about the non-profit, non-partisan work that they do at Pew. Once again, the benefits of the ability to analyze data was emphasized, as well as the importance of an advanced degree."
- "It was interesting to hear her (Rep. Kathy Castor) speak about the partisan dynamics within Congress and her interactions with representatives from the other party."
- "It was an amazing experience and I would recommend it to anyone who was considering going. I got the chance to meet so

many interesting people that do great work, visit possible grad schools and I also got some perspective on what I want to do once I leave UT."

Based on these reflections, we are content that the expectations of the course were met. Students were able to apply classroom learning to real-life situations. Further, they understood how the dots connected.

COURSE EVALUATION 2: FACULTY LESSONS

Relying on digital technology has both positive and negatives consequences. In our case, we relied heavily on real-time data that is contained in digital form at Congress.gov. This means we have up to the minute information on bills that are making their way through Congress. However, it also means that if (and when) Congress fails to move forward with bills, as was the case in the first half of 2017, then there is not much information for students to use to complete their weekly assignments and craft a legislative strategy memo. Hence, the first lesson we come away with from this endeavor is to be flexible. Reliance on digital technology means that we must be prepared to adjust our plan for the day. It also means that for each class meeting there must be a backup plan.

Second, once students have had a taste for digital technology as a mode for learning they may be resistant to going back to the books; using digital technology is much more exciting and reflective of how they learn and acquire information in their everyday life. This leads to the second lesson: it is a challenge to balance traditional classroom expectations and innovative methods such as digital technology.

Finally, global engagement is a winner. Out-of-classroom experiences coupled with advances in digital technology can help students make the connection between substantive content and real-world applicability. Therefore, the third lesson for us as faculty is to find ways to incorporate digital technology and engagement into all university courses. Students love it and learn from it in meaningful ways. Students connect the dots, and they can check that box.

NOTES

1. Kathy L. Brock and Beverly J. Cameron, "Enlivening Political Science Courses with Kolb's Learning Preference Model," *PS: Political Science and Politics* 32, no. 2 (1999): 251–256.

2. John Dewey, *Democracy and Education: An Introduction to the Philosophy of Education* (New York: Macmillan, 1916).

3. Association for Experiential Education, accessed May 9, 2018, http://www.aee.org/what-is-ee.

4. The American Presidency Project, accessed May 30, 2018, http://www.presidency.ucsb.edu/platforms.php.

5. David R. Mayhew, accessed May 30, 2018, http://campuspress.yale.edu/davidmayhew/datasets-divided-we-govern/.

6. Center for Responsive Politics, accessed May 30, 2018, https://www.opensecrets.org/influence/.

7. Congress.gov, accessed May 30, 2018, https://www.congress.gov/about/.

THIRTY-THREE

—ᴟ—

Using Digital Humanities to Reimagine College Writing and Promote Integrated and Applied Learning

PATRICIA TURNER

University of Wisconsin-Eau Claire

INTRODUCTION

The Association of American Colleges and Universities defines integrative and applied learning as "an understanding . . . that a student builds across the curriculum and co-curriculum, from making simple connections among ideas and experiences to synthesizing and transferring learning to new, complex situations within and beyond the campus." Integrative and applied learning pedagogies strengthen critical thinking and real-world problem-solving. They encourage lifelong learning by enhancing students' ability to apply their knowledge, experience, and skills to new situations. At a time when the rapid pace of technology is transforming work and public life, "developing students' capacities for integrative and applied learning is central to personal success, social responsibility, and civic engagement in today's global society."[1]

In the past few decades, institutions of higher education have promoted integrative and applied learning through linked or "bundled" courses, innovative "high impact" pedagogies, and experiential learning opportunities. It remains, however, a challenge to develop writing assignments that effectively invite students to apply multiple perspectives and methodologies to solve complex real-world problems.[2] In addition, integrative and applied learning pedagogies are often used in single-discipline courses, when, arguably, students would benefit most by bridging long-standing gaps between technical knowledge and writing skills.

Digital humanities is a natural venue to promote integrative and applied learning by reimagining college writing. As Kathie Gossett notes: "Digital Humanities is interdisciplinary; by necessity, it breaks down boundaries between disciplines at the local (e.g., English and history) and global (e.g., humanities and computer sciences) levels."[3] Within the virtual environment, students can use tools such as text mining, content analysis, multimedia composition, and hypertext to transform their writing in ways that enhance content knowledge and strengthen professional and technical skills.

COLLEGE WRITING IN THE DIGITAL ENVIRONMENT: MAKING IT WORK

Digital humanities can be used to reimagine student prose in any course, but it is ideal for courses in the humanities that require extensive written composition. Making it work requires that we first acknowledge that incorporating technology into a humanities course can appear daunting. Fortunately, traditional barriers such as steep learning curves for coding languages and limited server space have largely been overcome by new software and technical services. College learning management systems (LMS) used for online learning such as Blackboard, Canvas, and D2L offer user-friendly environments for hosting classroom projects. Many colleges and universities have dedicated server space for showcasing digital humanities projects. Educational site licenses enable campuses to provide cutting-edge graphic design, video editing, and web design applications that are menu driven and require little or no coding. Web design applications include templates that streamline the design process and facilitate the use of digital tools, allowing students and faculty to focus on the content. Campus IT departments commonly offer online guides, tutorials, and individualized training for supported software. Finally, introductory primers are now available to provide detailed technical guidance for using digital technologies in the humanities classroom.[4]

Beyond technical support, digital humanities projects require more scaffolding than standard writing assessments. In contrast to print-based assignments submitted by individual students, a digital humanities project is a shared endeavor; each individual text contributes to the project's collective design and objectives. Digital humanities projects are thus particularly well suited for collaborative group work. Here are the essential steps to completing a collaborative digital humanities writing project:

- First, prepare a detailed plan of the project's concept and product. This includes determining the preliminary research and writing needed to realize the project. In the early planning stage, it is extremely helpful to storyboard the project, in which a mock-up of each web page is created on paper. (There are numerous storyboard templates available on the internet.) A project storyboard enables students to visualize the project's overall design and flow as well as to identify gaps where additional content is needed.
- Second, if the project will result in a real-world application for public viewing, consider its intended audience when determining the project's design and outcomes. It can be challenging to balance the course objectives for the students who complete the project with the needs of those who may use and benefit from it.
- Third, decide on the software to be used to complete the project. Here, too, a project storyboard is very useful as it provides a guide for determining the digital tools needed to implement the project's design elements. If, for example, one or more of the web pages in the project requires custom animation, it is necessary to select a software package with this capability. Campus IT departments can usually provide guidance regarding which programs are suitable and available by site license.
- Fourth, arrange for students to get technical instruction on the selected software. Depending on what support is offered on campus, this can take place via classroom workshops or online tutorials created by the software provider. It is essential to tailor the instruction to the project's specific requirements; this enables students to work creatively within the digital environment without being overwhelmed or distracted by the technology.
- Fifth, determine the best option for hosting the project online: whether you use an LMS, a campus server, or a third-party website will depend on available institutional support and whether the project is strictly for classroom use or will be made available to the public.

• Finally, anticipate and resolve before beginning the project any potential legal issues such as copyright permissions and FERPA privacy restrictions. For projects designed for public viewing, students must give permission in writing for their work to be published online.

HISTORYTELLING: WRITING AND TEACHING HISTORY IN THE DIGITAL ENVIRONMENT

My lower division seminar, History in Fiction, Fiction in History, incorporates a digital humanities project designed to enhance the course's integrative and applied learning objectives. The course content challenges and blurs conventional distinctions between fiction and history through the comparative study of novels, primary sources, essays, films/plays, and other historical writings. Students analyze how historical perspectives inform fictional narratives and, conversely, how popular culture utilizes fictional techniques to represent historical events. For their final paper, students compose either a piece of short fiction related to a historical period or, alternatively, an argumentative essay focusing on representations in popular culture of a historical subject. Examples of student projects include: memoirs of a Guantanamo Bay inmate (short fiction); analysis of the play 1776 and its representation of the Continental Congress (essay); the depiction of revolutionary Boston in the video game series *Assassin's Creed* (essay); a day in the family life of the Mafia gangster Al Capone (short fiction); and the contested authorship of Shakespeare's plays (essay).

Once drafts of the papers are completed, we employ digital tools and web design software to transform the essays and short stories into interactive programs. Because public server space is not available at our institution, we created a hosted website, www.historytelling.org, to make the programs available for use by K–12 teachers and students. (See fig. 33.1.)

This project enables my students to apply the pedagogical objectives of the course to the real-world problem of how to effectively teach historical perspective, analysis of evidence, and critical thinking skills. Each program focuses on a history/social studies or English/reading topic. Elementary and secondary school teachers can assign the programs to be viewed independently or use them in class as instructional aids.

For the short stories, we utilize two digital tools: "pop-up" hypertext windows and multimedia timelines. These are incorporated into the text to juxtapose the eyewitness immediacy of the story with its broader historical context.

Figure 33.1. historytelling.org home page: http://historytelling.org/index.html.

Figure 33.2. Illustration of short fiction "Valentine's Day" with historical ("pop-ups") annotations: http://historytelling.org/methodology.html.

The result is a hybrid form of "creative nonfiction"; the digital environment enhances the narrative by embedding it within its unique cultural context, allowing the viewer to appreciate the importance of historical perspective. (See figs. 33.2 and 33.3.)

For the argumentative essays, we deconstruct them into interactive, inquiry-driven dialogues that, in lieu of standard citations, incorporate the primary source evidence directly into the text for viewers to compare and interpret. (See fig. 33.4.)

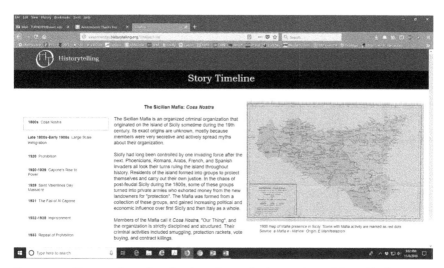

Figure 33.3. Historical timeline for short fiction "Valentine's Day": http://valentines day.historytelling.org/timeline.html.

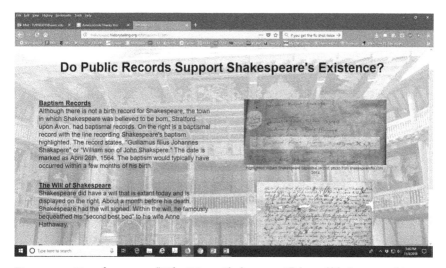

Figure 33.4. Page from essay "Who Wrote Shakespeare?": http://shakespeare.history telling.org/iaffirmation-1.html.

At the beginning of each program, the viewer is presented with an essential question, followed by documentary and multimedia evidence supporting various perspectives on the issue. Viewers evaluate the evidence and construct their own arguments in the form of thesis statements. The object of the essay-based programs is to use the digital environment to render more transparent

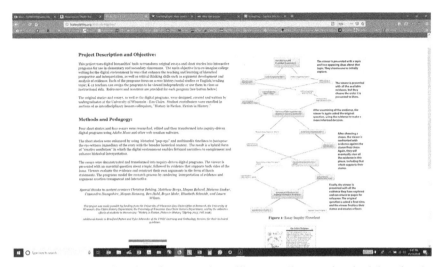

Figure 33.5. Inquiry flowchart for essays: http://historytelling.org/methodology.html.

and dynamic the research process as it relates to the interpretation of evidence and argument creation. (See fig. 33.5.)

All eight programs, as well as additional details on the project methodology and associated resources, can be viewed on the project website, www .historytelling.org.

CONCLUSION

As this project illustrates, digital humanities projects provide opportunities to reimagine college writing and enhance integrated and applied learning. Digital humanities also offers a unique environment for bridging the knowledge and skill gap between the humanities and information technology. In his 2017 book *Robot-Proof: Higher Education in the Age of Artificial Intelligence*, Joseph Aoun argues for the teaching of "humanics"; that is, the integration of human literacy skills taught in the humanities—such as writing—with technological skills emphasized in mathematics and the sciences.[5] Digital humanities, coupled with project-based learning with real-world outcomes, can provide students with the lifelong skills they need to thrive within a globalized and increasingly automated workforce.

ACKNOWLEDGMENTS

I thank Megan Henning, Bryce Mohr, and all my students in History in Fiction, Fiction in History for collaborating with me on this digital humanities project. The products of their work can be accessed at www.historytelling.org.

NOTES

1. American Association of Colleges and Universities, "Integrative and Applied Learning Value Rubric," https://www.aacu.org/value/rubrics/integrative -learning, accessed February 16, 2020.

2. Mary Huber, Pat Hutchings, Richard Gale, Ross Miller, and Molly Breen, "Leading Initiatives for Integrative Learning," *Liberal Education* 93, no. 2 (Spring 2007), https://www.aacu.org/publications-research/periodicals/leading -initiatives-integrative-learning, accessed February 16, 2020.

3. Kathie Gossett, "DH: Defining the Digital Humanities," in *Debates in the Digital Humanities,* ed. Matthew Gold (Minneapolis: University of Minnesota Press, 2012), 67.

4. Claire Battershill and Shawna Ross, *Using Digital Humanities in the Classroom: A Practical Introduction for Teachers, Lecturers, and Students* (New York: Bloomsbury Academic, 2017); Eileen Gardiner and Ronald Musto, *The Digital Humanities: A Primer for Students and Scholars* (New York: Cambridge University Press, 2015).

5. Joseph E. Aoun, *Robot-Proof: Higher Education in the Age of Artificial Intelligence* (Cambridge, MA: MIT Press, 2017).

THIRTY-FOUR

Early Indiana Presidents

Incorporating Digital Humanities, Public History, and Community Engagement

SHAWN MARTIN

Dartmouth College

CAREY CHAMPION

Indiana University Bloomington

CREATING HISTORICAL NARRATIVES FOR STUDENTS requires teachers to create three elements: historical knowledge, significance, and empathy.[1] Teachers lecturing on history in the classroom, however, often struggle to create such connections for students, and the creation of websites showcasing historical documents can help "enable students to use authentic historical resources for engaging meaningful content directed at learning about the usable past."[2] Leadership at Indiana University: Andrew and Theophilus Wylie, 1820–1890, (http://collections.libraries.indiana.edu/wyliehouse/) a bicentennial project funded by the Indiana University Office of the Bicentennial has allowed for the establishment of a new exhibits website to create just such a resource for teachers and community members interested in early Indiana history. The Wylie House Museum, in collaboration with the Departments of History and Information and Library Science, the Indiana University Archives, the Mathers Museum, and Indiana University Libraries, has brought together a wide variety of digital images of manuscripts, printed books, and museum objects that help students make connections between two of Indiana University's earliest presidents, and their relevance to students at Indiana University and within Bloomington even today.

The Wylie House Museum is a historic home and local heritage site that inspires community interest and engagement for Indiana University, the city of Bloomington, and beyond. The museum's interpretation and programming efforts are aimed at supporting the Indiana University curriculum and providing dynamic and informational offerings to the public and organizations that intersect with the museum. It is the repository for, and home to, archival collections, books, and many objects related to the Wylie families, including Indiana University's first president, Andrew Wylie (1789–1851), and his cousin, Theophilus Wylie (1810–1895), an administrator and faculty member for over forty years. Furthermore, the Wylie House Museum curates materials related to nineteenth-century life in the Midwest. These resources inform, supplement, and complement the interpretation of the museum, the on-site exhibitions, and the regularly offered outreach programs. The museum also draws from a variety of related collections and resources that are not managed by the museum but are available through other repositories, such as Indiana University Archives, Indiana State Library, and the Indiana Historical Society as well as archives and digital repositories across the country that have related holdings. In the past, the museum mediated these robust resources, distilling them for volunteers and the public through on-site interpretation, curation, and programming. The launch of this new exhibits site and some initial exhibits provide the museum a method for building classroom modules for instruction within Indiana University courses and for offering community members and partners within Bloomington and beyond an avenue for easy, direct access to archival resources and objects that were previously behind the scenes or involved independent research efforts.

TEACHING

Whether one is studying history as an undergraduate or to be a librarian with aspirations to help historians, it is essential to understand history's underlying requirement to create a coherent historical narrative.[3] From its inception, teaching this way of historical thinking was an integral part of the Leadership at Indiana University project. Two classes were chosen for initial teaching modules. The first of these was Digital History, an undergraduate elective class taught within the History Department at Indiana University. The second was Digital Libraries, a graduate-level class taught within the Department of Information and Library Science. In addition to formal teaching in the classroom, project staff were able to teach an undergraduate intern more informally and one-on-one. In all, these three teaching opportunities provided an excellent way for understanding how historical thinking and digital methods can be integrated in ways that help students utilize both historical research methods and technical skills.

Digital History

In the Digital History course, students focused on creating proposals for their own digital history projects. Primarily, digital history teaches students various digital methods for studying history including geographic mapping using Google Maps, textual analysis, and other approaches. The most effective way to help students connect these methods is to get them to think about their historical narratives as early as possible.[4] The Wylie Leadership project is an excellent case study for students. The site contains a wide variety of materials including manuscripts, printed texts, and museum objects and, eventually, archaeological artifacts. Thus, one can make any number of different kinds of arguments with these materials. Moreover, the students' final project in the class was to create a digital history site similar to the Wylie project. Having an example of a final project helped students think about how their evidence would be presented in an online platform.

Digital Libraries

The Digital Libraries course focused on building online collections, including digitization and creating metadata and a website. The focus of this class was quite different from that of Digital History. In this case, graduate students in library science were more interested in understanding organizational issues such as structure and the organization of data.[5] Therefore, the module on the Wylie Leadership project for the Digital Libraries course focused more on the platform, Omeka (a digital library platform), that the Leadership at Indiana University site is built on. In this class, the students had to create a final project utilizing the Omeka software. Like the Digital History class, it was helpful for students to see a practical example of how a digital history project meant to ask broader questions found ways to do so within the technological limitations of a platform that was not designed for that purpose.[6]

Interns

Another skill set all digital projects (in class or outside) require is project management.[7] Students in these classes had to manage small projects within the deadlines for the course, but the Wylie Leadership project was also able to teach some of the same skills to a student intern who was in charge of digitizing over one hundred manuscripts, helping create a data set of annotations for a nineteenth-century library, and performing some background research for the digital exhibits. To accomplish this work, the project intern had to understand project timelines and the long-term goals of structuring data within the data set and to shift work schedules and timetables to meet the needs of the library, Wylie House Museum, and other project partners.

COMMUNITY ENGAGEMENT

The Leadership at Indiana University project sought not only to work with students, however. One of the primary goals of establishing a digital exhibit space for the Wylie House Museum was to provide supplementary or complementary exhibits for the benefit of community users. Volunteer docents, gardeners, quilters from the community, K–12 students, Boy Scouts and Girl Scouts, local history clubs, camps, the county and city government, local and regional museums, as well as local artists and musicians on projects and events all collaborate with the museum. These groups, however, have different interests in the museum, ranging from volunteers invested in increasing their familiarity with all aspects of the museum and family histories to historic preservationists who want to know more about local architecture and city development. The museum has a role to play in serving as a resource for K–12 research projects on nineteenth-century children's lives and local garden clubs' knowledge of historic heirloom plant varieties. For each of these groups (and more), it is easy to imagine a digital exhibit or multiple exhibits that can focus on specific topics or themes, satisfying their interests, forwarding the research mission of the museum, and making the information easily available and accessible to anyone who has the ability to connect to the internet.[8]

CONCLUSION

Information that was previously limited by the physical constraints of the Wylie House Museum and bound by exhibit timeframes and location is made accessible to those interested in learning more—at any time and from any location. The digital exhibits in the Leadership at Indiana University site will serve as a reference archive of museum-related topics that is dynamic in nature, able to accommodate new understandings or incorporate new resources. The exhibits platform will also serve as a space for the faculty and students at Indiana

University and community partners such as high school interns and other local museums to develop and cocreate new scholarship efficiently and easily.

Digital humanities and digital history provide a tremendously effective way to engage students and the community with history.[9] Historical thinking requires the creation of a narrative argument. Historical narratives require gathering evidence, contextualizing it, analyzing it, and putting it all together to demonstrate how past decisions by historical figures such as nineteenth-century Indiana University presidents affect the school's evolution and the development of the present. Exposing people to this kind of historical thinking allows the museum to make connections, provide additional information, and extend the reach of the museum into the classroom and the community without necessarily requiring just a tour or program visit. For example, the Wylie House Museum can now supplement its annual textile exhibit with a digital exhibit that showcases digitized Wylie family letters and financial documents, provides images of garments too fragile to put out on display, and offers historical context by pulling from collections at other institutions related to broad topics such as the industrialization of cotton processing to specific topics such as natural plant dyes.

The amount and type of information shared during the typical forty-five-minute visit or program at the Wylie House Museum is incredibly small relative to the vast amount of related themes and materials with which the museum intersects. A digital exhibit space provides the opportunity to serve as a greater resource for faculty members, students, community members, organizations, and partners.[10] The efficiency and ease with which the museum can create and maintain exhibits related to numerous topics also allows for volunteers and engaged visitors to contribute ideas, ask questions, and experience a response related to their interest by simply returning to the website at their own convenience and from any location. The creation of this digital humanities platform and the initial exhibits created through the Indiana University Bicentennial Project Grant program are the beginning of a shift from a community heritage site to a community heritage resource for the Wylie House Museum.

ACKNOWLEDGMENTS

We acknowledge the funding of the Indiana University Office of the Bicentennial for providing a grant to help create a project called Leadership at Indiana University: Andrew and Theophilus Wylie, 1820–1890. The website is available at http://collections.libraries.indiana.edu/wyliehouse/leadership. We also acknowledge Kalani Craig, clinical assistant professor of history, and John Walsh, associate professor of information science, both at Indiana University, who provided time to teach these modules in their classroom.

Finally, we thank Brett Roberts, undergraduate in the School of Public and Environmental Affairs and the intern at the Leadership at Indiana University project, for all his hard work.

NOTES

1. S. G. Grant, "It's Just the Facts, or Is It? The Relationship between Teachers' Practices and Students' Understandings of History," *Theory and Research in Social Education* 29, no. 1 (2001): 102.

2. Brendan Calandra and John Lee, "The Digital History and Pedagogy Project: Creating an Interpretative/Pedagogical Historical Website," *Internet and Higher Education* 8 (2005): 323.

3. Sherman Dorn, "Is (Digital) History More Than an Argument about the Past," in *Writing History in the Digital Ages*, ed. Kristen Nawrotzki and Jack Dougherty (Ann Arbor: University of Michigan Press, 2013), https://quod.lib .umich.edu/d/dh/12230987.0001.001/1:4/--writing-history-in-the-digital-age?g= dculture;rgn=div1;view=fulltext;xc=1#4.1.

4. T. Mills Kelly, "Making: DIY History?" *Teaching History in the Digital Age* (Ann Arbor: University of Michigan Press, 2013), https://quod.lib.umich.edu/d /dh/12146032.0001.001/1:9/--teaching-history-in-the-digital-age?g=dculture;rgn =div1;view=fulltext;xc=1.

5. Arianna Ciula, and Øyvind Eide, "Reflections on Cultural Heritage and Digital Humanities: Modelling in Practice and Theory," *Proceedings of the First International Conference on Digital Access to Cultural Heritage* (2014): 36–37.

6. Allison C. Marsh, "Omeka in the Classroom: The Challenges of Teaching Material Culture in a Digital World," *Literary and Linguistic Computing* 28, no. 2 (2013): 279–282.

7. Edin Tabak, "A Hybrid Model for Managing DH Projects," *Digital Humanities Quarterly* 11, no. 1 (2017), http://www.digitalhumanities.org/dhq /vol/11/1/000284/000284.html.

8. Micah Vandegrift and Stewart Varner, "Evolving in Common: Creating Mutually Supportive Relationships between Libraries and the Digital Humanities," *Journal of Library Administration* 53, no. 1 (2013): 70–71.

9. Jack Dougherty, Kristen Nawrotzki, Charlotte D. Roches, and Timothy Burke, "Conclusions: What We Learned from *Writing History in the Digital Age*," in *Writing History in the Digital Age*, ed. Kristen Nawrotzki and Jack Dougherty (Ann Arbor: University of Michigan Press, 2013), https://quod.lib.umich.edu/d /dh/12230987.0001.001/1:10/--writing-history-in-the-digital-age?g=dculture;rgn =div1;view=fulltext;xc=1#10.3.

10. Chris Alen Sula, "Digital Humanities and Libraries: A Conceptual Model," *Journal of Library Administration* 53, no. 1 (2013): 10–16.

THIRTY-FIVE

—ᴡ—

Measuring the Anzacs

Exploring the Lives of World War I Soldiers in a Citizen Science Project

EVAN ROBERTS

University of Minnesota

INTRODUCTION

The centennial of World War I has been commemorated by a diverse range of public and scholarly explorations of the conflict. Digital initiatives by archives and museums have been a significant aspect of the commemoration, facilitating historical research and community engagement with artifacts, records, and exhibits. The pedagogical possibilities with these digital resources range from secondary research[1] on specialist topics to more complex and extended assignments with primary sources.

This chapter shows how instructors can use the Measuring the ANZACs (http://www.measuringtheanzacs.org/) website to work with primary sources for a better understanding of the experiences of World War I soldiers. But before doing that, many readers will want to know who are the ANZACs, and why are they being measured? ANZAC—Australian and New Zealand Army Corps—was a combined Australian and New Zealand command in World War I, serving primarily in the Middle Eastern theater. The personnel records of nearly all the soldiers from both countries have been preserved, digitized, and made publicly available. Measuring the ANZACs is a citizen science project to transcribe key information from all the New Zealand files, to support research on

the height, health, and postwar survival of soldiers.[2] The research and pedagogical possibilities with the files are much broader, with family networks,
military careers, and combat experiences all well documented. Because New
Zealand troops served alongside other Allied troops, their files can give broader
insights into the World War I experience.

Students' work with Measuring the ANZACs can support several learning
outcomes. The foundation of these is improving students' applied problem-
solving skills through the process of transcription. Many students today are
unfamiliar with reading historical handwriting. But the majority of documents
are mostly legible. Completing a transcription requires identification of a small
fraction of unclear letters or words that can be identified by context or matched
to other examples. To do this, students must take stock of what they do know
and then apply that knowledge to make a reasoned inference about the letter or
word they are unsure about. Extended assignments that ask students to analyze
and narrate the soldiers' records into a biography develop students' analytical
and written communication skills. All the material needed to write a short
profile of an individual is present in the file. Yet students must order events
described in files that are only partially organized and identify important
events or facts that are not always marked explicitly as important. They must
then articulate to instructors and peers why they have told the soldiers' story
in a particular way. Finally, students' engagement with the lives and deaths of
young men can be a powerful empathetic and moral experience contributing
to the development of citizenship.

DIGITAL RESOURCES FOR STUDYING WORLD WAR I

Scanning of World War I primary sources has been widespread. In Europe,
multinational portals to digitized material facilitate access to thematically
similar material from several countries.[3] Sources that have been scanned
include the easily legible, such as printed high-level political documents and
official bulletins. Greater insight into the lived experience of the war comes
from unique archival sources with handwritten records. Unit diaries—a key
primary source detailing troop movements and combat—have been scanned
to facilitate greater public and scholarly use.[4] The International Red Cross
has scanned and published online the records of five million prisoners of war,
providing a glimpse into the trauma of captivity.[5]

In Australia, Canada, Great Britain, and New Zealand, national archival
agencies have scanned millions of pages of personnel records detailing the

lives and experience of approximately five million service members.[6] American service records for World War I were largely destroyed in a 1973 fire.[7] Thus the British Empire files are the only option for large-scale exploration of English-language military personnel records from World War I. With introduction and context, they can form the basis of high school and college assignments in American classrooms. The digitized files for Australian, Canadian, and New Zealand forces are freely available for download, while British files require a subscription.[8]

Reflecting their origins in military bureaucracy and preservation by archival agencies, all of these collections are well organized and completely indexed on a small number of identifying criteria: name and serial number. But locked in all of the British Empire personnel files is an incredible trove of varied information on prewar lives and wartime experiences. Documentation of death from wounds or action is also included, presenting both a challenge for instructors to support students engaging with the material and an opportunity for students to understand the human horror of the great death toll. For those who survived, postwar pensions, disabilities, and deaths are documented. Many of the forms in the files are printed and standardized, asking the same questions and collecting the same categories of information for thousands of service members.[9]

MEASURING THE ANZACs

The digitized personnel records have significant potential for a "Big Data"[10] approach to the digital humanities. To realize this potential, Measuring the ANZACs is a collaboration of the present author and coauthors Kris Inwood and Les Oxley with the Zooniverse citizen science organization. Archives New Zealand has provided the scanned files. Measuring the ANZACs aims to eventually transcribe key demographic, health, and military service information from the 140,000 New Zealand personnel files. Between launch in October 2015 and the present publication, around 8,000 soldiers' files have been worked on, totaling more than twenty million characters, or the equivalent of five million words. Much work remains to achieve a complete transcription. Every piece of information must be transcribed three times and then verified for input into the final public database. Student's work with the website contributes immediately to learning and contributes incrementally to building shared resources for further pedagogy and research.

The design of Measuring the ANZACs is influenced by citizen science approaches from physics and ecology and pedagogy from the humanities. The principle of citizen science in Zooniverse projects is to design tasks and workflows that allow citizens to make valuable yet incremental contributions and minimize the impact of erroneous or malicious contributions. Thus, the work-flow on the site asks contributors to separately do three tasks: identify types of documents; identify text for transcription; and, finally, transcribe the text. These steps reproduce in a structured way how humanities scholars work with manuscript documents. Teachers assigning work with Measuring the ANZACs can emphasize the site's fidelity to the original layout of documents. On opening a manuscript, humanities scholars assess what the pages contain. They then identify what parts of the text they are interested in and, finally, transcribe or take notes from the relevant sections.

Assignments based on Measuring the ANZACs are primary source assignments. These give students the opportunity to go beyond the sources their teachers or peers have looked at as well as exploring original documents from the past. Assignments like this can rapidly develop students' skills in independent analysis and original writing composition—both vital skills for further education and the workforce. But the benefits of exploring unknown sources are offset by some risks. A topic interesting in the abstract or exciting to students may not have enough accessible material to complete work in a timely fashion. Measuring the ANZACs provides instructors with a corpus of primary sources where students can explore documents as yet unseen by the instructor and make their own independent discoveries. The extensive collection of files available means instructors can be confident students will soon find something interesting to research and write about. The site features tools to share links to records, so instructors and students can easily look at the same material. Instructors can thus easily supervise and check the work students are doing.

RESEARCH IN THE CLASSROOM WITH MEASURING THE ANZACS

Measuring the ANZACs has been used in classrooms around the world. It can be used with students from about age fourteen onward through college and graduate school. Topically, the site can support instruction in history and the digital humanities. A less obvious application is for teaching about health and illness, because of the extensive documentation of wounds, medical assessments, and death.

The major barrier to entry is being able to read old handwriting. Instructors should take time with students to review strategies for reading cursive and script writing. An effective beginning is to look at a page as a class and work together through reading the handwriting. It is common for students to initially be frustrated with this aspect of the site. Reassure students that within twenty to thirty minutes they will find the handwriting significantly easier to read. Key tactics for deciphering handwriting that instructors should review are:

- Recognize the question or prompt that the handwritten answer is a response to, and think about valid answers. A question about a man's "trade or calling" is more likely to have responses like "Labourer" than "London."
- If a letter is unreadable within one word, look for that letter elsewhere on the page in a known word to infer what it is.
- Write down the letters of the word that are legible, placing a dash where a letter cannot be read. The physical act of writing most of the word can trigger recognition of what it is.

Before assigning students work with Measuring the ANZACs, instructors will also benefit from knowing about the structure of the sources. Armies might have marched on their stomach, but they also consumed vast quantities of paper. Every man in the NZ Forces had at least four pieces of paper describing his life, physical characteristics, and military career. Most files were even larger, averaging twenty-six pieces of paper. The key documents are:

- *Attestations* describing social, economic, family, and demographic characteristics and prior military service. Attestations changed format incrementally during the war, with more than thirty different versions.
- *History Sheets* summarizing the experiences a soldier had, including being wounded, when he served abroad.
- *Statements of Service* that provide more detail on the units a man served in, his promotions and "reductions," and extensive documentation of misconduct and punishment.
- *Active Casualty Forms* that provide detail on wounds, sickness, transfers between hospitals, and deaths in service.
- *Death Notifications* for men who died in service, and postwar deaths for most men dying before 1990.
- *Ballots* that indicate if a soldier was conscripted.
- *Miscellaneous Papers* describing hospital stays, postservice pension assessments, and correspondence.

Not every document is available for transcription. Currently, Measuring the ANZACs is only transcribing the History Sheets, Statements of Service, Attestations, and Death Notifications. (See figs. 35.1 and 35.2.)

Based on our experience in introducing high school and college students to the Measuring the ANZACs website (and other citizen science websites at zooniverse.org), we suggest three basic approaches to working with the website

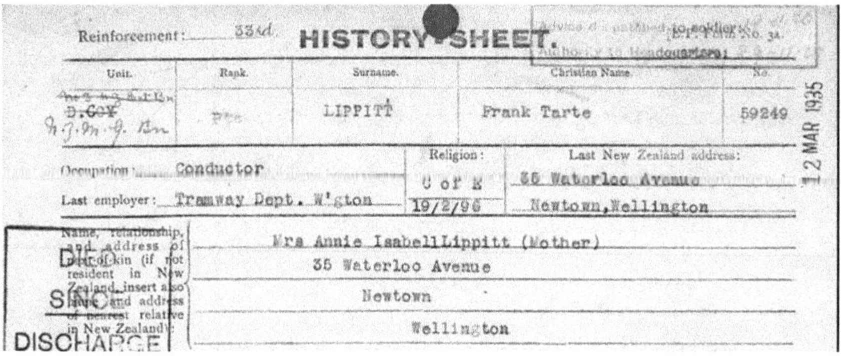
Reinforcement: 33rd HISTORY SHEET.

Unit.	Rank.	Surname.	Christian Name.	No.
D. COY / N.Z.M.G. Bn	Pte	LIPPITT	Frank Tarte	59249

Occupation: Conductor
Last employer: Tramway Dept. W'gton
Religion: C of E 19/2/96
Last New Zealand address: 35 Waterloo Avenue Newtown, Wellington

Name, relationship, and address of next-of-kin (if not resident in New Zealand, insert also name and address of nearest relative in New Zealand): Mrs Annie Isabell Lippitt (Mother) 35 Waterloo Avenue Newtown Wellington

12 MAR 1935

DISCHARGE

Figure 35.1. Military history sheets provide information on where someone lived, next of kin, and religious affiliation. In this example, we see the date of baptism is included. This image is licensed by Creative Commons 2.0 through Archives New Zealand.

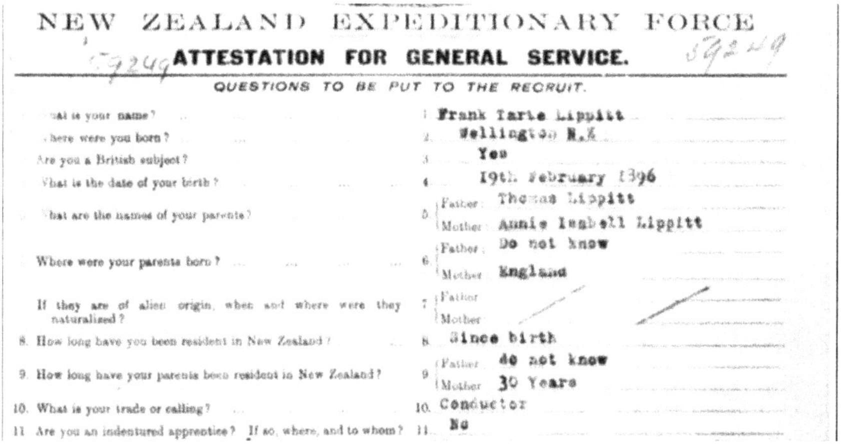
NEW ZEALAND EXPEDITIONARY FORCE

59249 ATTESTATION FOR GENERAL SERVICE. 59249

QUESTIONS TO BE PUT TO THE RECRUIT.

What is your name? — 1. Frank Tarte Lippitt
Where were you born? — 2. Wellington N.Z.
Are you a British subject? — 3. Yes
What is the date of your birth? — 4. 19th February 1896
What are the names of your parents? — 5. Father: Thomas Lippitt; Mother: Annie Isabell Lippitt
Where were your parents born? — 6. Father: Do not know; Mother: England
If they are of alien origin, when and where were they naturalized? — 7. Father: —; Mother: —
8. How long have you been resident in New Zealand? — 8. Since birth
9. How long have your parents been resident in New Zealand? — 9. Father: do not know; Mother: 30 Years
10. What is your trade or calling? — 10. Conductor
11. Are you an indentured apprentice? If so, where, and to whom? — 11. No

Figure 35.2. Attestations include significant information for genealogists including parents' names and origin. The attestation form changed over the course of World War I, so the available information differs for different soldiers. This image is licensed by Creative Commons 2.0 through Archives New Zealand.

in classroom and homework assignments. We have made copies of these assignments available so you can download the Word file and adapt it for your own classes.[11]

Explore the website: This assignment is suited to history classes that focus on or pass through World War I. In a class period, students explore the documentation and blog, with prompts to answer straightforward questions about

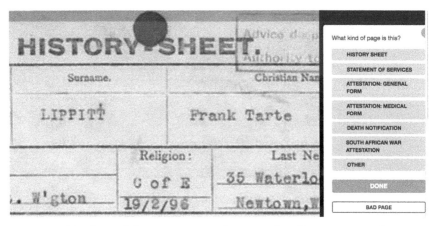

Figure 35.3. The first task for citizen transcribers is to classify pages as one of six key documents. Many pages are easily identified by their title.

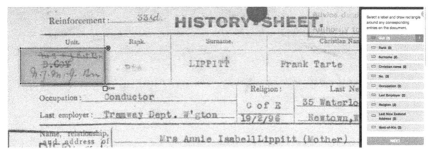

Figure 35.4. Citizen transcribers can then mark the fields that need to be transcribed if other transcribers have not identified them. The marking is done by tracing a box using your computer mouse. This image is licensed by Creative Commons 2.0 through Archives New Zealand.

the website, the research, and World War I soldiers. This will give students a deeper understanding of the motivation for the research, and their contribution. Students then return to the home page and work through the different steps of identification, marking, and transcription. To focus students' attention, ask them to summarize the story of the person they encountered, providing key details such as name, background, and wartime experiences. (See figs. 35.3–35.5.)

Biographical profiles: With two to four hours of student time, students can complete a biographical profile of a soldier. These can be found randomly for

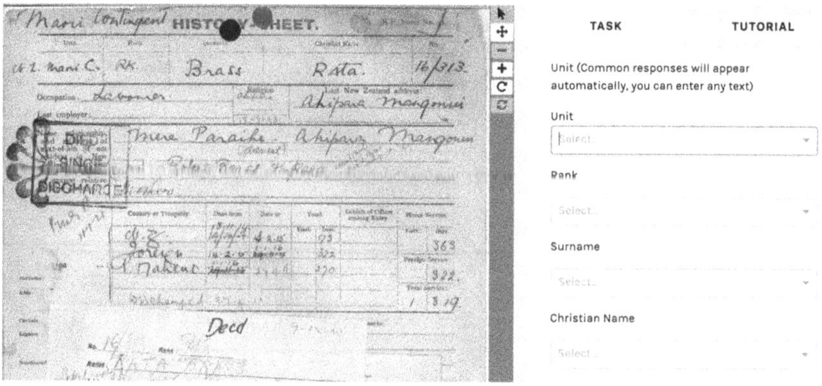

Figure 35.5. Fields that have been marked are then available to transcribe. Every field will be transcribed three times to create the final database to ensure a high level of accuracy. This image is licensed by Creative Commons 2.0 through Archives New Zealand.

each student, by starting at the Measuring the ANZACs home page. However, we encourage you to contact the research team for customized links to particular soldiers to facilitate this assignment. Students should first complete the transcription of the required pages and note key details for themselves. Although the documents in the files generally appear in a standardized order, the chronology of a soldier's life from birth to death is not linear across the pages. Birth and death dates are often on page 1, but intermediate events from childhood and young adulthood appear later in the file. Thus, students need to move back and forth in the file, to construct a soldier's life. This assignment can be adapted to family history and historical methodology classes as well. Students completing a biographical profile are often struck by the similarity of the soldier's life stage to their own, as soldiers were seventeen at the youngest and averaged twenty-four years of age. This assignment often raises student questions about changing life courses, and historical patterns of work and education that are evident in the files.

Case reports: With six to ten hours of student time, a more complex assignment is to give students the files of four to six soldiers. After transcribing the key data fields for each soldier, they write a memo from the perspective of a doctor or social services case worker who is assessing these men as returning veterans. The memo summarizes the set of files for an imaginary colleague who will be taking over the care of these veterans. This assignment has been successfully deployed in a medical sociology class and could be adapted to the history of medicine or social welfare history classes. It is effective in encouraging concise writing and identifying social patterns across a set of documents.

NOTES

1. For example, the *International Encyclopedia of the First World War* provides access to authoritative overviews of more than 1,200 aspects of the conflict and references to secondary sources, http://www.1914-1918-online.net/, accessed May 30, 2018.

2. Kris Inwood, Les Oxley, and Evan Roberts, "Physical Growth and Ethnic Inequality in New Zealand Prisons, 1840–1975," *History of the Family* 20, no. 2 (2015): 249–269; "Physical Stature in Nineteenth Century New Zealand—A Preliminary Interpretation," *Australian Economic History Review* 50, no. 3 (2010): 262–283.

3. See http://www.europeana-collections-1914-1918.eu/, accessed May 30, 2018.

4. Richard Grayson, "A Life in the Trenches? The Use of Operation War Diary and Crowdsourcing Methods to Provide an Understanding of the British Army's Day-to-Day Life on the Western Front," *British Journal for Military History* 2, no. 2 (2016).

5. 1914–1918 Prisoners of the First World War, ICRC Historical Archives, https://grandeguerre.icrc.org/, accessed May 30, 2018.

6. Kris Inwood and J. Andrew Ross, "Big Data and the Military: First World War Personnel Records in Australia, Britain, Canada, New Zealand and British Africa," *Australian Historical Studies* 47, no. 3 (2016): 431–433.

7. Walter W. Stender and Evans Walker, "The National Personnel Records Center Fire: A Study in Disaster," *American Archivist* 37, no. 4 (1974): 521–549.

8. Australia, discoveringanzacs.naa.gov.au/; Canada, www.bac-lac.gc.ca /eng/discover/military-heritage/first-world-war/; Britain, Lives of the First World War, livesofthefirstworldwar.org/; New Zealand, archives.govt.nz, accessed May 30, 2018.

9. Inwood and Ross, "Big Data and the Military," show the similarity across the British Empire of these files. Yet, within each country, the forms changed slightly over the course of the war.

10. Myron P. Gutmann, Emily Klancher Merchant, and Evan Roberts, "'Big Data' in Economic History," *Journal of Economic History* 78, no. 1 (2018): 268–299.

11. See http://z.umn.edu/anzacwork, accessed May 30, 2018.

THIRTY-SIX

—⚬⚬—

Global Foodways

Digital Humanities and Experiential Learning

LAUREN S. CARDON

University of Alabama

FOOD GENERATES DISCUSSION AND REFLECTION—we talk about what we like, what we have tried, where we have tried it, and what it means to us. Food provides a multisensory experience: we struggle to find the right diction to describe it, often relying on figurative language and onomatopoeic words like "sizzling" and "crackling." Food generates topical debate as we consider the ethics of eating meat or specific types of meat, the damage wrought by the industrial food complex, the ways that globalization has impacted local foodways, and the treatment of workers in the food and food service industry. And food teaches us about culture, for eating can be a form of anthropological research. Through savoring a meal at a family home, attempting a new cooking technique, sampling an unfamiliar spice, experimenting with a recipe from an international cookbook, or browsing a local food market, we expand our knowledge of various foodways and reflect back on our own.

I first began teaching a writing seminar on discourses of food because of the topic's pedagogical benefits. The "discourses of food" theme has also, in the past, allowed me to incorporate both digital humanities (DH) and experiential learning elements into the curriculum. These techniques not only enhance students' technical abilities and better prepare them for careers but also establish students as curators of their own knowledge: students envision themselves as part of a discourse community as they create online content, reflecting on their target audience and how they can tailor their writing in a meaningful way for that audience. The DH emphasis of the class immerses students in professional scenarios as they write blog posts, promote events, draft technical instructions for re-creating a recipe, or write a restaurant review.

However, in past iterations of the course, the curriculum felt segmented, lacking a global coherence. Each assignment targeted a different skill but did not feel connected to the previous one. Each unit focused on a different element of food discourse (e.g., "the ethics of eating" and "food as community"), but one unit did not follow seamlessly after another. The DH component of the course, too, felt disconnected from the other course objectives. I collaborated with the Alabama Digital Humanities Center (ADHC) to design and create the website for the class, and, while the students learned how to upload content and format with visual elements, they had little say in the overall design.

The class felt too safe and, to some extent, too easy. The assignments gave students a taste of the professional writer's experience, but I wanted to immerse students in that experience, destabilizing their expectations for a writing seminar and leaving the course's success up to them. For the fall 2017 semester, I redesigned the course with a Global Foodways emphasis, and I altered the curriculum to amplify the experiential learning component through three methods. First, the students were required to select one regional or national cuisine for the entire semester to research and write about, facilitating more in-depth engagement; they were given funding for ingredients to allow them to research the cuisine by cooking it in addition to reading about it. Second, students were responsible for the Global Foodways website design, including formatting, conceptualizing the anchor page, and generating visual content. And third, I ensured that every assignment would be integrated into the website and have a professional dimension—that is, it would emulate the type of writing students may do as professionals.

Of these three major changes, giving the students control over the website design required the most preparation. Knowing little about site design myself, I relied heavily on the input of the digital scholarship librarian and IT specialist. We had an initial project meeting before the semester began, putting together an array of sample sites (including other DH projects) to give students a sense of the possibilities for design. In preparation for the class strategy session in the ADHC, students worked in groups to focus on different aspects of the site design—color themes, accessibility, and individual page layouts, to name a few. These groups consulted various popular food blogs and websites for inspiration, making note of the most and least successful elements. The students made sketches or used design software to format sample pages, writing down the ideas generated by their group. When we met with the ADHC faculty, the students were fully prepared to share their ideas.

The student meeting at the ADHC mirrored the initial project meetings I, as project leader, typically hold before a semester begins. During the student session, the groups presented their ideas to the ADHC faculty, drawing their designs on the whiteboard or projecting graphics from their laptops. They debated best practices and directed questions about the feasibility for various design elements to the IT specialist, adapting their plans in response. As an example, the students liked a feature from a different DH project, in which the landing page had a series of plated dishes that linked to different sections. They asked the IT specialist if they could have each cuisine represented by a photographed signature dish on a plate that would flip over as a user hovered over it, revealing the cuisine link on the back. This idea became a part of the final site design. In other instances, students focused less on dynamic design and more on streamlining and consistency. They recognized the potential for dissonance and confusion if the individual pages diverged from a strict model, so they created headings and icons that would link to the various class assignments.

As students were completing these assignments over the course of the semester—their oral histories, their informational overviews, their recipe narratives, etc.—they could visualize how each piece fit into the web framework. No assignment was merely completed and forgotten; students had to continually assess how to present their information and analysis digitally, knowing the content would remain online even after the semester ended. The design and execution of the Global Foodways site, therefore, provided the primary experiential learning component of the course. Students gained a deeper understanding of how to compose a compelling website, including anchor page, menus, layout, color schemes, individual page design, themes, navigation, and accessibility options.

The class officially launched the website as part of a Food Exhibition. As the final experiential learning activity of the semester, students designed poster presentations about their selected cuisines and cooked a signature dish. We had a poster of the anchor page as well as two laptops, allowing guests to peruse the site while they sampled the dishes. As students presented their posters and dishes to faculty, staff, and peers, they discussed their research with confidence and professionalism.

While the website looked professional and beautifully formatted, and the course redesign successfully addressed the issues of cohesion from previous semesters, both the site and the course underwent additional changes in the spring semester and will continue to do so in future iterations of the course. During the last official class meeting of the fall 2017 semester, I initiated a collective discussion in which students could offer suggestions for changing the course and DH project in future iterations of the class. Although the next Global Foodways course did not start the project from the beginning, I positioned the website as a minimum viable product (MVP), to allow agile development in ADHC project meetings. I presented the class in a similar way. Students offered suggestions for changing the order of assignments, for example, arguing that the literature review should go first so they immediately learn more about their cuisine and have a range of sources to consult throughout the semester. Incorporating this evaluative session at the end of the course allows for its continuity and redesign, so that the course evolves alongside the website. During the spring semester, students again collaborated with the ADHC to make formatting suggestions and changes based on their design analysis of our site and other food-related websites. The tighter organization of the spring course more successfully aligned the course content with the writing and professionalization objectives. Students, often on their own initiative, sought training in programs like Adobe Photoshop and Canva to strengthen the visual impact of their web content and poster presentations. In the fall iteration of this course, I will collaborate with one of the media center resources on campus to make training in these programs more readily available to interested students, and the class will again approach the current website as an MVP.

The course model that I use for the Global Foodways writing seminar can apply to any range of topics in a number of disciplines: a class might contribute to a website on local tourism, civil rights history, or American music. The instructor must ensure, however, that the selected topic allow students to explore something in which they have a personal interest and that the course objectives take precedence over the topic (unless they are the same). The website should echo these learning objectives so that all activities relating to the website seamlessly connect with these objectives, whether that means the site design, web copy, visual elements, or the research that goes into any of these components. The success of this holistic DH approach hinges on students being invested in the process, and this investment, in turn, hinges on their understanding of each activity's purpose.

This type of course model also places a burden on the instructor, for it requires meticulous organization and extensive collaboration. The instructor takes on not only the usual prep work associated with new course development but also the technical responsibilities of maintaining and troubleshooting a website and the coordination with other faculty involved in the course. For example, in the Global Foodways seminar, I coordinated with the ADHC faculty for the initial project meeting and web development, with another faculty member who led a photography workshop to help students with the visual content of the site, with the special collections librarian so students could look through primary source material for their research, and with multiple administrators to secure funding for the course. This burden, however, lessens with each iteration of the course and leads to many pedagogical, service, and scholarly benefits that outweigh the initial challenges. The MVP version of the course is an opportunity to build a network of faculty collaborators on campus, and this network can generate innovations and partnerships in future courses, panels at conferences, and on-campus pedagogical workshops. These collaborations also enhance the student experience in a time when pedagogy is changing very rapidly. This course model takes students out of the classroom, placing them in multiple professional scenarios. As a result, the students learn to network, to initiate strategy sessions, to participate in agile development, and to gain new skills (e.g., those related to IT, graphic design, and archival research) that will enhance their professionalism as they approach graduation.

CONTRIBUTORS

David Ainsworth
University of Alabama
dainsworth@ua.edu

Mary Alexander
University of Alabama
malexand@ua.edu

Rebecca Amato
New York University
becky.amato@nyu.edu

Clifford B. Anderson
Vanderbilt University
clifford.anderson@vanderbilt.edu

Mary R. Anderson
University of Tampa
mranderson@ut.edu

Sofiya Asher
Indiana University
soasher@indiana.edu

Edward L. Ayers
University of Richmond
eayers@richmond.edu

Lisa Siefker Bailey
Indiana University-Purdue
University Columbus
lsiefker@iupuc.edu

Christine Berkowitz
University of Toronto Scarborough
chris.berkowitz@utoronto.ca

Samantha J. Boardman
Boardman Consulting
sam@samanthajboardman.com

Camden Burd
Andrew W. Mellon Postdoctoral
Research Fellow at
the New York Botanical Garden
camden.burd@gmail.com

Stephen Buttes
Purdue University Fort Wayne
buttess@ipfw.edu

Joy H. Calico
Vanderbilt University
joy.calico@vanderbilt.edu

Lauren S. Cardon
University of Alabama
lscardon@ua.edu

Carey Champion
Indiana University Bloomington
crbeam@indiana.edu

Adam Clulow
University of Texas at Austin
Adam.Clulow@austin.utexas.edu

Zach Coble
New York University
zach.coble@nyu.edu

Mary Angelec Cooksey
Indiana University East
mcooksey@iue.edu

Chad Crichton
University of Toronto Scarborough
chad.crichton@utoronto.ca

Juilee Decker
Rochester Institute of Technology
jdgsh@rit.edu

Jacqueline H. Fewkes
Florida Atlantic University
jfewkes@fau.edu

J. Michael Francis
University of South Florida,
St. Petersburg
jmfrancis1@usfsp.edu

Scot A. French
University of Central Florida
scot.french@ucf.edu

Robin D. Fritz
Indiana University-Purdue
University Columbus
rwinzenr@iupuc.edu

Julia M. Gossard
Utah State University
julia.gossard@usu.edu

Samuel Horewood
Duke University
samuel.horewood@duke.edu

Hélène Huet
University of Florida
hhuet@ufl.edu

Connie Janiga-Perkins
University of Alabama
cjaniga@ua.edu

Bernard Z. Keo
Monash University
bernard.keo@monash.edu

Brian Kokensparger
Creighton University
BrianKokensparger@creighton.edu

Armanda Lewis
New York University
al861@nyu.edu

Justin B. Makemson
University of New Mexico
jmakemson@unm.edu

Rhonda J. Marker
Rutgers University
rmarker@rutgers.edu

Shawn Martin
Dartmouth College
shawn.j.martin@dartmouth.edu

Elizabeth Matelski
Endicott College
ematelsk@endicott.edu

Lisa M. McFall
Hamilton College
lmcfall@hamilton.edu

Anne Milne
University of Toronto Scarborough
anne.milne@utoronto.ca

William M. Myers
University of Tampa
wmyers@ut.edu

Alejandro Paz
University of Toronto Scarborough
alejandro.paz@utoronto.ca

Theresa Quill
Indiana University
theward@indiana.edu

Evan Roberts
University of Minnesota
eroberts@umn.edu

Natalie Rothman
University of Toronto Scarborough
natalie.rothman@utoronto.ca

James Roussain
University of St. Michael's College
james.roussain@utoronto.ca

Rachel L. Sanderson
University of South Florida,
St. Petersburg
rsanderson@mail.usf.edu

Kirsta Stapelfeldt
University of Toronto Scarborough
kirsta.stapelfeldt@utoronto.ca

Serenity Sutherland
State University of New York,
Oswego
serenity.sutherland@oswego.edu

Anya Tafliovich
University of Toronto Scarborough
anya.tafliovich@utoronto.ca

Laurie N. Taylor
University of Florida
laurien@ufl.edu; hhuet@ufl.edu

Molly Taylor-Poleskey
Middle Tennessee State University
mollygtaylor@googlemail.com

Patricia Turner
University of Wisconsin-Eau Claire
turnerpr@uwec.edu

Hannah Tweet
University of South Florida, St.
Petersburg
htweet@mail.usf.edu

Silvia Vong
University of St. Michael's College
silvia.vong@utoronto.ca

Robert Voss
Northwest Missouri State University
robvoss@nwmissouri.edu

Carmen Walker
Bowie State University
cwalker@bowiestate.edu

Katherine Wills
Indiana University-Purdue
University Columbus
kwills@iupuc.edu

Emma Annette Wilson
Southern Methodist University
eawilson@mail.smu.edu

INDEX

The Faculty Academy on Excellence in Teaching (FACET) was established as an Indiana University Presidential Initiative in 1989 to promote and sustain teaching excellence. Today, FACET involves over six hundred full-time faculty members, nominated and selected through an annual campus and statewide peer review process.

MICHAEL MORRONE is Director of the Faculty Academy on Excellence in Teaching (FACET) and is Senior Lecturer in the Kelley School of Business at Indiana University Bloomington.

EMMA ANNETTE WILSON is Assistant Professor of English at Southern Methodist University.

THOMAS C. WILSON is Professor and Associate Dean for research and technology at the University of Alabama Libraries.

CHRISTOPHER J. YOUNG is Assistant Vice Chancellor for Academic Affairs, Director for the Center for Innovation and Scholarship in Teaching and Learning, and Professor of History at Indiana University Northwest.

Lightning Source UK Ltd.
Milton Keynes UK
UKHW010352040920
369273UK00013B/60